A NEW TIME FOR MEXICO

FARRAR
STRAUS
GIROUX

A NEW TIME FOR MEXICO

. . . .

Carlos Fuentes

. . . .

Translated from the Spanish by
Marina Gutman Castañeda and the author

. . . .

Farrar, Straus and Giroux
New York

Translation copyright © 1996 by Farrar, Straus and Giroux, Inc.
All rights reserved
Originally published in Spanish under the title *Nuevo Tiempo Mexicano*
by Aguilar Nuevo Siglo © 1994 by Carlos Fuentes
Printed in the United States of America
Published simultaneously in Canada by Harper CollinsCanadaLtd
Designed by Fritz Metsch
First printing, 1996

LIBRARY OF CONGRESS CATALOGING-IN-PUBLICATION DATA
Fuentes, Carlos.
    [Nuevo tiempo mexicano. English]
    A new time for Mexico / Carlos Fuentes ; translated from the
Spanish by Marina Gutman Castañeda and the author.
        p. cm.
    1. Chiapas (Mexico)—History—Peasant Uprising, 1994– 2. Mexico—
Politics and government—1988– I. Title.
    F1256.F8413 1996 972'.75—dc20 96-10540 CIP

Contents

. . . solamente lo fugitivo permanece
y dura.

. . . only the fleeting lasts and endures.

A Roma sepultada en sus ruinas
Francisco de Quevedo (1580–1645)

A NEW TIME FOR MEXICO

1 : MEXICO
. . . .

The Face of Creation

To see Mexico from the air is to look upon the face of creation. Our everyday, earthbound vision takes flight and is transformed into a vision of the elements. Mexico is a creation of water and fire, of wind and earthquake, of the moon and the sun.

Not just one sun but the five suns of ancient Mexican cosmogony. First comes the Sun of Water, which presides over the creation of the world and ends in the storms and floods that foretell the coming eras—Sun of Earth, Sun of Wind, and Sun of Fire—each ending in catastrophe until we arrive at the fifth sun, our own, which awaits the final cataclysm.

Sun of Water

Coursing through Mexico are serpentine rivers, mere threads of fertility in the midst of deserts, opulent tropical undulations pouring slow and wide into the sea. Over the flowing waters of the Papaloapán, river of butterflies, over the still waters of Lake Pátzcuaro, furrowed by dragonflies, flutters the goddess Itzpapalotl, a star in the Aztec pantheon. Her very name, Obsidian Butterfly, resounds with the ambiguity of all the elements, her fragile multicolored wing at once a fearful sacrificial knife.

She is the first sign of creation, proclaimed by the fleeting liquid element. It is not the nature of water to be always placid, and when it lies as calm as a mirror locked in the crater of a volcano, its image is ominous indeed, for its supernatural tranquillity promises an imminent commotion. What are our years when seen against the mountains' millennia of stone? Who can really believe that these rock-encircled lakes in the craters of Toluca and Puebla always wore, and always will, this same metallic, motionless sheen?

Now everything moves again. The Usumacinta River flows on, inseparable from the forest it waters, equally inseparable from the clouds that gather over both jungle and river, as if they, too, were drawn along by the current. We know that all three—sky, river, and jungle—hide and protect the civilizations that slumber beneath them, pretending to be dead, giving signs of life only in the mystery of the figures drawn on the rocks beside the Planchón River and in the ghostly processions of the frescoes at Bonampak.

The stillness of the waters is illusory. Majestic waterfalls cascade, washing away the land and its history. Mountains collapse into the sea. Sandbars break the very waters of the sea. And the surf on the coast of Jalisco shows the earth as a dark-clawed monster, besieged and battered by the fury of the sea.

The land is a portrait drawn by the sea. But we have only to turn the picture around to imagine the contrary. Is this not rather the portrait of the sea as it is attacked by a hungry, ferocious land, an ambitious, aggressive, imprisoned land that challenges the sea, ruler of the greater part of the planet's surface, for its dominion?

Unquiet, tremulous, and insatiable, fearful and defensive, land of teeth and nails, jaws and talons—for a moment the land of Mexico shakes. The earth is about to speak. Earth will come to dominate water. The second sun comes to life amid awe and terror.

Sun of Earth

From the heights, the dead volcanoes—Popocatépetl, Iztaccíhuatl, the Nevado de Toluca—signal that their silence is no insurance against catastrophe, but rather a portent of the next tremor. Paricutín, the youngest volcano, smiles like a mischievous child, warning us that one day a curl of smoke may appear in a Michoacán farmer's field, spiraling up from the bowels of the furrowed earth that shakes its shoulders, vomiting flame and ash until, in a matter of hours, it reaches the sky.

And there is more: Chichón, that dark, active giant, proclaims that its quaking and smoking will cease only in foreboding of the next great commotion of this restless land, where creation has not yet ended its labors. Each volcano ends only to pass the flaming baton to the next.

Sun of Water, Sun of Earth. From the air, we can see the origins of the land and all that flows over its surface. We can take a picture of the very point where the Sierra Madre Oriental begins, proudly abandoning plains and deserts as it starts its climb, then shoots toward its vibrant coupling with the western chain in the Nudo Mixteco. Linked forever, the two chains then run on together to their ultimate extinction at the southern extreme of the continent in Chile and Argentina, where the Andes bud off from the chain like frigid grapes. We can also take a picture of the source of the Conchos River and see the birth of its waters from the womb of the land.

As we see all of this, we are present at the creation of nature. Not as something that happened *illo tempore*, in the age of the gods, but as something that is happening to us now, in our own time and before our very eyes.

The Nevado de Colima shows itself a mature gentleman, a bit gray around the temples, reminding us of the ambiguity of nature in Mexico. But neither he nor any of the great slumbering patriarchs watching over the earth can deny us our own time in this land.

For it is we—you and I—who see and touch and smell and taste and feel today, even as we witness the perpetual rebirth of the land here and now. We are the witnesses to creation, because of the mountains that watch us and in spite of their warning: "We will endure; you will not." Our response to this warning can be as sinful as pride, but also as virtuous as charity. We take the earth in our hands and re-create it in our own image.

Geometry, Einstein said, is not inherent in nature. Our mind imposes it on reality. Man's geometric imagination can be marvelously observed, from the air, in the incomparable clash of jungle and architecture in Palenque and Yaxchilán. It is at these sites that the primeval struggle between nature and civilization seems to have taken place; indeed it is still going on. Nature embraces architecture, but the human creation suffers because, while desiring to give itself up to nature's almost maternal tenderness, it also fears being suffocated by it. And as human beings, we also fear that we will be expelled from that great, moist womb that nurtures and protects us, cast out into the shelterless world.

The great art of ancient Mexico is born from this tension between nature and civilization, between fear of enclosure and fear of exposure. The splendors of the great acropolis at Monte Albán and the sacred spaces of Teotihuacán are the triumphs of but an instant of human domination over nature, yet also of human equilibrium with it. In these places, man has met time and made the shapes of time his own.

Nevertheless, man looks around him and sees the seductive threat of the sierras' deep gorges, the devouring tangle of the jungle, and the latent tremor of the mountains. He responds by gently caressing the slopes of the mountains, festooning them with terraced gardens; by stroking the plains and planting them with wheat and maize; and by building cities, shelters of his own making to substitute for the protection of trees, caves, and craters.

Mexico is a land of walls. Like all other peoples, we built them first to defend ourselves against inclement weather, marauding animals, and enemy attacks. Soon, however, architecture found other motives. First was the need to distinguish the sacred from the profane. Then came the need to segregate the conqueror from his subjects. And finally it becomes necessary to distance the rich from the poor.

In spite of these divisions, our cities transcend their limits and, with the very walls that divide and separate, create movement, a circulation that reunites us in the public square—the common place, the central site—and later in atriums and naves, chapels and portals, patios and gardens, until a network of communications is established that defies, and sometimes even defeats, the walls of isolation.

This is so because the human creation of the city acquires, in the Iberian New World, a sense of paradox. Civilization means living in the city, in the *civitas*. But in Ibero-America the paradox is that the city is simultaneously a creation of the will and a product of chance. Perhaps this is true of all cities, simply because the *civitas*—the place of civilization, the space where we coexist—is also the *polis*, the place of politics, the space where we debate. And both civilization and politics, much as they may imagine themselves to be projections of the will, are also the result of necessity and chance.

The cities of Mexico, I hasten to add, temper these characteristics with powerful admixtures of tradition and novelty. First tradition: the energetic plan of the new Spanish city replaces its Indian counterpart, supplants the traditional ceremonial, political, and religious functions, only to find itself obliged to take them on anew. And then novelty: the Spanish-American city offers the opportunity to create new, regular, chessboard cities, as rectangular as the grid on which Saint Lawrence burned.

During the Renaissance, Leon Battista Alberti dreamt of making the ideal Platonic city real. The novelty of America permitted such a thing. Here one can leave the walled agglomeration of the medieval city behind. But the past does not allow itself to be buried so easily. On the one hand, the previous tradition—the Indian center—struggles to reassert itself from under the very foundations of the new city, as recently happened in Mexico City when the Aztecs' Templo Mayor was uncovered in the central square, at the heart of the modern metropolis. On the other hand, racial novelty transforms both the Indian and the European city into a mestizo city, a city of mixed bloods. And economic demands—mining, the haphazard topography of gold and silver—also cause the Renaissance city to revert to the medieval hive of narrow alleys, tunnels, stairways, and pits.

From the air, Puebla, Oaxaca, and Morelia display their checkered innovations as well as their mestizo ambiguity, while Taxco, Zacatecas, and Guanajuato yield to the serpentine cityscapes called for in the mining districts. Like the gold seekers themselves, these cities scramble up mountainsides, tumble down slopes, and sniff out the precious metals there. When they find them, they adorn their altars with them, pave the streets with silver when their daughters get married, or lose their gold forever on a bet, on a whim, at a fiesta.

There is a splendid photograph by Michael Calderwood, the distinguished British artist, of the Barranca del Cobre, the Copper Gorge, in Chihuahua. Like the other canyons of the Americas, especially the most glorious of them all, the Grand Canyon, this great Mexican abyss bears witness to the two extremes of creation, birth and death. If this is a picture of the first day of creation, it is also a portrait of the last. Nevertheless, the drama of these places does not end in an affirmation of the beginning and end of the earth: their greatest effect lies in how they define our frame of reference step by step as our vision moves through space. In Arizona or Chihuahua, the reality of these natural wonders is actually determined by our movements. A step to the right or left and the great stone abyss that we see changes so fundamentally that we never look on the same gorge twice. The movements of our body, our change in point of view, transform what on the surface seemed an unalterable monument of nature.

Am I not defining the Baroque and searching for its specific American form? The Baroque is always an art of displacement, requiring the movement of the spectator if the work of art is to be seen at all—and, perhaps even more important, if it is to see itself. For the Baroque is a circular, not a frontal, art. The Byzantine icon must be seen from the front. Bernini and Michelangelo, on the other hand, invite the spectator to see the icon in the round. And when, in *Las Meninas*, Velázquez liberates painting from sculpture—to use Ortega y Gasset's phrase—his instrument of liberation is that circular gaze which enters the painting and observes the painter at work, as it were, from behind his back. In this way, the Baroque painting paints itself a second time.

In Mexico, as throughout Spanish and Portuguese America, the Baroque goes well beyond the sensual intellectual reason of the Europeans. For among us, the Baroque is a necessity, a vital, re-sounding affirmation—or, better yet, the affirmation of a necessity. A devastated, conquered land, a land of hunger and of dreams, finds in the Baroque the art of those who, having nothing at all, want everything. The Ibero-American Baroque is born of the abundance of need; it is an art desiring what is not there, a triple somersault over the abyss of desire with the hope of landing on one's feet on the other side and touching at last the object of desire: the fraternal hand, the body of love. The harsh, abysmal landscape of Mexico is, in its savage solitude, the picture of the Baroque hunger for its opposite, abundance and sharing.

The Sun of Earth, seemingly the most solid, the most long-lasting, thus shows that it, too, is a passing phenomenon. Its true image is that of a cloud in the artificial heaven of a Baroque altar. But the real heaven of Mexico offers more clouds than any altar does. Clouds are the crowns of Mexico's second geography.

Sun of Wind

Mexico is a country of prolonged, tranquil, luminous clouds. And clouds are the favorite daughters of the next sun, the Sun of Wind, which erodes coastlines and mountain peaks, that sculpts the stones and reshapes the tilled land.

At times, Mexico's opulent clouds are like a shroud tenderly shielding our eyes from a stiff or moribund body. Clouds hide from us the agony of the Lacandón rain forest and its people. Both are destined to extinction. At times, though, clouds are but the veil of civilizations unwilling to be disturbed. Most subtle of shields, the Sun of Wind protects all things in our country that await another time, a better time, to become manifest. In the meantime, clouds disguise the persistence of a sacred, magical world that the active, Faustian will of the West strives to annihilate.

Yet the clouds of Mexico carry out another, more disinterested task: they constantly soften the harder contours of the elements. Sea and land, volcano and air, ancient ruin and jungle, river and desert all clash head-on in Mexico. Here the elements war among themselves for their moment in the sun, and whole eras are named after each—water, fire, earth, and wind.

Everything in Mexico vibrates simultaneously, perhaps because the clouds constantly soften the harshness of the imperious Mexican elements, so none truly triumphs over the others. Wind pushes the clouds, the airy spray dissolves the roughest peaks, clouds intertwine surf and shore and commingle waterfalls with cascades of flowers—hibiscus, bougainvillea, yellow marigolds for the dead. The cloud is an all-embracing mist, a smoke dissolving all things and rendering all distances deceptive.

An encounter and a coupling, at times a confusion, a triumph of light, a blurring of the slashing strokes so often present in Mexican art. The hardest lines of Rivera or Siqueiros are as fearsome as the brutal natural encounters we see in the Mexican landscape. The Isla Tiburón with its point—appropriately named Chueca, Crooked—is like a shadowy wing menaced by a dagger-colored sea. It is as if the island wanted to fly away and the sea were holding it down, reminding the island that its destiny is to live between land and sea in perpetual confrontation.

The Sun of Wind then intervenes to dissolve all borders, to still

every quarrel, to silence all shouts. The Sun of Wind ruffles the
sand, softly caresses the face of the water, reveals the texture
of the undersea depths, and pulverizes the many varieties of stone:
porous, basalt, chalk, and sand. In Mexico this region of the air
belongs to the painter Ricardo Martínez, in Europe to J. M. W.
Turner. The Sun of Wind has been photographed by Gabriel Figueroa here, by Michael Calderwood there.

In this way, the Sun of Wind reveals a third Mexico within the
very element from which we see the country: the air. The wind that
blows through the mouths of two twin gods, one Mediterranean
and the other Mexican, Aeolus and Ehécatl, dissolves the rigidity
of the earth and the immobility of the sea as they confront each
other. The wind is a gift, a godly one. But like all other divine
offerings, it is ambiguous. And it has three names. The first is metamorphosis. The second is harmony. And the third is death.

The Sun of Wind transforms the unmoving landscape into a
movable passageway. Things that seemed eternal prove to be
changeable. Forms come together and pull apart to create new
forms. The Pinacate crater in Sonora becomes a delectable woman's nipple. A river in Baja California acquires a surprising shape:
a pink scorpion nestling in a bed of black earth. Are those real
cows crossing the lagoon at Mexcaltitán or merely a mirage?
Aren't those fishing boats anchored around a buoy at Puerto Pe-
ñasco really a butterfly freshly emerged from the chrysalis of the
sea? Are the cupolas of Cholula mushrooms? Are the tiger cages
in Chapultepec Park made only of air?

Sun of Wind, my sun. On the cover of the geography book I
used in school as a boy was a picture of Mexico as a horn of
plenty, out of which flowed an overwhelming wealth of fruit as
well as a long stalk of wheat that turned into the Baja California
peninsula. That cornucopia appeared to be floating in midair. No
hand, no land held Mexico up in the sky. It was like a free-floating
planet of infinite riches.

I had to believe in the powers of the god of wind, Ehécatl, in
order to hold in my imagination that Mexican cornucopia floating
in the sky, scattering its fruits and fertilizing the fields with wind-
borne seeds.

To penetrate the wealth of Mexico is to discover at one and the
same time its permanence and its transience. For one moment,

nothing changes and all the elements unite harmoniously. White birds resting in the waters of a power dam rob it of its engineered coldness. Cattle and wheat fields, derricks, hotels, haciendas, modern cities, and beach resorts—these are all names for abundance. But do they express harmony as well? Perhaps real serenity is far more modest and intimate. I find it in an aerial view of Tlacotalpán, with its peculiar knack for harmonizing gaiety and reserve. Here is a livable sensuality, the very definition of life in Veracruz.

Abundance also means the flight of the flamingos coming to feed, the pink blur of the birds on an orange sea, the silhouette of the jungle's green shadows. The shock of Mexican colors and the mutable hues of nature come together in a recently repainted village church or in the haven of a Oaxaca hamlet. This is perfection, the harmony we long for, the peace of the elements.

Sun of Fire

Peace does not last. The fourth sun, Fire, is ready to scorch the earth, to make it resemble those craters that—only because whimsy is more necessary than need itself—allow themselves the luxury of surrounding a cornfield near the sky. From the air we can see a soccer field, its outlines burned into the asphalt of the city like the burning graphics of that portrait of the sky on the earth at Nazca, in Peru, which can only be seen from the air.

There is a stony place in Chihuahua called Rocas de Lumbre, Rocks of Fire. Only, the fire is not necessarily a visible flame but rather, at times, the paradox of burning water—the *atl tlachinolli* of the Nahuas—the inner conflagration that we know, that knows itself, as death. As in the prose of the Mexican novelist Juan Rulfo, the lowest-lying field and the highest mountain have a hole in them through which escapes the heat of sexuality and death. Eros and Thanatos are both entryways into the invisible underworld, the Mictlán of the ancient Mexicans, where we enter wearing masks. We need another face for death, a mask that makes us acceptable for the other life—a better face perhaps than the one we had when we lived on earth, when we were bathed by water and animated by wind.

To see the Temple of Inscriptions at Palenque from the air is to look upon death. This pyramid was erected by Lord Pacal, first to anticipate and then to commemorate forever his own death. From above, the extensive fields of *zempazuchil*, the yellow flower of the Day of the Dead, are a sign of the service nature always provides for death. Flowers the color of fire associate death with an invisible fire disguised as life: the Sun of Fire that proclaims death does not exhaust itself in death, even though it brings it, as it were, to life. For life in Mexico foresees death; it knows that death is the origin of all things. The past, the ancestors, are the source of the present. Now the craters are lakes, are cornfields; once they were boilers filled with fire. Could they be that again? Of course—just as life will come back again, because death precedes it.

The Sun of Fire is not, then, an omen of inexorable destruction and catastrophe but a link in a circle where fire consumes air only to become its opposite, and then earth and then air again, before it burns and starts the cycle over.

Again, the Sun of Water

From on high, the four suns are consecutive but also simultaneous. As our gaze descends to the earth, it assigns precise names and places to each of the suns of creation. The name of Water may be Acapulco or Careyes, Puerto Escondido or Mazatlán, Veracruz or Cancún. Three seas—the Pacific, the Caribbean, and the Gulf of Mexico—surround our land with more than six thousand miles of coastline. And these seas, although they are ours, bring news from the outside world on every wave.

From the gulf coast the god Quetzalcoatl journeyed to the Dawn, promising to return to see if the people had put his principles of peace and brotherhood into practice. To that same coast came the Spanish conquistadors on the day prophesied for Quetzalcóatl's return, thus appropriating to themselves an omen that was theirs only by chance: the gods have returned to settle accounts with us. . . .

The Gulf of Mexico became from that day on the last cultural port of call of the Mediterranean in the Americas. Soldiers and monks, scribes and merchants, pirates and poets, invaders and ex- iles brought with them and carried through Veracruz the news of two worlds: America and Europe, Gulf and Mediterranean. Final resting place of the waves of the Bosporus, the Cyclades, Sicily, and Andalusia, the Mare Nostrum of European antiquity comes to an end in Tampico, Villahermosa, and Campeche.

But the waters of Mexico also send back their waves through the Atlantic to the Mediterranean, and their message is the news that the New World so desired by Europe is yet to be discovered, is yet to be imagined. It harbors mankind's oldest myths, its most secret truths, its dreams of the creation of the world and of man amid violence, pain, hope, and joy.

"Let the day break!" exclaims the Popol Vuh. "Let the dawn appear in the sky and on the earth. There will be neither glory nor grandeur until the human creature exists."

In Mexico's second sea, the Caribbean, an invisible sentinel stands guard at Tulúm, waiting for the impossible return of the god. Sun and sea meet here. The watch is sleepless and eternal. But no god will return, because the earth is demanding that its children rebuild it, that they themselves be the creators now.

Finally, on the Pacific coast, the waves tell of a world even more distant than Europe—Cathay, the Kingdom of the Middle Earth, Cipango, the Land of the Rising Sun, and our vaporous sisters in the shadows, the Philippines. Each of these islands and kingdoms sends us its wealth—"Japan its silks, the South Sea its treasure of rich pearls, China its mother-of-pearl," as the colonial poet Bernardo de Balbuena says in his *Grandeur of Mexico* (1602).

In you are their grandeurs condensed,
For you supply them with gold and fine silver,
While they give you things more precious still.

The Sun of Water does not enclose us. It opens us, puts us in communication, breaks down the barriers of isolation; it makes us circulate within and without. We receive, we give, exchange, prepare the passage of water to land, of land to air, of air to fire, of fire to water again.

Mexico is a portrait of the cycles of creation, a portrait of the skies and a succession of suns and elements that give no quarter. The portrait of the Mexicans is the portrait of creation.

That is why human victories are greater in Mexico. No matter how harsh our reality may be, we do not deny any facet of creation, we do not deny any reality. We try, instead, to integrate all aspects of the cosmos into our art, our way of seeing, our sense of taste, our dreams, our music, our language.

From the roof of Mexico, one can better appreciate this way of being. We are like Calderwood's picture of Rivera's sculpture of a god that can be truly seen only at a distance, from on high.

This is a portrait of a creation that never rests, because its work is not yet complete.

2 : ON MEXICAN TIME

. . . .

Kierkegaard in the Pink Zone

In an essay as intelligent as it is amusing, Søren Kierkegaard explains his personal strategy for staying alive and preserving his independence of spirit and movement in a Copenhagen that, a century and a half ago, had something like Mexico City's Pink Zone—a cluster of meeting places, coffeehouses, shops, libraries, squares; they were traditional habits, as Nietzsche would explain it, become modern, universal fashions. The place, in sum, where you saw and were seen.

Kierkegaard, by appearing every day at the same time in the cafés, streets, and theaters of his Pink Zone (call it Greenwich Village, St.-Germain-des-Prés, the Via Veneto, King's Road), convinced his contemporaries that they were dealing with a consummate loafer. His apparent availability provoked sympathy and tamed the envy and anger that would have fallen on his head if, absent and secluded, he had given the impression that he was a writer ensconced in an ivory tower (a term, lest we forget, coined by Sainte-Beuve about the Romantic poet Alfred de Vigny).

What to do with the time allotted us? Such is the problem posed by "that individual," as his Danish brethren called Kierkegaard, forced by the customs of his time to nourish his anguish privately and to flaunt his indifference in public. More precisely, he was forced by his time to do exactly the contrary of what the spirit of the time demanded. Time is always a version of another time, even when it flows on oblivious of us, as in Newton's sublunar consideration. We defend ourselves from timeless time by investing in time, reverting to time, diverting, subverting, and converting time. The pure version of time is a time without humanity. Diversion, reversion, inversion, subversion of time are the human responses, the stain—*la mancha*—of time. The corruption of its immaculate, fatal indifference to us. To write is an untimely struggle against time. We are out in the streets with Kierkegaard when it rains; we are with him in the basement when the sun shines. Writing is a countertime, an obstacle in Romance languages, *un contretemps, un contratiempo*. Writing in Spanish is indeed a rebellion against a time out of sync, a countertime opposed to the usually oppressive official time, a stain on the calendars of dogmatic rule, religion, race: *la mancha*, the stain, is the space of Don Quixote and the time of our tradition.

Is the Kierkegaard gambit possible in Mexico? I start by doubting it. The European author writes with a sense of linear time, time progressing forward as it both directs and assimilates the past. Even the great literary and philosophical violations of purely lineal continuity—Vico's *corsi e ricorsi*, Joyce's vicocyclometers—presuppose that a linear time does exist, that it is the central tradition and can thus be creatively disrupted. In Mexico, on the contrary, there is not and never has been one single time, one central tradition, as in the West. In Mexico, all times are living, all pasts are present. Our times appear before our eyes dressed in impure cloaks, charged with resistant agonies. We face a double battle: against a time that also diverts us, reverts back against us, subverts us, and converts us constantly.

The coexistence in Mexico of multiple historical levels is but the external sign of a deep subconscious decision made by the country and its people: all times must be maintained, all times must be kept alive. Why? Because no Mexican time has yet fulfilled itself. We are a horizon of latent, promising or frustrated, never fully achieved potentialities. A country of suspended times. The poet López Velarde saw in Mexican history a series of "subverted Edens" that we would like, simultaneously, to recover and to forget.

As a child, I used to travel by car every summer between my father's diplomatic post in Washington, D.C., and my grandmother's home in Mexico City. I felt even then a ruined quality in both countries, the United States and Mexico. But I also felt that in the United States the ruins were merely mechanical, the ruins of promises kept and accomplished and then left behind. For me, as a Mexican, it was depressing to contrast the progress of a country where everything worked, everything was new, everything was clean, with the inefficiency, backwardness, and dirt of my own country. Today I can see the destiny of U.S. progress—with abandonment, inefficiency, danger, and crime invading the citadels of what I admired as a child. And I have rescued my Third World infant pride and realized that while U.S. progress has produced garbage, Mexico's backwardness has produced monuments. Mexico's ruins are the vital ruins of the nation's origin, the debris of projects promised and then abandoned or destroyed by other projects, natural or human, but always proximate to something that an innocent look can only identify as a perpetually original force. That is the difference between the ruins of Mexico and those of classical antiquity. A Toltec temple has no descendancy; it is a ruin in itself and for itself. I have already alluded to the most pristine and permanent of Mexico's original forces, nature itself. And while it remains true that U.S. ruins are the debris of promises kept and then left behind, of objects eagerly bought, used, and thrown away—enormous piles of garbage, automobile graveyards, suffocated cities, blackened factories—since my youthful trips Mexico, too, has industrialized and a lot of these features have also become daily garbage in Mexico.

The paradox of time in Mexico is that when its promises are kept they self-destruct and when they remain unfulfilled they go on living forever. The basic example is the Spanish Conquest, which to Indian eyes signified the accomplishment of a benevolent myth: the return of the good god, Quetzalcoatl, the plumed serpent, at the precise time foreseen by the calendars of religion and mythology—Easter 1519, the Indian Year of the Reed, *Ce Acatl*. With the arrival of the Spaniards the time of Indian Mexico fulfilled its promise only to find its death. The era during which Mexico was a Spanish colony was an anachronism that tried to prolong fictitiously the world order and the mind-set of the Middle Ages, denying the time both of Indian antiquity and of European modernity (rationalism, mercantilism, free inquiry). What it did marry was the authoritarian traditions of the Aztec world and the needs of Spanish royal absolutism.

Both submerged times came back perversely, the Indian time as sentimental nostalgia, the modern time as exploitative capitalism. Nevertheless, the colonial centuries did create a new time, mestizo, based on the mixture of Indian, black, and European bloods, and a new culture, Baroque, a culture of disguise and dissatisfaction, protecting the persevering religious faith of the Indian world under Christian domes, compensating for the people's poverty and uncertainty with altars of gold, shrines of silver, and carved stone. By the time independence was won from Spain three centuries after the Conquest, we did have a new, mestizo culture but did not give ourselves credit for it; we wanted to become just like France or the United States as quickly as possible. We wanted to become "modern." The dreams of Mexican modernity in the nineteenth century—liberalism and positivism—were achieved only partially and always at the expense of the communitarian bonds, the dignity, the rights, and the culture of the peasant and indigenous peoples, as I attempt to describe in Chapters 3 and 5. Benito Juárez's dream of a nation of small property owners ruled by market values becomes the Porfirio Díaz nightmare: severed from their traditional links and the protection given them by the Spanish crown, the Indian and agrarian communities dissolve into the big belly of the latifundios, the haciendas, sometimes as large as Holland, where the laborer is chattel. The will to modernity of Juárez and his companions in the Reforma movement of the mid–nineteenth century ignored the simultaneity of Mexico's times, leaving us with pure actuality, deprived of deep historical or cultural identities. That is why the freedoms won by Juárez so easily became forms of subjection under Díaz.

Only the Revolution made present all of Mexico's pasts—and that is why it deserves a capital *R*. I will extend this idea throughout this book. The Revolution revealed the plurality of times instantaneously as if it knew that there would be little time for ceremonies of reincarnation. Mexico's heavy tradition of centralized power, the inveterate mental tendency to paternalism and strict economic pragmatism soon transformed the Revolution into an institution—an institution that pays homage with words to the Indian and revolutionary pasts while expressing its capitalist creed in its acts. Again, the cult of actuality has been translated into forms of internal authoritarianism and external dependency.

The rhetorical kowtow to simultaneity in Mexico's history thus has a double meaning: it numbs, justifies, depoliticizes; but it also keeps the ancient aspirations of the Mexican people alive. The national tiger takes siestas, but it is not dead, as recent events in Chiapas have proved.

Instantaneity: the Mexican response to time. When André Breton called Mexico the chosen land of surrealism, he was saying that in Mexico desire finds an immediate response precisely because, the necessities being as enormous as they are, it needs supra-real instruments to achieve satisfaction. This explains much of Mexican art and literature—the paintings of Tamayo, for instance, and the novels of Rulfo. In the land of need that is Mexico, desire is a central fact of life and imagination. Western civilization, in a certain sense, has been one long road toward the encounter of desire and its objects. In our time, we realize that a permanent contradiction has presided over this journey: the desire of the Western world diminishes in inverse proportion to the number of objects capable of satisfying it. The desires and the objects have often been false, and today they are in any case diminished: smaller desires, smaller objects. Much of modern Western art—including surrealism—was a rebellion against this order of things. The greatest European artists—Picasso, Braque, Ernst, Buñuel, Joyce, Kafka, Broch, Lawrence, Akhmatova—make dazzling but desperate attempts to discover, through memory and the imagination, all that Europe had forgotten. Their warnings were timely but went unheeded. Europe became the stage for the most brutal—because less expected, less rationally forecast—of all holocausts.

In Mexico, the impossible distance between desire and the thing desired has given both yearning and object an incandescent purity. The bridges drawn from the shore of aspiration to the shore of satisfaction must override, by force, all "realistic" contingency. In Mexican popular life, in our definitive acts of love and death, passion and revolution, art and celebration, opposites meet and desire is nothing but the acknowledgment of the estrangement previous to the reunion. It is, perhaps, even the condition for the reunion to take place. Death shall become life, revolution shall be a fiesta, passion shall become art, spirit matter, accident essence, and body soul. You shall be I. A mask, a word, a greeting, or a farewell, a way of walking or looking will be enough for the meeting to occur: any celebration that ensures that we come closer—before sickness, death, separation, or distance triumphs all over again. A disguise, a dance are sufficient to obtain the desired beauty, courage, sensuality, identity: I shall be You. For after all, desire is love for something else; it is transfiguration. Desire must assail reality to meet its object, to recover the unity of the subverted Eden that is our country. The nostalgia of paradise lost, the impossibility of paradise future leave most Mexicans with no possibility other than paradise in the present, the most difficult of all paradises to inhabit because so fugitive—the past one instant, the future the next.

After the great catastrophes of our century, the modern world can perhaps better understand Mexico's ageless conviction that danger is just around the corner, in a lost bullet, a casual encounter, a burst of anger, in sickness, in hunger, in bondage. The violence of centuries has taught us this. The so-called Mexican love of death is really a double resource of life. Death is the other half of life, completing life. But death is part of life only if it becomes a conscious part of life, a permanent companion, an object of celebration and tragic resistance. Life and our sense of history are intimately linked to our sense of death once we realize that we descend from death, that death is the origin of life, that without the death of our ancestors we would not be here in the world at all.

Even more: death is the resource of transfiguration. It is, of course, the way out of life as well as into life, and life, says the popular Mexican song, is worth nothing, *no vale nada*. But it is also the entry into life, since life is as valuable as our conscience decides it is.

The Mexican *mañana* does not mean putting things off till the morrow. It means not letting the future intrude on the sacred completeness of today. There is nothing more distant, I agree, from the Anglo-Saxon sense of expediency—and nothing more attractive, either, to the Anglo-Saxon rebel. In any case, when a total past throbs so powerfully in the present, future time can become something of an abstraction and lose a lot of its value. Perhaps *mañana* is empty, but surely today must be fulfilled. This is the greatest paradox of Mexican time: the instant is retained and eternalized within its fugitiveness. A line from the great Spanish Baroque poet Quevedo that I often quote comes to mind:

. . . solamente lo fugitivo permanece y dura.
. . . only the fleeting lasts and endures.

All the commonplaces (that is, the meeting grounds) of Mexico repeat this. The sugar skulls, the black earthen sirens, the straw angels, the cardboard skeletons, the fragile candelabra that are the tree of life, the fireworks that glow while consuming themselves, the hollow Judas figures made to be destroyed during the ceremonial instant of Resurrection, Easter Saturday—all these fragile figures, fascinating in their very provisionality, are the reminder, grave and smiling, that beauty can be fashioned in the image of its object, the passing instant, retaining it, redeeming it.

Does not this Mexican time, sacralized and profaned and maintained at maximum intensity, offer us, the men and women of Mexico, the temptation of becoming, we ourselves, time? Does it not push us to the brink of opposing, to our personal time, all those versions of time that the far too diverting, subverting, inverted, reverted, converting, and controverting Mexican time both offers and denies us? All too often, Mexican time, totalizing yet latent, tries to substitute itself for our own personal clocks, simply because this time of ours, more than a recipient of our personalities, pretends to substitute itself for them and is occasionally richer, more varied, and more powerful than they. We city-dwelling middle-class Mexicans, ferocious individualists with a collective bad conscience, are as troubled by the time of Mexico as we are by our desire to be rid of it and by our fear of being overwhelmed by it. We exorcise it. Maybe this book is one more attempt at literary witchcraft. The fact is, the time of Mexico reaches us charged with all that we could become, but the charge precedes us and is so enormous that at moments we would like to become pure time, so as to defeat the historical time that denies, mocks, defies, and besieges us. This book is a chronicle, at many levels, of such a time and its troubles, such a time and its figures.

Wouldn't it be nice to be a Yankee, a Brit, a Frenchman, even a Dane? Kierkegaard was talking about time on the European scale, a malleable time. He could mock time and play with it, hide from it, do nothing whatsoever, and yet be seen as a most active individual. He could show himself, expose himself to time, do a

million things, and pass for a vagrant. He could be free. But in
Mexico, time mocks individuals, and particularly writers. The
writer partaking of his times may be seen as frivolous or demagogic; retiring from time, he becomes an inmate of the ivory tower
condo. It is easy in Latin America to be seen not as a writer but
as a bloodsucking vampire, exquisite aesthete gringo, or frog imi-
tator. Kierkegaard, in Mexico, would have ended his days crying
at the intersection of Insurgentes and Reforma, two typically revolutionary names for sedate city avenues. His public presence
would be the only admissible testimony to his private anguish; his
gesture, solitary proof of his *gesta*; his presence, sufficient confession of his absence.

   We turn on the television sets of the Mexican mind, and every
night we hear the same evening news. Top of the news: THE SPAN-
ISH HAVE CONQUERED MEXICO. Second item: THE GRINGOS STOLE
HALF OUR TERRITORY. After that, murders, arson, kidnappings,
and five-legged calves. We try to understand the fabulous totality
and instantaneity of true Mexican time. We cannot disguise ourselves as what we are not, so as to live that total, instantaneous
time which we can perhaps understand but not fully experience.
For ours is a demanding time; it wants us to live it completely,
with hands and dreams, with desire and dust. We are citizens of a
region where once the air was clear, suburban inhabitants of a city
whose founding hieroglyph is as fearful as it is paradoxical: *atl
tlachinolli*, burnt water. Mexico City denizens, our tongues are on
fire; ashes make our mouths water. Garrulous sphinxes, prophets
of the past, Oedipuses without a mother because someone else—
others, everyone—has been fucking her forever. Narcissuses condemned to gaze at ourselves in the bottom of a cup of instant decaf.
Prometheuses chained to the shrink's couch, to the priest's confessional, to the multiple little thrones that the Institutional Revolutionary Party distributes to offices, congresses, and unions. The
past contains all of our images, all of our desires, all of our solutions. The present undresses us. The future, over and over, deceives
us.

   What a bore, says Julio Cortázar of Argentina, to have all the
time in the world in front of you. How uncomfortable, say I of
Mexico, to have all of the past behind you . . . and to be, precisely,
a writer of the Mexico City upper middle class, bereft of the trans-

missible values of a cardboard Judas or a black earthen siren; to lack all instantaneous salvations; to write. How very uncomfortable. Quick, let us advance—there is no time left. We must go forward to 1910; we must make the Revolution. Stop, draw back; we have all the time in the world: the PRI knows what it's doing; there's no need to be impatient. There's a Moctezuma in your future; put a Cortés in your motor. Confession in church or psychoanalysis on the couch: heal the past. Art: paint the past. Revolution: restore the utopian past, found the utopian future. Politics: invoke the revolutionary past while practicing the conservative present. Religion: believe in our holy mother the Virgin of Guadalumpen. Culture: we are one seamless civilization from Quetzalcoatl to Pepsicoatl. Invert: without a past what have I to confess? Subvert: without the Revolution what institutional stability do I have? Revert: Paradise, here I come. Divert: I can well remember the year 2000.

In writing this book, I accept Kierkegaard's lesson. I show myself struggling with time. That is, I show myself countering time, shelterless, and then I withdraw to write in seclusion, knowing full well that each line is a countertime.

3 : INDIAN MEXICO

· · · · · · ·

A Trip to the Center of the Origin

I

Travel is the original movement of literature. Words are the origin of myth; myth is the first name of home, forebears, and tombs. It is the word of that which abides. The word of movement tears us from the hearth. Its name is epic, and it throws us into the arms of the world, of the different, of the voyage. During this trip from mythic hearth to epic strangeness, we discover our tragic fissure. We then return to the land of the origin, there to tell our tale and renew our dialogue with the myth of the origin, asking it to have pity on us.

This fiery circle of literature, which in the Mediterranean world has the generic names of myth, epic, and tragedy, is what propels the narrative of travel. It is a wide gyre indeed. It springs from the identification of voyage and language and gives form to poetry— from Homer to Byron to Neruda. Politics has been determined as much by Herodotus as by Pericles, and the best guides for any contemporary summit meeting between Russian and American leaders continue to be the travel books of the Marquis de Coustine in Russia and of Alexis de Tocqueville in the United States in the nineteenth century.

Movement and stillness: thanks to language, a voyage can be purely internal, confessional, subjective—from Saint Augustine to Rousseau to Freud—or it can be a trip outside our own selves and toward a recognition of the world; such is the history of the novel from the moment that Don Quixote leaves his village and goes out to compare the truth of his books with the truth of his world. Traveling can also be the immobile voyage of Jules Verne, who rarely left the confines of his own village yet was capable of traveling to the moon or twenty thousand leagues under the sea. A voyage can be a vast symbolic journey in search of the Golden Fleece or the Holy Grail, and Xavier de Maistre can take us on a trip around his bedroom, Thomas Mann to the magic mountain, or Virginia Woolf to the lighthouse. Yet Thomas Wolfe reminds us that "you can't go home again."

In any case, voyage and narrative are twins because both signify a displacement, an abandonment of the place, the *plaza*, a farewell to the common place and a plunge into the territories of risk, adventure, discovery, the unusual. Voyage and narrative are surely all of this, yet finally they are simply voices telling us that the world is ours but that world is alien. How shall we explore it, how shall we make it our own? How can we travel around the world without losing our souls but, rather, discover ourselves as we discover the world, realizing that we lack an identity if forsaken by the world, though without us the world itself would become faceless?

This is, perhaps, the common cipher that unites personal destiny with the art of travel. I address others, my life, my work, my love, my world. And nothing permits me to think that these, my life's truths, will come to me if I do not go toward them.

II

Three contemporary authors of travel literature particularly seduce me. Bruce Chatwin died tragically at the age of forty-six, leaving at least half his work unfinished. His books *In Patagonia* and *The Songlines* take us south to Argentina and to the vast Australian hinterland. In them, Chatwin gives powerful examples of his two great literary virtues: an unparalleled capacity to distinguish an object and bring it into relief, infusing it with singular luminosity yet never separating it from its context, and the art—also incomparable in contemporary literature—of skipping two out of every three probable sentences, thus giving us an essential text driven by great elliptical power. In *The Songlines*, these literary virtues, from a man one must consider one of the best writers of the second half of the twentieth century, come together as an inquiry into the movements of Australian aborigines. The nomadic life, not the sedentary life, is the normal life, Chatwin informs us.

In his book *The Snow Leopard* the American novelist Peter Matthiessen transforms his trip to Nepal in search of the blue sheep of the Himalayas into a spiritual pilgrimage toward the Crystal Mountain and its Buddhist sanctuary; the awaited reward for this quest is a vision of the snow leopard. Like Chatwin, Matthiessen is in possession of an essential prose, and like him he, too, asks why our idea of the world depends so much on movement and stillness, on staying put or displacing ourselves. Is it true, as Chatwin points out, that for the nomad the world is already perfect, while the sedentary being vainly agitates himself trying to change the world? And is it not equally true, as Matthiessen finds out on his trip to the great mountain range, that movement is but the search for the perfection forever fixed in a single holy place?

The Mexican writer Fernando Benítez tried to answer these questions from the center of a paradox pertinent to Mexico and Mexicans. The paradox consists in knowing that the meeting with the sacred place is an illusion, that to find it is only proof that we must go forward, renew, begin all over, continue searching. Chatwin and Matthiessen also arrive at this truth, but only when they become pilgrims in their own lands, when they discover the other, the strange, in the bosom of their own countries. Chatwin wrote the indispensable novel of Wales, *On the Black Hill*, and Matthiessen has found the North American other in the remnants of the Indian world of the United States, in alien territory, the reservation, but also a forbidden territory. (*In the Spirit of Crazy Horse*, one of Matthiessen's Indian books, was for a long time besieged by an army of legal suits.)

Mexico has been a favorite hunting ground for the Anglo-Saxon writer, from Thomas Gage, who made his colonial voyages in the eighteenth century, to Fanny Calderón de la Barca, the Scottish wife of the first Spanish ambassador to independent Mexico. More recently, we have been visited and described by Aldous Huxley, D. H. Lawrence, Graham Greene, and Malcolm Lowry. (Evelyn Waugh permitted himself the sick prank, worthy of the author of *Vile Bodies*, of writing a libel against the nationalization of oil in Mexico, paid for by the British petroleum companies, as if he had really been in Mexico and witnessed its horrors; in truth, he never went farther than the London bank where he cashed his check.)

Books by United States writers on Mexico have abounded, historical, sociological, and touristical, and many gringos have skillfully incorporated the Mexican theme into their novels and poems—from Hart Crane to Harriet Doerr, from Katherine Ann Porter to Jack Kerouac. A great French writer, Antonin Artaud, is, however, the author who came closest to (and whose descriptions are almost indistinguishable from) the other Mexico, Indian Mexico, in his trip to the Tarahumara.

This is the world that Fernando Benítez explores in his great books on the Indians of Mexico—the world of the Coras, the Tarahumaras, the Huicholes and the Tepehuanes, a world, as foreign in a way, to the Mexican Benítez as to the Englishman Huxley or the Frenchman Artaud. The difference is that this is Benítez's world, part of his country, his identity, his heritage. His drama is as acute as Matthiessen's among the Sioux or Chatwin's among the Welsh: these people are other, but they are mine. The extraordinary quality of Benítez's books is that he can see the Indians with objectivity yet participates with them in a drama of conflictive subjectivity. The Indians are his yet also not; he cannot be a complete man without them, even if they go on with their lives, totally indifferent to him.

Why does this happen? Benítez is the bearer of a pluralistic cultural conscience. He knows that Mexico cannot be only one of its parts but must be all of them, though some of them, such as the Indian regions, are slowly dying, victims of all kinds of abuse, of injustice, misery, solitude, alcohol. . . . How do we maintain the value of these cultures and save them from injustice as well? Can Indian values coexist with those of Western progress, with modern conditions of health, work, and social protection? Is it worthwhile to maintain those original values if the price is continuing poverty?

These are some of the anguished questions that run through Benítez's books, giving them, apart from their literary excellence, immense moral value. The author's literary ethics opens up a series of burning options, only superficially dualistic, since we soon realize that each of their terms is inseparable from the others: each option is the mirror of another, reflecting it without touching it. But it is also its twin, its carnal pain, its mysterious destiny.

III

The Indian world of Mexico offers an opposition between the visible and the invisible. The modern history of Mexico, Benítez reminds us, has powerfully conspired to make the Indian population invisible. The Europeans' conquest of Mexico left the Indians a defeated people, and sometimes a defeated people prefer to go unnoticed. They become at one with darkness, wishing to be forgotten so as not to be struck once more. But after the colonial period, independent Mexico was menaced by foreign wars and dismemberment; it had to protect and reinforce the parts of the nation most threatened by foreign powers—Spain, the United States, France—and consign large fragments of its territory to oblivion. The Indians became part of a terra incognita; nobody, at any given moment, knew where the Huicholes, the Coras, or the Tarahumaras really were; nobody, notes Benítez, really cared whether they existed or not.

There is a memorable scene in a film by Rubén Gámez, *The Secret Formula* (about the formula for making Coca-Cola), in which a Mexican tries to place himself within camera range so as to be photographed, but each time, the camera moves away from him, always leaving him outside the frame. It is as if this character wishes to win for himself the identity of the picture and as if the camera repeatedly denies him that wish. Do both of them—camera and subject—fear they might lose their souls in the act of making or not making a photograph? Who knows? But Benítez's books can be read as one vast and disturbing effort to make the invisible visible. He finds striking comparisons between the supreme visibility of Western painting and the actual appearance of a group of Tarahumaras; their Renaissance-page haircuts, their naked legs, their bulky codpieces make them look like Brueghel figures lost in the high tropics; a young Tezltzal shepherd carries a lamb across his shoulders like Donatello's figure of Saint John; and the orgiastic confusion of the Coras during Easter week becomes as clear as the memory of Bosch's *Garden of Earthly Delights*.

But once the eye of the city traveler goes away, one cannot doubt that invisibility reclaims this forgotten mimetic world. How can it make itself visible? The answer is fleeting and mutable; its name is Myth, its name is Magic, its name is The Sacred. Can it someday also be named Justice? Benítez does not divorce the two realities. Magical reality makes Indians visible to themselves; the possibility of justice can also make them visible both to themselves and to others.

This idea opens up yet another series of oppositions that Benítez tries to unite. The Indian world, in order to become visible, struggles between movement and stillness. Both are names of the extremes of metamorphosis. Without it, there would be no change, no movement toward the sacred that Benítez quite correctly observes in most of the truly vital activities of the Indian world; a "turning upside down of the order of daily life, altering the usual rhythms of the world, giving the world different authorities and naming things all over again."

How can we make a safe transition from the profane to the sacred? The answer lies in a ritual universe where the masters of the magic arts, the shamans, those who know, those who name, those who sing, occupy the privileged space. María Sabina is the best-known of these ritual actors.

They speak, they sing. The passage from the invisible world to the world of images is also a passage from silence to voice, from the forgotten to the remembered, from stillness to movement. Benítez warns that the Huichol people know that in their rituals they "reconstruct" the deeds of their gods, which took place in the original time of creation. Present-day Indians know ritual down to the smallest details. Yet the pain of this knowledge is that it is not self-sufficient. On the contrary, it demands for itself movement, wrenching itself from something, exposing itself to lose the very thing it was searching for: the original unity of humanity and of the world.

The Indian runs the risk of going mad as he faces these choices. He hurls himself into the abyss but creates "an immense ritual" that will become the wings of his mythical flight. Metamorphosis is the name of the ritual. The Indian sings a poem so that the gods may become flowers and enter a mother's womb and come out as clouds and that the clouds may then rain on the cornfield.

Movement and voice. Stillness and invisibility resemble silence; movement and visibility resemble voice. Benítez perfectly captures the tone of Indian voices, so much like their silence: pathos and edginess of modern urban life are unknown here, he says. Indians talk in caressing, mute tones. It is in bad taste to let the voice betray irritation or disdain. Their voices are "white, impersonal," and they are not underlined by gesture or confirmed by look.

The contrast is indeed very striking between the world of Indian silence and the verbal resurrection that a Mexican writer, writing in Spanish, finds in such a forgotten nature. Facing the varieties of geographic accident and the rich correspondences between nature and its Spanish place-names, Benítez writes, "Words buried in dictionaries become animated, acquire their color, their nuance, their harshness, their depth, their relief, and their drama."

Most dramatic of all is that this verbal wealth not only opposes the writer, who owns his tongue, to the Indians, who own silence, but baptizes the world, naming the New World for the first time. Benítez repeats this feat in his books on the Indians, the feat that the Cuban novelist Alejo Carpentier attributes to Latin American writers in general. Yet the marvelous élan that the writer both inherits and resurrects is diminished not only by the silence surrounding him but by the mortal danger that the use of his language, Spanish, may signify for Indians.

A Mixtec Indian says this: "They want to kill me because I speak Spanish. The killers speak only Triqui, and they think I am signing documents denouncing them." Benítez realizes that by speaking Spanish the Mixtec has "violated the secret of his people, he has left his own group by speaking the foreign language." Nothing illustrates as terribly as this Indian's words—they want to kill me because I speak Spanish; they think I am denouncing them in a language they don't know—the distance between two cultures within the same nation. Is that distance unbridgeable? Language, Vico tells us, is the first communitarian reality of culture, the first thing that we share, the first thing that unites. Here, it separates, menaces, divorces people. What is the place of justice in a world such as this, "where victims and executions unite to defend with impenetrable silence the intimacy and secrets of their lives"?

The stranger, writes Benítez, "is the eternal enemy," and enmity begins at the basic level of language. To be sure, he offers numerous examples of the cultural distance between the oral and the written word. A man is capable of speaking only if his words do not become "papers." Even in urban Mexico the oral is a surer thing than the written, and the tradition of old-fashioned Mexican politicians is to leave nothing written down. But in the case of the Indians, the denial of writing is not only a form of self-defense but also a form imposed by violence and slavery. The educational effort of the first Christian missionaries was short-lived. The crown and the clergy reserved for themselves a monopoly on the written word, thus to increase their power "over the illiterate masses of the New World."

Baptized with the name of negation, words led fatally to violence. These are mute men, says Benítez, "who recover speech only with alcohol." Violence and its daughter, Death, atrociously sear the Indian world of Mexico. Collective degradation through alcohol, murders, and wars without limits—these scenes are described by Benítez with the starkness of a Goya engraving, of a charcoal line by Orozco, of a mortal phrase by Rulfo: "They killed his parents and one of his little sisters on the way. Of all the family, only this boy is alive, as well as another little brother called Pedro. . . . If they do not find the man they are looking for, they kill the wife and the children, that's for sure. . . . If people aren't killed here, then nobody's happy."

Alcohol breaks silence but inaugurates violence. "Some were totally drunk and I defended them because there was no other reasonable way of going thirty or forty kilometers across the mountains with a cadaver on their backs in an almost total state of decomposition."

IV

In the reader's memory, this decomposed cadaver recalls another dead body, that of a jailed Indian showing his face between the crude, heavy bars of his cell, all the light in the world concentrated on his teeth: "Their razorlike brilliance expressed the impotent desperation of a caged animal in a way that his elemental Spanish could never express." This also prefigures, in its openmouthed, jailed muteness, another body, not carnal or singular but symbolic: the body of the God, be he called Christ or Deer. Between the divine body and the abandoned, imprisoned, mute, sick bodies, the Indian response is called ritual, mystery, myth. To the individual deaths of human beings and to the universal death of God, the Indians of Mexico respond by traveling from the profane to the sacred, from the body of man to the body of God.

Traveling from one reality to the other requires not only a knowledge of ritual but an understanding of what myth unites, of what has been separated and of what myth remembers, of what has been forgotten. These are not disguised tautologies but essential movements of the soul, visibly manifesting themselves in ritual. Benítez makes us see how the ceremony of eating peyote has the purpose of halting the dispersion of the self, of allowing communion with the All, attention to the song of inert objects, and a return to the original time, the time of creation, "the virginal age of first ideas, where the Farmers of the World reigned, surrounded by green and blue feathers." Original unity, immediate dispersion —the consciousness of this movement is expressed in the spoken texts of the Huicholes, where the gods, barely born, disperse "and run like water through the jungle."

Within this sacred circle live the fear and the nostalgia of the aboriginal soul, for as they recover the original time, the Indians also preserve its immobility, thanks to myth. "They are the prisoners of the eroded mountains, and God is their jailer." Custom, which gives the Indians a spiritual and mythical universe no longer available to modern Mexicans, also gives them the habit of lowering their heads, consulting witch doctors, buying candles and firecrackers for the saints, being exploited, drinking themselves to death, believing in spirits, doubles, and flying skeletons. Custom, that hard cord of vice and superstition which ties them hand and foot, is at the same time the source of their unity, "the tie that preserves their character and their life."

We all live within a process of constant choice between diverse options, between negations and affirmations, knowing that each decision we make sacrifices a plurality of alternatives. In spite of silence, immobility, and custom, the sense of alternatives and of sacrifice due to choice is even more dramatic in the Indian world. Or perhaps the Indians of Mexico are simply more conscious than we, their modern urban brethren, of the possibility so eloquently described by Jacob Bronowski writing about chess: the moves you don't make are as much a part of the game as the moves you do make.

William James wrote, "The mind is at every stage a theater of simultaneous possibilities." We can both understand this thought and share it with the aboriginal world. It is equally valid for María Sabina and for Rainer Maria Rilke. The indigenous world expresses it through all these dramatic oppositions—visibility and invisibility, voice and silence, memory and oblivion, violence and death.

Yet there is one more duality that masks this spiritual movement of the plural and the simultaneous: the duality of the provisional and the permanent. Life, faith, ritual are permanent, but things tend to be provisional, as in the village of Copala, described by Benítez, where everything, with the exception of the church, "is provisional and is marked with the seal of violence and death." I do not know if this provisional character merely disguises a kind of virtuality of the absent yet potential movements in the indigenous world; I do not know if, when we travel into Indian Mexico, we are spectators in a theater of simultaneous possibilities. But I do believe that what we see there is a will to survive in spite of catastrophe, injustice, and the hostility of nature.

Nobility and misery meet in the Indian communities, while the vulgarity and pretensions of the urban world disappear. The Indians of Mexico are the only aristocrats in a country of provincial imitations, shabby colonial hidalgos, haughty republican Creoles, and corrupt, cruel, and ignorant revolutionary bourgeois. The dignity and beauty of the Tarahumara region's severe witnesses, of the Tzotsiles, whose "virility is a triumph over the fragility of childhood," are constantly devastated by poverty, alcohol, fatality: "Everything goes wrong for us everywhere."

Yes, as Fernando Benítez says, they deserve another destiny. For the time being, they meet their fate in isolation, through atavistic wisdom and mythologies, decking themselves out in the regalia of the gods, worn atop ragged clothes and rubber-soled huaraches, for they wish to recover the mystery, the distance, the ritual purity, the contact with the gods—and to do so without losing sight of the suffering imposed on their humanity.

Do they deserve another fate? "Once the coherence of the fiesta is broken, the vision of fraternity and abundance dispelled, what remains is the dusty desert, the sloth, the hunger never satiated by the fruits of the cactus. . . ."

Do they deserve another fate? The answer must also be ours. It is up to us to decide if we are interested in participating in the life of Mexico's indigenous communities, sharing their fruits, their ritual purity, their closeness to the sacred, their memory of all that has been forgotten by urban hedonism, making it ours, on our own terms, while respecting their terms and the values they attach to their culture. It is up to us to decide whether we are able to respect the values of the Indian world, saving it from injustice rather than condemning it to abandonment.

The Indians of Mexico are part of our polycultural and multi-racial community. To forget them is to forget ourselves and condemn ourselves to eventual oblivion. The justice they receive will be inseparable from that which governs the rest of us. The Indians point the way to our own possibility as citizens of a free society. We shall not be just men and women if we do not share justice with them. We shall not be satisfied men and women if we do not share bread with them.

4 : REVOLUTIONARY MEXICO

....

History Out of Chaos

The Mexican Revolution of 1910–21 was at least three revolutions. Revolution number 1—fixed forever in pop iconography—was the agrarian, small-town movement led by chiefs such as Pancho Villa and Emiliano Zapata. This was a locally based revolt, intent on restoring village rights to lands, forests, and waters. Its program favored a decentralized, self-ruling, communitarian democracy, inspired by shared traditions. It was, in many ways, a conservative revolution.

Revolution number 2, more blurry in the icons of the mind, was the national, centralizing, and modernizing revolution led originally by Francisco Madero, then by Venustiano Carranza after Madero's assassination in 1913, and finally consolidated in power by the two forceful statesmen of 1920s Mexico: Álvaro Obregón and Plutarco Elías Calles. Their purpose was to create a modern national state capable of setting collective goals while promoting private prosperity.

Somewhere between the two, and definitely dim in the collective memory, an incipient proletarian revolution number 3 took place, reflecting the displacement of Mexico's traditional artisanal class by modern factory methods. Radicalized by anarcho-syndicalist theories and leaders, the nascent working class staged the two greatest challenges against the Porfirio Díaz dictatorship: the strike of the textile workers in Río Blanco in 1906 and, a few months later, the miners' strike at Cananea. During the Revolution itself, workers banded in so-called Red Battalions and helped Carranza, but retained their autonomy under the organization called Casa del Obrero Mundial, an alliance of self-governing labor unions. In general, the workers looked down on the peasants as primitives and reactionaries, and looked beyond the middle-class leadership and its respect for private property toward worker control of factories and expulsion of national and foreign capitalists.

Revolution number 2 finally triumphed over revolutions 1 and 3 and established, between 1920 and 1940, the institutions of modern Mexico. How this came about, and from what social and historical depths modern Mexico has emerged, is the subject of John Mason Hart's probing and passionate book *Revolutionary Mexico*.

The United States' relationship with Mexico is, perhaps, secondary only to its relationship with Moscow, yet the disparity between the attention given to the world of the former Soviet Union and that granted to Mexico (and, by extension, to Latin America) is flagrant. As the power of both the United States and the former Soviet Union diminish and a post-Yalta multipolar world emerges, Mexico and Latin America are becoming less dependent on either great power, more closely allied to Western Europe and the countries of the Pacific Basin, and more closely knit among themselves as an Ibero-American community. Relations between the Americas will be vastly restructured in the next years and the next century, and nothing will be gained by mutual ignorance. Hart's book goes a long way toward dispelling myths and clarifying the process of Mexican history.

Mexico's history is sometimes presented as a layer cake: you can slice it evenly and in well-cut segments. The Indian world was conquered by the Spaniards in 1521, followed by three centuries of colonial rule. Political independence was achieved between 1810 and 1821, and dictatorship, anarchy, and the loss of half the national territory to the United States in 1847 ensued. The liberal reform led by Benito Juárez in the 1850s was the first attempt at modernization, but it was interrupted by conservative reaction, French intervention, and Maximilian's short-lived empire. Modernization without democracy was the hallmark of the long-lived Porfirio Díaz dictatorship, which began in 1876 and was finally overthrown by the revolution of 1910. The revolution itself went through an armed phase until 1920 and then through what has been called a constructive phase until 1940. A stage of growth and equilibrium seemed to have been reached, until the economic crisis of the 1980s, preceded by the political crisis of 1968 (the

Tlatelolco massacre), again threw the whole matter of Mexican history and its direction into question.

As in all layered pastries, nevertheless, beneath the icing lie the real goodies: jams, doughs, and chocolate creeks running up and down the cake. Hart's book is not about the icing or the slicing of the Mexican cake but about the way it is filled. Several ingredients are immediately perceived. One is the continuity of the social struggle in Mexico: the Mexican Revolution, one could argue from reading Hart, actually began the day after the fall of the Aztecs to the conquistador Hernán Cortés. The second is the tension, within that continuity, between the dynamics of modernization and the values of tradition. This implies, at every stage of Mexican history, an adjustment between past and present whose most original feature is admitting the presence of the past. Nothing seems to be totally canceled by the future in the Mexican experience: styles of life and legal claims dating from the Aztec or colonial centures are still relevant in our times.

It is one of the strengths of Hart's book that he not only understands the presence of the past in Mexico but organizes the mutual responses of traditionalism and modernization so clearly. He does this by distinguishing, beyond neat chronological slices, Manichaean melodrama (Mexico as a history of heroes and villains), personal theatrics (Mexico as the story of powerful personalities), and even changes of political administrations, a continuity of social groupings whose interests, at times concurrent, at times inimical, truly explain the dynamics of revolutionary Mexico.

I hope I am not simplifying too much when I single out the four groups that Hart subjects to intensive study: peasants, urban workers, middle class or petty bourgeoisie, and provincial elites. Hovering over them, at times distant and unconcerned, at times intrusive and often repressive, is the central state in all its guises: autocratic Indian empire, Spanish monarchy in its two phases—Habsburgs from 1521 to 1700, paternalistic, removed, but extremely wily at undercutting the colonial elites, and Bourbons from 1700 to 1821, interventionist, modernizing busybodies, convinced that the role of the state was to promote development. This triple tradition—Aztec, Habsburg, and Bourbon—was lost by the independent republic as, along with the rest of Spanish America, Mexico launched into its extralogical imitation of the laws and institutions of Britain, France, and the United States. The Mexican Revolution can, in a way, be seen (in this and many cultural matters) as a return to the source. The modern Mexican state—authoritarian, paternalistic, teleologically geared toward the achievement of the common good and therefore more interested in unity than in pluralism—is nearer to Aquinas than to Montesquieu.

Hart concentrates on the social and economic movements of Mexican history more than on the development of the national state, and he is right to do so, since his method permits the reader to grasp seldom-understood processes. The peasantry of Mexico, for example, is correctly seen as a traditionalist class, interested in restoring communitarian rights of land tenure and production derived from the pre-Conquest era and later confirmed by the monarchy's own legal vision of eminent domain. The relative equilibrium of the colonial era, as oppressive and as protected as it came to be, was radically destroyed by liberal activism in the nineteenth century. The liberal laws outlawing communal property led to massive land seizures and the dispossession of village lands by local landed elites; from this eventually sprang the *latifundia* system of the Porfirio Díaz regime, which vastly benefited the Mexican oligarchy and foreign, mainly United States, landowners.

Revolutionary Mexico minutely researches a little-known area, that of United States landed property in Mexico during the Díaz dictatorship. By 1910, it amounted to 100 million acres, including much of the most valuable mining, agricultural, and timber land and representing 22 percent of Mexico's land surface. The complexes owned by William Randolph Hearst alone extended to almost eight million acres. But by 1910, 90 percent of the peasants had become landless.

The Díaz regime began, in 1876, as a dynamic and modernizing administration. Hart describes it as broadly based in a country of 9.5 million people (Mexico today has ten times that number of inhabitants) and enjoying the general support of the middle class and the provincial elites until the end of the nineteenth century. But as the *porfiriato* permitted the development of Mexico to be defined, more and more, from abroad, the middle groups saw themselves cut off as major profits went to foreign companies. These foreign groups had a great interest in promoting exports but little interest in expanding the internal market.

This scheme, imposed on a basically agrarian society with a strong landowning class, resulted in a weak bourgeoisie, in crushed peasant and labor movements, and, finally, in a failure to incorporate the new groups—businessmen, professionals, administrators, ranchers—that the regime itself had originally fostered. The Díaz government transformed thousands of traditional peasants and artisans into agrarian and industrial workers. But it also had to establish powerful security forces to see to it that workers stayed deunionized, that strikes were broken, and that labor remained cheap. Repression, lack of opportunities, nationalist sentiments, susceptibility to economic contractions from abroad, claims to the land, and new claims to power finally brought peasants, workers, the middle class, and the provincial elites together in revolution. As often happens, the society had outgrown the state and the state did not know it.

Hart's lapidary statement that "the deeper significance of the Mexican Revolution" was that of being "a war of national liberation against the United States" distracts from the overwhelming fact of Mexico as a nation searching for itself through the contradictions and revelations of revolutionary upheaval. The Revolution as self-knowledge, the Revolution as a cultural event, is the most lasting legacy of what went on in Mexico between 1910 and 1940, and this event would have happened with or without the United States. It continues to nourish the arts, the literature, the collective psyche, and the national identity of Mexico more than any other single factor of the Revolution. Yet every other factor includes the cultural perception of self, searching back into precolonial times.

But Hart is correct in saying that Mexico's claim to revolution is justified by the transformation of property ownership that took place, from absentee to local control and from foreign to national ownership. The story of the political and economic transformation of institutions is told on simultaneous national and international planes. What the middle class and provincial elites of Mexico, engaged in revolution, finally faced was a campesino-and- worker-led revolution to establish a radical state based on popular power. The workers in the Casa del Obrero Mundial, over 100,000 strong, in 1916 defied a government that had just triumphed on the battlefield by staging the largest general strikes in Mexican history. Their aim was workers' self-government, a program that continues to send shudders down the spines of capitalists and totalitarians alike, since it shuns them both. Villa and Zapata were adamant in demanding wholesale land redistribution and direct self-government for the agrarian communities. As Hart describes it, "In the Villistas' wake, dozens of pueblos seized nearby estates and established collectives." Villa emancipated peasants, promulgated land distribution; in his name, thousands of lower-class rebels assaulted United States– and Mexican-owned haciendas.

Zapatismo proved to be incorruptible and undefeatable, and it constantly demonstrated its "capacity to replace the state with decentralized self-government" through a federation of free municipalities. And both the middle-class modernizing and centralizing leaders (Madero, Carranza, Obregón) and the United States saw in these movements the ultimate threat to their own interests. They tacitly banded against them, but naturally their respective sets of options differed. For the Wilson administration, revolution in Mexico came to represent an unwanted choice between two extremes. Washington had to accept the triumph of a collectivist, anti–United States, radical, and experimental, but also confusingly traditionalist peasant and workers' revolution on the southern border—or it had to accede to demands from powerful United States factions that intervention against Mexico, and even annexation of Mexican territories, become Washington's official response to revolution.

These were no idle threats. Between March and September 1913, the United States made enormous shipments of arms to the dictator Victoriano Huerta, in the hope of stopping the Carranza, Villa, and Zapata revolts and of giving Huerta a chance to reestablish those two gringo fetishes order and stability. The Wilson administration, Hart points out, repeatedly signed exceptions to President Taft's earlier embargo on arms to Mexico and only admitted the prohibition when it became obvious that Huerta, an incompetent and bloody tyrant, could not restore order.

The frontier was then opened to arms purchases by rebels, and this influx ensured the recovery of central Mexico by the revolutionaries and the overthrow of Huerta. Along with this, the Wilson government occupied the port city of Veracruz in 1913 and there amassed a huge arsenal of weapons. But as it faced a popular revolution it could neither understand nor control, the Wilson presidency also faced the pressure of United States interests affected by the Revolution and impatient to intervene. Foremost among these were the above-mentioned Hearst, William F. Buckley Sr. of the Texas Oil Company, and Senator Albert B. Fall, who asked for outright seizure and annexation of Mexico.

These extremes beheld their own imaginable catastrophes—not only a fear of lower-class collectivism, but a pre-Vietnam intuition of endless war, already foreseen by two generals, Zachary Taylor and Winfield Scott, in 1847, when they withdrew from the heavily populated regions of central Mexico they had conquered, against the advice of those other two noted interventionists, Marx and Engels, who believed, like Buckley and Fall, that the only good Mexico was a Mexico ruled by the United States.

Engels, writing in 1848, greeted, "with due satisfaction, the defeat of Mexico by the United States. This, too, represents progress. For when a country until then perpetually embroiled in its own conflicts, perpetually torn by civil wars and with no way out for its development . . . is forcibly dragged to historical progress, we have no alternative but to consider it as a step forward. In the interests of its own development, it was convenient that Mexico should fall under the tutelage of the United States. The evolution of all the American continent will lose nothing with this." The right to intervention that the superpowers have taken unto themselves in our time (the so-called Brezhnev and Reagan doctines) has deep historical roots in the nineteenth century.

Poised between pressures, Wilson chose the lesser evil: the middle-class and provincial elites led by Carranza. The Marines turned over the aresenal at Veracruz (artillery, carbines, bayonets, machine guns, rifles, pistols, cartridges, grenades, barbed wire, poison gas, and dynamite) to Carranza. United States ships supporting the Carranza faction entered the ports of Mazatlán, Manzanillo, Acapulco, Salina Cruz, and Guaymas, assuring the flow of supplies. Villa and Zapata were thus defeated. And so—as one reads Hart—was the myth of an immaculate Mexican Revolution that never received (as Cuba or Nicaragua did in more recent times) armed support from abroad.

But if Wilson had a problem, so had the middle-class leaders of the second revolution. They faced the double threat of a radical, self-governing, lower-class movement making it to power and, if Buckley, Hearst, and Fall were to be heard, partition, annexation, or at least the creation of a United States protectorate over Mexico. The middle-class leaders had to reformulate, in contemporary terms, yet another strand running through the Mexican cake like chocolate through a Sacher torte. This issue was nationalism, and even Díaz, who gave so much to the North Americans, felt toward the end of his regime that he had some redressing to do. He went out of his way to help the Nicaraguan nationalist president, José Santos Zelaya, against President Taft's interventionism, and, much to the chagrin of Standard Oil, Texaco, and sundry Harriman and Stillman interests, he gave the British the upper hand in what until 1907 had been United States preserves in the Mexican economy: oil and railroads.

President Taft was not pleased. The United States then backed Madero against Díaz. But as Madero had to ensure his own nationalist legitimacy, United States backing, as noted, shifted to Huerta and then to Carranza against the Villa-Zapata revolutionaries. But Carranza, who was forced to admit Brigadier General John J. (Black Jack) Pershing's punitive expedition against Villa in 1916–17, also had to balance that act with blushing coquetry toward Kaiser Wilhelm (as recounted in Barbara Tuchman's *The Zimermann Telegram*) and with refusals to reassure United States banking, mining, and oil interests of continued concessions in the future. Again, Senator Fall (who was to fall indeed as President Harding's secretary of the interior during the Teapot Dome scandal) was not pleased. The Obregón government, while more radical ideologically than the preceding Carranza administration, nevertheless reassured North American companies of their place in Mexico. The so-called Bucareli Accords of 1923 went so far as to guarantee the United States that Mexico would not apply its constitution retroactively in matters regarding property of the subsoil. Yet again, in 1938, President Lázaro Cárdenas fully restored the constitutional mandate and went on to nationalize all foreign oil holdings.

The conflicting class interests made apparent by the Mexican Revolution did not come to an end with the defeat of Villa and Zapata and the assimilation of their surviving leadership, as well as that of the Casa unions, into the second revolution. The constitution of 1917 was indeed, as Hart indicates, a result of the solidarity between provincial elites and the rising middle class. Yet that document had to make concessions to all social classes. The Mexican Revolution then went on to consolidate itself in government or, as a revolutionary general famously remarked at the time, "This revolution has now degenerated into a government."

Out of necessity, or through sheer political genius, President Obregón, in the early 1920s, gave the triumphant elite the chance to prove themselves as state builders, creating political institutions that would unite the defeated peasant and proletarian groups with the victorious middle groups. The new government needed to continue its alliance with peasants and workers because it continued to face challenges left and right, from restless campesinos, from the church, from army dissidents, from the remnants of the ancien régime, from the United States, and from the foreign companies. Throughout the administrations of Elías Calles and Lázaro Cárdenas, between 1925 and 1940, the army and the church were brought under control, the central government established its authority over rebellious military leaders, enormous advances were made in health, education, and communications, a modus vivendi was reached with the United States during the Roosevelt administration, and the former Villa, Zapata, and Casa leaders were given a say in the umbrella organization that survives under its present title: Partido Revolucionario Institucional (Institutional Revolutionary Party, PRI).

What would have happened in Mexico if Villa and Zapata had prevailed? What if the workers in the Casa had achieved their ends? What if the Revolution, indeed, had not occurred, and Mexico had been left to its own tides of evolution? Indeed, what if the United States had continued as a British colony into the twentieth century, or Russia had evolved under the czars? The questions are tantalizing but finally useless. As Hart comments, through the Mexican Revolution "the masses made striking gains, eliminating most of the vestiges of caste and archaic social relations that still plague much of Latin America and opening society for public education and individual mobility."

Nearly seventy years after the death of Zapata, Mexico again faces crisis and the need for change. Enormous development has taken place, along with great injustice. Again, as Mexico searches for solutions in economic modernization, it must also find them in political modernization. The society, as in 1910, has outstripped the institutions. But, once more, modernization cannot be achieved at the expense of the small agrarian communities, the forgotten world of Villa and Zapata. *Revolutionary Mexico* is a timely reminder that if Mexico is to achieve lasting growth, it must, at last, permit the strong central state to meet the peaceful challenge of self-government from below. The cultural element again becomes paramount, since the continuity of Mexican history implies an effort to admit the presence of the past, joining tradition with development.

5 : AGRARIAN MEXICO

. . . .

The Death of Rubén Jaramillo

On a lonely height, like a Mexican equivalent of the Inca fortress of Machu Picchu in the Andes, the ancient Toltec ceremonial center rises amid the ravines of Xochicalco. You can listen to the silence. The cicadas sing at dusk. Rapidly, hooves of goats descend the steps of the ruins. The buzzards caw over the remains of a dead dog. They do not manage to destroy the silence. It is a silence that protects and, in complicity with the setting sun, gives shape to the vast extension of the valley of Morelos. Xochicalco is a stone belvedere that dominates the undulating canvas of the valley, its lights and shadows, its various green hues. The pyramid seems to hang from the sky, and the sky seems made of huge dark blocks of fast-moving clouds. All of it, land and sky, is bounded by the clearly cut mountains, which have the shape of the breasts of the Roman she-wolf. Here Rubén Jaramillo died.

Who Was Rubén Jaramillo?

"He was one of us. He fought for us all his life. That's why he died, because he created powerful enemies. Listen, way back in 1938 Jaramillo was president of the board running the cooperative at the big Zacatepec sugar mill created by General Cárdenas for our benefit, for us, for communal farmers. Jaramillo decided to put an end to the old vices. He talked, he pleaded, he convinced the peasants to stop drinking, until he had to go into hiding, because the gunmen for the alcohol merchants threatened to kill him. Don't let them tell you tales! We'll always remember Jaramillo because he tried to help us and see that we got a square deal. He never asked a cent from us. He spent what little he had on us. He wrote down our pleas. He went with us to face the authorities.

He counseled and organized us. That's the truth. All of us in this region owe a lot to him.

"I met Rubén Jaramillo in 1942, but I had heard his name before. Back in 1934, at the convention of the ruling party in Querétaro, he made an appearance and spoke out for the peasants of Morelos. General Cárdenas, who was the party's candidate, spoke with him and said he would set up a cooperative for the cane workers in the fields of Morelos if he became president. Cárdenas kept his promise, and Zacatepec began functioning as a workers' cooperative in 1938. Things went well at first, but soon they went wrong. In 1942, when Ceferino Carrera Peña was manager, we peasants and workers got together to demand that he publicly explain how our money was being used. Rubén Jaramillo was our leader. Then the governor, Elpidio Perdomo, intervened and said, 'Hit the scum hard.' That's what we are to them, scum. After that, Rubén could not live in peace. The government sent people at night to menace and insult him. He fled to the mountains to protect himself, and about eighty or ninety of us went along with him.

"We were all defending ourselves, but of course when the army attacked we got tough and struck back. But we did not rise up in arms against the government. We were only defending ourselves. If we had stayed in the cities, they would have broken us. We also had a program like the government's, the difference being that they just talked about it. We had a program so that no one could accuse us of being bandits. And all the people in the hills were with us, helped us, gave us food, warned us when troops were near.

"In 1943, during a brush with the army, I was wounded in the leg. They took me to Mexico City and presented me to President Ávila Camacho. The president said he wanted to avoid bloodshed, wanted to solve the problems of the Morelos peasantry, and wanted to grant Jaramillo amnesty. I was taken care of in the military hospital, sure—well taken care of. And just listen to this: Jaramillo visited me several times. He disguised himself, came down from the mountains to Mexico City.

"Once, when state troopers were after us, Jaramillo and fifty-two of us went to Mexico City to see the Independence Day parade, and we mingled with the soldiers in front of the palace. Jaramillo had nerves of steel and he was courageous—as couragous, let me tell you, as his wife. He could be felled only by treachery. When I left the hospital I saw President Ávila Camacho once more and he asked me tell Jaramillo to visit him and gave his word of honor that nothing would happen. A few weeks later, there we both were. Jaramillo, respectful but firm, told the president that he was not a bandit, that he only defended the peasants. Ávila Camacho told him to go home, that his demands would be attended to. The president's military chief of staff, General Luis Viñals, said that first Jaramillo had to lay down his arms, to which the president answered, 'They will keep their arms to defend themselves against their enemies.' Jaramillo was not a man to cave in. One of the governor's cronies at that time told him to give up fighting and added, 'How much do you and your family need to live on?' Can you believe it, to ask such a thing of Jaramillo? Rubén simply was not one of them. He could have been one of those who grow rich and steal from the people, like Eugenio Prado, the worst manager Zacatepec ever had. But he refused.

"Things only got worse, so Jaramillo kept on fighting: two governors, Castillo López and Escobar Múñoz, persecuted him. In 1946, he ran as an independent candidate for governor. Soon after that, the army and the rural defense, at the service of the big landowners, tried to grab him during a peasants' assembly, but he managed to escape to the hills, which saved his life. For many years he was on the move, from Morelos to Guerrero to Puebla to Mexico State, always protected by people on the land. In 1952 he supported General Henríquez Guzmán for president. So over the next six years, while Ruiz Cortines was president and López de Nava governor, Rubén again had to be on the defensive, menaced and persecuted as he was. They tried to get rid of him at any price. But he just went on.

"I think there is no one living on these lands who does not love and respect him. When some of us became desperate because things just went on the same, Jaramillo would calm him and say, 'Have faith. New people are coming into the government.' But the people in government, old or new, always leave things for tomorrow. At first Señor Barrios at the Agriculture Department listened to our grievances; later he refused to see us and his aides wouldn't let us come in. They said he had gone to the opening of a new school, that he was having lunch with the president, so come back tomorrow, *muchachos*. We acknowledged he was busy, so we went on waiting, always waiting. But then we decided we were tired of waiting. Here in Zacapetec, things were going from bad to worse. We heard a lot of promises and then nothing. Jaramillo was demanding that the fields of Michapa and El Guarín be distributed to landless peasants—this had been agreed to. But this February the army came and threw the people out. The law was set aside— here the law is always set aside, especially when it favors us.

"I don't know who killed Jaramillo, but I think it was everybody with power, the rich, who want everything for themselves and don't care about anyone else."

The speaker is an old communal farmer from Tlaquiltenango. He is sitting at dusk in his miserable patio at the far end of a miserable hut. The hut is used for everything—cooking, eating, sleeping.

"The Chief Is Dead"

You can hear the silence. You can hear it even better when the guns crackle at the foot of the ruins, in the hidden place at the foot of the mountains. Perhaps Rubén Jaramillo, his wife, and his children knew that this was it, that so much silence was meant to be broken only in a lost ravine by the road to Teclama. They must have felt that crushing supernal silence preceding death, from the moment the lead-colored car stopped at the crossroads and turned away from Cuernavaca, where they told them they were going, and took the road to Xochicalco. Jaramillo tried to get up when the car accelerated. They hit him with the butt of a rifle but, propped up by his wife, he did not fall. Her name was Epifanía. Then the son, Filemón, aggressively defied the abductors.

"Shut up, kid, or we'll cut your tongue out."

"No, let's just fill his mouth with dirt."

In spite of his pain, Jaramillo refused to close his eyes. He needed them wide open to see, see until the end, see the land that rushed by hotly, brightened by the afternoon sun. How many times, returning to the hills, mounting his horse and taking his rifle as his sole defense and that of the campesinos who believed in him, had he not said, "This time they nearly got me"? This time they really got him. They were taking him away with his pregnant wife and his children. Maybe they thought that by killing off the entire Jaramillo family there would be no more Jaramillos to go on fighting. They did not realize that the death of five Jaramillos was the best fertilizer for the next five hundred, the next five thousand Jaramillos. That's what a campesino told us today:

"They killed our leader. Now we are all Jaramillos."

What Did He Fight For?

"Come in, please come in. If we had known, we would have prepared something. But please, be seated. I think we can offer a ranch tortilla, a salted dumpling. Later we'll go see how the rice is doing. Hurry up, ladies, something hot for these gentlemen. Now, don't worry, we do have cornmeal. Besides, our women are strong. Just look at that girl—she can make tortillas all afternoon. Yes indeed, we are very happy to be receiving you. When we receive guests, I almost feel like dancing.

"But today we are in mourning. Our leader is dead, though the problems are alive. And our problems, *señores*, are very ancient. They are the problems of all peasants without land. We've been fighting for a long time to achieve justice here. We have even lost whatever fear we had at the beginning. Like Valentina in the revolutionary ballad, I'm not afraid of dying; if they want to, they can kill me right away. We'd grieve for our families, for our friends—that's the only reason to fear death. But I tell you in truth, things are very hard in these parts. There's a lot of government these days prowling around Morelos. Now, after they killed Jaramillo, we are being watched more than ever, as if peasants as humble as we could be dangerous.

"Look at it this way: today you're here talking with me about my little rice paddy; well, this very evening your visit will be known to government agents. I knew the late Jaramillo when we began to fight the Zacatepec sugar mill. He came here many times, right where you're sitting he sat, and from where you are he told me what we had to do and what we would do when justice was done to us. The worst was the time of Eugenio Prado. Many campesinos were killed and we never received accounts of our earnings in the cooperative. That man Prado is still running around, he owns a lot of land.

"See, *señores*, if you look for them you'll find many large estates, many latifundios, and the peasants are still very poor. I owned barely half a hectare with the little rice you came to see. Is that what Zapata fought for? Is that why Zapata died? The sugar mill here has become exactly what the hacienda was in the times of Porfirio Díaz. The late Jaramillo used to say that the cooperative was created by President Cárdenas for the peasants and workers, but now the truth is very different. The truth is, we're worse off than in the old haciendas. No, maybe not. The truth is that the new manager, Merino Fernández, wants to help us. But he can't do anything—the board is the same, the people running things are the same. We don't get to elect the members of the board of administration and oversight. They should defend us, but they don't, because they're not part of our people; they are 'unconditionals' for the authorities. They're put there by the people who run things.

"Now they are saying that we're what they call Communists. Maybe we are. If demanding lands and saying that we don't want to be robbed anymore is Communism, then maybe we're Communists. Because all these guys do is steal. They have things pretty well arranged. They cheat us on the scales. We know what we take in to be weighed, but the scales at the sugar mill give different numbers. In the last ten years, the price for a ton of cane has risen only two pesos. Even after they took away Cuban sugar we didn't get a better price. The U.S. has given Mexico a better sugar quota, but we don't see anything. Only the managers make money. They cheat us on the weight of the cane, and we can't control the yield in sugar, alcohol, pressed pulp, molasses. The chemistry man at Zacatepec always 'discovers' that our cane is less sweet. We know it isn't so, but what can we do? All this means that we get lower and lower prices. They control everything, and we never know how much we earn or how much we save. And this is supposed to be a co-op! Every year they build some little thing—any old private house is worth lots of money—and since the manager says it is destined for 'social use,' we end up paying for it. The law around here has two standards, just like those scales.

"We have no democracy here. Promises are never kept. Our kids never get their scholarships; we never get health services. Sometimes they tell us to take our own representatives to the board, but it's useless. The manager only accepts the weak ones, and when a stronger guy comes around they soften him up with money. Jesús Vega is now our representative. We don't even talk to him.

"We met Jaramillo in the course of our struggle and we also met a certain José Martínez. I recall that Prado brought him all the way from Chihuahua, and he began to rise very quickly. Jaramillo had formed a cane workers' defense committee to fight Prado. First they tried to buy off the committee members, and then when that didn't work they tried to frighten us off. This guy called José Martínez was only a lieutenant then. He broke up our meeting in Zacatepec with rifle butts. He caught me and wanted to put me in jail but I screamed right into his ugly face: 'As Vicente Guerrero once said, death is unimportant when one is right!'

"On top of this, we were threatened by the military commander, General Cornejo Brun: 'Don't even think of getting together, *muchachos*, or we'll just machine-gun you.'

"In those days they killed Ocampo, the engineer who was our friend and told us about the crooked doings at the mill. When they killed him, they said the soldier on duty had accidentally shot off his gun. That's how hard things are around here, *amigos*. I don't care if they take me before a judge. If the government says the time has come for me to go to jail, I'll go quietly. I'll even go quietly if they tell me I've been sentenced to death. What I don't want is to be killed in the dark, with my family, like Jaramillo. Well, *señores*, don't let me keep you. I know you only came here to look at my little rice field. Who killed Jaramillo? I think you know. He was killed by the fight he led for justice for the campesino. Up there in Mexico City they talk a lot about freedom. Some fucking freedom!"

The speaker labors on half a hectare of rice and he talks to us in a small adobe hut, near a fire.

We're Not Afraid

No one cries. No one seems frightened. Maybe the only frightened men—though they try to hide it with their crooked smiles—are those criminal officers of an army that likes to call itself popular and revolutionary, those police agents in the service of local political bosses, big landowners, big businessmen. Rubén Jaramillo, his wife, Epifanía, and his sons, Ricardo, Filemón, and Enrique, never showed fear. All the men and women of the region told us so, all the people we interviewed in Tlaquiltenango, El Higuerón, Galeana, and Zacatepec. They knew how to laugh, they knew how to work, but they did not know how to fear.

The Whimpering Boss

"Once, when we were up in arms with Jaramillo, we caught the political boss named Angel Abúndiz, a man who does dirty rice deals and who set the police against us. When we caught him he began to shiver and cry. Jaramillo just stared at him, and later on he said, 'Don't be afraid, Don Angel, we're not going to kill you. We're only going to have you around for a little while.'

"The boss was so frightened he couldn't eat. Jaramillo just went on staring at him and then he said, 'Come, Don Angel, eat your tortillas. But if you go on crying, we'll shoot you.'

"Later, when we came down from the hills, we set him free. He learned nothing. He is still there, the little angel, robbing the campesinos blind."

The speaker, an old comrade in arms of Jaramillo's, lives in a hut near El Higuerón.

And Now Who?

The car leaves the paved highway and turns right, along a narrow road, toward Teclama. But it quickly stops beside a dry ravine, among the shrubs, the stunted trees, the dusty ferns, the abandoned sticks, the little piles of stones. It's four o'clock in the afternoon, and the mountain, crowned by the Toltec temples, courtyards, and ball courts, begins to cast its shadow over this hidden place.

They shove them out of the car. Through Rubén Jaramillo's eyes passes a river of memories and hopes. He must ask himself: And now who is going to defend them? Who is going to demand that the communal lands of Michapa and El Guarín be turned over to the five thousand landless campesinos whose rightful property it is, and not to the political bosses of Puente de Ixtla, Amacuzac, Huajinclán, Coatlán del Río, Tetecala, and Mazatepec? Who is going to see to it that when the new dams multiply the value of our land the bosses don't sell it to other *señores*, to new absentee landlords, new exploiters, eternal lords of agrarian Mexico? Who is going to fight so that the workers and peasants in Zacatepec have the right to elect their representatives freely? Who is going to clamor, day in day out, for schools, health services, profit sharing? Who, if they kill the bandit Jaramillo, the murderer Jaramillo, the delinquent Jaramillo, Jaramillo the criminal since birth, fighting since the time of Zapata for all of this?

He must have thought these things for only an instant. And then must have banished them, for they had nothing to do with his true faith, a faith shared with the thousands of men and women who followed him: that now all of them together would demand, oppose, fight, defend. The leader is dead. Now we are all Jaramillos. The so-called bandit died, killed by the real bandits.

Why Did Jaramillo Die?

"The hard part began in February, right on the fifteenth, when the soldiers threw us out of the fields of Michapa and El Llano. We had already been to the Agriculture Department in Mexico City and they were going to give us the land. But every time, something new came up—postponement after postponement. We had taken our census and we were ready. But when the politicians found out that these lands were going to be irrigated by the new dams, they found new pretexts and threw us out at bayonet point. There are 27,000 hectares of field. We were nearly five thousand men. We asked for only 14,000 hectares, and the rest should be given, we said, to other people as needy as we, poor and landless peasants. We would all have become friends. When the land is cultivated with love, it makes friends of strangers. We wanted the land for everyone."

The speaker is a young campesino. He is standing in a rice paddy near Galeana, water up to his ankles.

The Crime

They push him down. Jaramillo cannot contain himself. He is a lion of the fields, this man with a weather-beaten face, gray mustache, suspicious bright eyes, firm mouth, straw hat, denim jacket.

He throws himself against the gang of murderers. He defends his wife and children, especially his unborn child. They knock him down with rifle butts; they pop out one of his eyes. The Thompson submachine guns fire. Epifanía hurls herself against the assassins; they tear off her shawl, her dress. Filemón curses them, they fire once more, and Filemón doubles up, falls next to his pregnant mother, near the stones. He's still breathing when they open his mouth, take fistfuls of earth, fill it with dirt. Now everything happens quickly. Ricardo and Enrique fall, riddled with bullets; the submachine guns spit against the five fallen bodies. The gang awaits the final death throes. These people are taking too long. The men draw near with their pistols and point at the heads of the woman and the four others.

Once more the silence of Xochicalco.

The car drives away.

The buzzards flap their wings; the goats run.

"There's Nothing I Can Do"

"There was Rubén, on the patio, sawing a board to build a chicken coop. I saw the soldiers coming. One of them pointed at him with a machine gun. I ran and embraced Rubén.

" 'Don't be a coward,' I screamed at the soldier. 'My father has done nothing.'

"Heriberto Espinosa the Painter, who in other times had been my father's friend, came into the house and I blocked his way. 'You can't come in without a warrant.'

" 'You're right, girl,' he answered, laughing. 'You ought to be a lawyer.'

" 'You've sold Rubén out,' I answered. 'You're worse than Judas because at least Judas was not a murderer.'

"Captain José Jiménez called from outside: 'If Jaramillo doesn't come out, we'll burn the house down.'

"Our neighbors who were with us protested. A strong, hatless man wearing a yellow shirt and carrying a cocked pistol in his hand said to Jiménez, 'There's a family in there. You can't do this.'

"My sister-in-law, Filemón's wife, opened the door and a bunch of soldiers poured into the room, pointing at my father with their guns. The soldiers were distracted for a moment, so I managed to escape and run to the town hall.

" 'Ah, *señor!*' I cried at the mayor, 'they're taking Rubén off. We must defend him.'

"He answered, 'There's nothing I can do. They have orders from the attorney general's office. They're only detaining him. He'll be back in half an hour.'

"This happened on Tuesday at two o'clock. On Thursday people came to tell us that they had been killed, and on Friday I went to fetch them at the hospital in Tetecala. My mother and Ricardo were on stretchers; the others were just thrown on the floor. They smelled awful. Filemón, who was a very brave boy, had been disfigured and his mouth was full of dirt. They had given my mother twelve bullets, one of them in the forehead. Her shawl, her dress, were all ripped, bathed in blood. . . . They say that even the unborn baby was shot."

The speaker is Raquel, Epifanía's daughter, whom Jaramillo adopted. She was in her parents' house in Tlaquiltenango.

Xochicalco, the Altar of Death

At the peak of the mountain, in the center of the public square, rises the great temple of Xochicalco. A river of stone runs around its four sides: it is the frieze of the god Quetzalcoatl, the plumed serpent. The streams of liquid feather, the viper's long tongue, the thread of violence, embrace and devour the human figures of the frieze, as well as the sculpted jaguars and cedars. Life itself seems a prisoner of the deity. The eagles, carved on timeworn granite, cannot escape the serpent's coils. Rabbits fall dead at the touch of the poisonous forked tongue, and jaws devour suns the shape of seashells. The spirals, necklaces, shields, headdresses yield before this plenitude of barbarism: the centuries have not managed to fully erase the yellow pigment of this long, all-powerful symbology of death. An altar of stone, an altar of death, a bowl of sacrifice —what distinguishes this altar from the one rising at a bend in the road, next to the ravine, where five bodies lie in silence, where even the trees have been hit by .45-caliber bullets? Night falls on us. We look at one another without speaking. Epifanía had said to Heriberto the Painter, Jamarillo's Judas, "You feed on the blood of your brothers, and now our turn is come to be eaten by you."

The judges, the dignitaries, the priests are different; the barbarous part of agrarian Mexico remains the same, the terror of Mexico identical, nocturnal or daylight. On their golden thrones, the new powers of Mexico act out the old ceremonies of death. The governor. The general. The political boss. The deputy. The businessman. The crooked official. But they do not demand blood, as the powers of old did, to nourish the gods, the sun, or even nature. They do not kill to pacify the forces of the indomitable. They want blood to fatten their bank accounts, blood to steal the land of those who till it, violence to maintain in hunger, in sickness, and in ignorance the millions of Mexican campesinos for whom the Revolution is still a promise in the future and a lie in the present.

But this is not the barbarous fatality of the gods. This is injustice men and women can fight against. The injustice that killed Rubén Jaramillo and his family.

"When a Bandit Dies . . ."

"I have lost my son-in-law, Rubén, who supported my life; I have lost my daughter, Epifanía, and my three grandsons, Ricardo who was twenty-two, Filemón who was eighteen, and Enrique, sixteen. Rubén was sitting at a table when they came to get him.

" 'How are you going to take him?' I asked.

" 'My word of honor that no harm will come to him. Don't worry,' said the man with the cocked gun.

" 'He has habeas corpus, a paper from the president,' I answered.

" 'Well, those papers are worthless.'

"My grandson Filemón showed him the papers and the man took them and put them in his pocket, screaming at Rubén, 'Walk, you motherfucker.'

" 'How cowardly can you be, how vile?' I spat out at them, unable to contain myself.

" 'We're going to kill all the broads.'

" 'I don't care. You're a bunch of cowards.'

"Rubén had crossed his arms, like a lamb taken to slaughter. I knew they were going to be killed. I know them. They are vile, *señor*, they are cowards. That was the way that Rubén's brother

Porfirio died. That was the way they took Don Pedro López, Rubén's son's godfather. I knew they would never come back, and when they took them away, surrounded by soldiers, I prayed: 'Father, I give up the souls of your children unto your most holy hands. Thy will be done.' Rubén used to say, yes, he used to say: If you become a redeemer, you'll end up crucified. He was murdered because he helped the poor. The needy were always asking him, Please travel to Mexico City for us, please defend us; our lands have been stolen. He worked tirelessly for them. Sometimes when Rubén himself was poor they gave him a few coins for his trip or for the costs of the lawsuit. He never asked anything from the campesinos. He supported himself with his plot of land, planting a few tomatoes, a little corn, a little rice. The boys worked in the fields and Epifanía sewed and sold dresses. That's the way we got along. The governor would call him in and advise him, 'Look, Rubén, don't get mixed up in this business of the land. You've got enough to eat. You have your plot, your home. Let the fucking campesinos go to hell.'

" 'No, governor,' Rubén would answer, 'if I eat meat, I want others to eat meat too; if I have a plot of land and a home, I want others to have the same.'

"Not long ago a police agent who was not a bad sort said to him, 'Scram, we have orders to bust you.'

"Rubén didn't want to be a fugitive all his life. He wanted to live in peace and defend the campesinos. Now, in the Mexico City papers they paint him as a bandit, as a beast, but that's just another lie. When a bandit dies, he dies alone, but five thousand mourners followed Rubén to his grave. The mayor of Jojutla signed a check for 1,300 pesos to pay the funeral parlor for the five coffins; the check was covered by Reyes, Rubén's brother, who kept the plot and the rice harvest. They've stolen all our papers; they have cut off those who were the arms and legs of the unprotected. My daughter, ay, *señor*, was my only daughter. Last night I slept sitting up because if I lay down feeling so heartsick I knew I'd never get up again. I'm more on the other side than on this one and I need nothing, I want nothing. My people have given their lives to defend the poor, and I am content, but I have other grandchildren and must support them. Rubén's land is our land. We shall fight for it."

The speaker is Rosa García, Epifanía's mother, a woman of eighty paralyzed by deforming rheumatism and seated like a rag doll on a bench outside Rubén Jaramillo's bedroom.

The Sacred Writ

In the summer of 1962, a group of Mexican writers—Fernando Benítez, Víctor Flores Olea, León Roberto García, and I—visited the villages and rice fields of Morelos. We went to investigate and denounce another of the many crimes silenced by the corrupt Mexico City press: the death of Rubén Jaramillo. Now, decades later, I have transcribed some of the testimony we heard there. Let me add a little more.

Jaramillo's secretary received us in a simple adobe house. He was a middle-aged man, bald, with a big, curly mustache and the hands and face of a soft, dark Buddha. It was not easy to distinguish him from the peasants around him, except for two details that singled him out as a lettered person. The night was hot and sticky, yet he wore a black waistcoat and from one of its pockets jutted a gold-nibbed ballpoint pen. He was a gentle, proud man, sad and firm in both word and attitude.

Yes, the state authorities had told him to keep quiet. But he knew those who were responsible: an untouchable financier had colluded with the state governor, who, according to some versions, had been present forty-three years before at the assassination of Emiliano Zapata. All the interests ranged against justice were covered by the mantle of the Institutional Revolutionary Party. These were the financiers and investors who wanted to take over the lands defended by Jaramillo for the community, the political powers named from the center—local political bosses, shopkeepers, owners of bars and brothels, managers of sugar mills and corn mills. They were all good Mexicans. Honorable men. All good revolutionaries, all PRI members. Jaramillo had to die. The investors had already invested a lot. Projects had been planned, officials paid, political bosses persuaded. The lands would become a big country club with a big golf course and modern condos. Yes, they'd probably won once more. Yes, the secretary would probably have to flee and hide.

We were restless, indignant. He maintained complete calm, a

headstrong serenity. He looked at us, observed our city clothes, our blue Renault parked near the tropical patio bursting with geraniums, where hammocks slowly swung.

"Don't be nervous," he said. "You can't eat anxiety."

He got up and entered the house. A few minutes later, he returned with a worn-out black leather portfolio in his hands. He placed it on the table, untied the knot that held it closed, opened it. With extreme care, he unfolded and caressed the sheets of paper, old, almost golden with age.

"These are our titles to the communal lands of Tlaquiltenango. The land was always ours, since Indian times. The king of Spain recognized this. But then the lands were taken from us. Zapata fought to restore them. Here is his signature. They do not have these papers. We do. They prove our right to exist. They are now in my custody and I shall never lose them, even if it costs me my life."

He put the papers back in the leather folder and went back in the house. The next day, when we came back, he was no longer there. Where had he gone? No one knows! *¿Quién sabe?* The last Zapatista had fled with his holy writ, as if he knew that the enemies of the agrarian movement, by murdering Jaramillo, had achieved nothing. They had not been able to murder the papers, the sole concrete proof of a total reality: the papers so jealously kept by the little bald man meant shared life and work, memory, hope. Stronger than crime, the titles to the land were even stronger than justice, since justice itself could only be rooted in this piece of paper signed by an ancient father, the king, and by a sacrificed brother, Zapata.

I imagined the little secretary as an errant keeper of the seals, humble, hidden, anonymous, but secure in his knowledge that he held true power and sure of his eventual triumph, because he held between his hands the final proof of legitimacy: the written word.

6 : THE MEXICAN POLITICAL SYSTEM

. . . .

Seeds and Ruins

On a rainy Friday night in August 1988, following the national elections of July, Félix Salgado Macedonio, the Frente Democrático Nacional (National Democratic Front, FDN) candidate for deputy in the second electoral district of the state of Guerrero, went up to the podium of the national congress, which was meeting in its function as Mexico's electoral college, with two burlap sacks on his shoulders. From the podium, he emptied them, and thousands of ballots fluttered out and down. They had all been marked for him by the voters and then totally or partially burned by the authorities; Salgado had been deprived of his victory, which had gone instead to Filiberto Vigueras, candidate of the longtime ruling party, the Partido Revolucionario Institucional (Institutional Revolutionary Party, PRI).

Emptying his cinder sacks, Salgado was throwing a handful of volcanic dust in the face of Mexico's traditional politics, for the PRI, under three different names, has been in power continuously since its creation in 1929 in the aftermath of the Mexican Revolution.

His Ash Friday was successful. The electoral college corrected the official results, gave Salgado his legitimate seat, and consoled his PRI opponent, Vigueras, with another spot awarded according to proportional representation.

Remembering Salgado's ashes, I also recall the brilliant first chapter of Alfred de Musset's *Confessions of a Child of the Century*. Observing the transition from the Napoleonic era to the Bourgeois Monarchy of Louis Philippe, the poet reminds us that past and present are never totally divorced; both coexist in our own time. With each step we take, writes Musset, we tread both a ground of ruins and a field of seeds.

Ruins and seeds—Salgado's ashes fall on our Mexican land with a double meaning. One is premonition, the other remembrance. They are the ashes but also the long furrows of a vast political tradition fed by many other traditions and nurturing many fires. Behind the emptied sacks of the deputy from Guerrero stands the whole history of Mexico. And even if we wanted to throw the ashes to the winds, we could not extinguish the volcano of our political history or promise, as only the Bible can, that we shall demolish the mountains and elevate the plains.

Call it tradition, call it the past, call it, even better, the tension between past and present, between tradition and renewal—this is the way that the heart of Mexican history beats. Its systole and diastole have been, on the one hand, a centralizing, conservative, authoritarian, religious impulse, and on the other, a decentralizing, modernizing, secular, and democratic impulse.

The first, centripetal impulse originally appeared under the mask of the Aztec monarch, whose official title, the Hueytlatoani, or Lord of the Great Voice, described his authoritarian attributes. Moctezuma was the absolute proprietor of words; he had the monopoly on speech. The Spanish monarchy, after the Conquest, gave Mexico a vertical and authoritarian system not very different from Moctezuma's, but with an important difference: the central metropolis was far from the peripheral colony. Between 1521 and 1700, the Spanish Habsburgs were remote, paternalistic rulers of Mexico, although extremely astute in undermining any pretension to rank or to autonomous power among the Creole colonial elites. Then, between 1700 and 1821, their successors, the Borbon kings, were true dynastic busybodies, intervening, modernizing, centralizing, convinced that the function of the Spanish crown was to promote the development of the Iberian Peninsula and that of the American colonies was to furnish raw materials and cheap labor for the greater prosperity of Spain.

Under the Habsburgs, the colonial elites matched wits with the monarchy and created local systems of exploitation in the mines and haciendas and in the use—or misuse—of Indian and black labor. While Charles V showered the Mexican viceroyalty, New Spain, with laws proclaiming the eminent domain of the crown over land, water, and subsoil, as well as protecting the Indians and their communities, the Creole oligarchy proclaimed its own credo: the laws are to be obeyed but never implemented.

The distance between crown and colony, between official legality and concrete reality, between authority legitimately exercised and abused de facto, created a tremendous vacuum in the colonial institutions of Mexico. But politics, even more than nature, abhors a vacuum, and Mexico's was quickly filled by local political bosses and their clans—families, associates, cronies, bodyguards, hitmen, lovers—who actually governed most of Mexico, far from the will of the king in Madrid or even of the viceroy in Mexico City, imposing their personal whim on public laws and institutions. This system of patrimonialist patronage, as Max Weber calls it, continues to be rife throughout Mexico and Latin America at all levels.

The Children of Caesar and Saint Thomas Aquinas

There are two more factors, far more philosophical, to account for Mexico's political tradition. The first is that for three hundred years Mexico, along with the rest of Spanish America, went to just one political school, that of Saint Thomas Aquinas. The teachings of Catholic Scholasticism are engraved in the very soul of Mexican politics. Aquinas proposes a superior goal, the common good, as the true purpose of politics. To achieve that goal, all other values must be subjected to it, especially individual values. The community is superior to the individual. And the values of the community can be obtained not through electoral choice but by virtue of the unity imposed by one man—the monarch—in the name of all. Political grace, like divine grace, is not available directly. It requires intermediaries. The mediation of divine grace is the function of the religious hierarchy, affirms Saint Augustine in his historic dispute with the heretic Pelagius, for whom God's abundant grace was accessible to all mortal beings. Martin Luther and the Anglo-Saxon world are heirs to Pelagius, Rome and Latin America heirs to Augustine.*

The second defining factor of our political tradition is Roman law and Roman imperial practices. The great juridicial revolution

---

* See Glenn Dealy's original work on this subject in "The Tradition of Monistic Democracy in Latin America," *Journal of the History of Ideas* (July 1974).

that took place in Rome was the publication of the Law of the Twelve Tables during the fifth century B.C. This revolutionary act requires the law to go public and be known by all, instead of being subject to ignorance, whim, and tradition. In fact, the ruling principle behind the Twelve Tables was that ignorance of the law did not excuse noncompliance. But publication of the laws was also meant to eliminate authoritarian whim, even if sanctioned by custom.

Under the Caesars public law underwent a remarkable modification. The Lex Trebonia gave all power to Caesar, but Augustus, the first Roman emperor, also had to face socioeconomic realities and a basic political need: the law also promoted a meritocracy faithful to Caesar. Caesarean bureaucracy became the center of imperial power and the prod in Caesar's effort to strengthen imperial rule by encouraging strife between the nobility and the plebeians in observance of the ageless adage of *divide et imperas*. Thus Caesar could favor the patricians one day so as to undermine the populist demagogues and favor the people the next day so as to undermine the noblemen. Manipulation, but also compromise.

Imperial Roman policies, blessed by Catholic political philosophy, legitimized the Spanish empire. The price that was paid was the sacrifice of Spain's democratic medieval culture—its Cortes, or parliament, its independent judiciary, its protection of nascent middle-class economic interests. Spain's budding democratic tradition was thoroughly defeated by Charles V in 1521, at the battle of Villalar, where he suppressed the revolution of the Castilian communities. That very year, Hernán Cortés, a forceful representative of that same middle class, conquered the Aztec capital of México-Tenochtitlán. Its self-made men, defeated in the Old World, were triumphant in the New World. But if ever a conquistador wished to create a democratic system in the Americas, he never showed it, nor would the crown have allowed him such autonomy.

When Mexico achieved independence from Spain in 1821, three centuries after the Conquest, its liberal and modernizing thrust left the past behind. All new Latin American republics plunged into wholesale imitation of British, French, and United States laws and institutions, believing that simply transferring them to their own poor, exploited, and unjust soil would instantly create prosperity and democracy. This exercise in Nescafé democracy neglected one thing and consecrated another. What it neglected was that there cannot be a democratic society without cultural continuity. Independence meant the denial of a triple heritage: the Indian and African pasts, judged barbarian, and the Hispanic past, judged retrograde. Forced to improvise a nonexistent democratic culture, we ended by consecrating the idea of the nation as a compromise between defeated Spanish imperialism and separatist fiefdoms (*republiquetas* in South America) stimulated by the collapse of the Spanish empire (much as is evident in Central Asia and Chechnya, say, with the fall of the Soviet empire today).

Challenging the liberal dream, the Mexican conservative party supported the continuation of the colonial order. The liberals wanted a legal country, but their constitutional facades merely disguised the real country that the conservatives wished to conserve. In the ensuing tug-of-war, a politicial vacuum developed. It was filled by anarchy and discord, alternating with dictatorship and more discord. Mexico, says the historian Enrique González Pedrero, became the country of a single man, the despot and anarchist Antonio López de Santa Anna.

A nation adrift, Mexico lost half its territory in an unjust war begun by the United States of America in the name of Manifest Destiny and was about to lose the other half, assailed by the world's strongest army, that of Napoleon III's Second Empire. But a crown of shadows, set by the French on the heads of the unfortunate imperial couple Maximilian and Carlotta, was a hollow crown, and the conservative party, allying itself with the French and Maximilian, self-destructed as a political movement in Mexico and remained inactive for many years to come. The loss of Texas and California marked the final dissolution of the Spanish empire on the mainland of the New World. Only the islands— Cuba, Puerto Rico—were still Spanish and still to be lost, also to the United States. Spain and Spanish America, instead of forming the Hispanic commonwealth envisaged by Count Aranda in the Bourbon court of Charles III, became a pulverized victim of the ambitious and potent young lion the United States. The conquerors and conquered of the sixteenth century were united in defeat by the American colossus in the nineteenth.

The reaction against Santa Anna's grotesque and feckless dictatorship was the liberal revolution whose principal political figure was Benito Juárez. His success, first against the conservatives, then against the French and Maximilian, was the greatest triumph of the secular, modernizing, procapitalist faction in Mexican history. Juárez separated church and state, established the supremacy of civil institutions, stripped the church of its worldly goods and the army and the aristocracy of their privileges, which they had retained as part of the Spanish imperial legacy of colonial Mexico.

Juárez wanted to transfer these powers and privileges to a democratic, individualistic, and capitalist Mexico, headed by an entrepreneurial middle class. But two prices had to be paid, and they were so high that they frustrated the good intentions of the liberal republic restored by Juárez. First, the communal rights of the peasants and of the Indian communities were denied in favor of capitalist expansion. Peasant and Indian were once again reduced to slavery, this time in the name of liberal progress. Second, the centralist republic had to be defended, initially against the French intervention and the Habsburg empire, then as a political necessity. Progress had to be imposed from above on a dirt-poor population that was devastated by war and civil strife: democracy had to be postponed yet again so that an ancient, traditionalist, miserable, invisible nation could finally prosper, guided by its liberal elite.

Mexico's liberal republic became as centralist as the earlier conservative order. What Juárez managed to create—it is yet another of his multiple merits, perhaps the greatest of all—was a national state in place of chaos. Porfirio Díaz then masterfully milked this state for all it was worth, giving it an authoritarian, despotic, and yet progressive caste, which began by protecting the interests of the middle class but ended up by alienating foreign interests in Mexico. These, however, cared little for the country's social development and a great deal for obtaining quick returns on their exploitation of raw materials and cheap labor.

Díaz ended up a straw man for these interests, repressing the new social forces born of the nineteenth-century turmoils—local entrepreneurs, a proletariat, but also a very traditionalist peasantry. The result was strikes at the Río Blanco textile factory in Veracruz (1905) and in the copper mines of Cananea in Sonora (1907), genocidal campaigns against the rebellious Yaqui and Mayo Indians, slave camps at Valle Nacional, political prisoners held in the dungeons of the fortress of San Juan de Ulúa. Barbarous Mexico, as the U.S. historian John Kenneth Turner called it, had triumphed. Or, in the words of the Mexican historian Francisco Bulnes, the thirty years of the Díaz regime became a frozen chaos.

When the chaos melted, it became the Revolution.

The Revolutionary Compromise

The Mexican Revolution was an attempt—the biggest in our history—to recognize the cultural totality of the country, none of whose components should be sacrificed. The epic cavalcades of Pancho Villa's men from the north and Emiliano Zapata's guerrillas from the south broke the barriers of the traditional isolation among Indian and colonial Mexicans. And the revolutionary momentum of all the people the length and breadth of the nation created a sense of mutual recognition, of acceptance of everything that Mexico had been, and of the contributions that made Mexico a multicultural nation in a world itself grown more varied and pluralistic every day.

Make no mistake: the Mexican Revolution was as profound and decisive for the destiny of my country as the French, Russian, or Chinese revolutions were for their nations or the North American revolution in its two phases (first in 1776, then in 1861) was for the United States. The Mexican Revolution, says the historian Enrique Florescano, "was not an ideological mirage of change; it was real change, revolutionizing the state, violently displacing the old dominant oligarchy, promoting the rise of new political actors, and establishing a new time, the time of the Revolution."

Revolutionary time springs from deep wounds: one million dead in ten years of fratricidal struggle, an incalculable destruction of wealth. . . . Many of these wounds healed through the process of national self-recognition—the greatest achievement of the Revolution—the discovery of a cultural continuity that has survived all the accidents of history though it has never been faithfully reflected in Mexico's political institutions.

If nothing else, the Mexican Revolution was a cultural revolution. In thought, literature, painting, music, film, it showed its best face. Unlike the revolutions in China and Russia, the Mexican movement did not silence the voices of its creators or, indeed, of its critics. Mexico understood that criticism is an act of love, a manifestation of concern, and that silence is a form of indifference, even a death sentence. We are what we are thanks to the self-discovery of the revolutionary years. We are what we are thanks to the philosophy of José Vasconcelos, the prose of Alfonso Reyes, the novels of Mariano Azuela and Martín Luis Guzmán, the poetry of Ramón López Velarde, the music of Carlos Chávez and Silvestre Revueltas, the paintings of Orozco, Siqueiros, Diego Rivera, and Frida Kahlo.

Never again can we hide our Indian, mestizo, European faces: they are all ours.

Nevertheless, the time of the Revolution undeniably established compromise—in essence, to organize a country devastated by war and anarchy. The order of the day was clear after the promulgation of the revolutionary constitution of 1917 and the consolidation of revolutionary governments in the 1920s: Let us create institutions, let us create wealth, let us create progress, education, health, and a modicum of social justice. Yet, since we are good Catholic Scholastics, let us maintain unity against internal reactionaries, against the imperialist pressures of the United States, in order to reach the goals of the Revolution, the Thomist common good made possible by the intercession of the Augustinian hierarchy, this time incarnate in the revolutionary state and the revolutionary party.

Divine grace (that is, democracy) is not available to the faithful by themselves (that is, the citizenry), but tyranny is avoidable, military dictatorship is avoidable, perpetual permanence of men in power, the bane of the Latin American republics, could and should be avoided. The army must become subject to civilian authority. The presidency, though not renouncing the vast executive powers of the Indo-Hispanic tradition, should also be limited by a constitutional proviso: no reelection; all power to Caesar, but only for six years and only once. This is what Madero demanded when he began the Revolution in 1910. But along with no reelection, Madero's revolutionary banner demanded free elections. And these—transparently fair, credible—we have not yet established as normal, predictable events. Democracy in Mexico is still the exception, not the rule. Our people are fighting to make it the rule. We shall not rest until it is.

How the Compromise Worked

The Revolution, first an epic struggle against tyranny, became the tragedy of the Revolution against itself, devouring, like Kronos, its own offspring. The unity against the tyrant Huerta's usurpation was followed by a war of factions: Carranza against Villa and Zapata, Obregón against Carranza, and then, in the 1920s, a breakup into myriad guerrilla bands and numerous coups headed by disaffected generals, followed by countercoups, political assassinations, and round-the-clock work for firing squads.

After the assassination in 1928 of President-elect Álvaro Obregón—or rather, President-reelect Álvaro Obregón, after a reform of the relevant constitutional article—the former president, Plutarco Elías Calles, Obregón's comrade in arms and the self-styled Maximum Leader of the Revolution, tried to balance the warring factions. The Partido Nacional Revolucionario (National Revolutionary Party, PNR) was his brainchild, and his purpose was to make concessions to the defeated Carranza, Villa, and Zapata followers. While consecrating classic liberalism, the new regime opposed various exceptions to capitalist principles: it reclaimed the state's eminent domain over subsoil, land, and waters and made private property a concession determined by the public good. It recognized the rights of Indian and agrarian communities and, for the first time in Mexican history, gave the working class constitutional protection. This was the dynamic novelty of the revolutionary constitution of 1917, inherited by the Obregón and Calles administrations after the assassination of President Carranza in 1920.

I am implying, of course, that behind these extraordinary exceptions to the liberal model, whether the pure Juárez model or perverted Díaz model, lay continued homage to the Catholic philosophical tradition. Paradoxically, this was at the same time that Calles violently persecuted the Catholic Church. But the Revolution secularized Saint Thomas and gave to the national state the Scholastic attribution of the common good as the teleology of power. The supreme value was to be reached through national unity against internal reaction: against hacienda owners who welcomed the first rural schoolteachers with knives and sent them back, earless and noseless, to Minister Vasconcelos in Mexico City;

against foreign oil companies that paid mercenaries (known as White Guards) to attack union leaders and workers; and against the pressures of the Harding, Coolidge, and Hoover administrations.

Equally germane, the Roman heritage imposed itself on the Mexican revolutionary conscience in a most practical manner. There were, it is true, excellent written laws that publicly declared the ideals of the Revolution as well as its legitimacy. But a government has to deal not only with the legal country but with the real country, educating it, communicating with it, financing it, shaping it politically. The unwritten Lex Trebonia of the Mexican Caesars was very similar to that of Augustus: it created a powerful official bureaucracy, promoted entrepreneurial and worker organizations, and manipulated all three in favor of the executive's political power.

I am not implying that today's PRI was founded on the unholy marriage of Caesar Augustus and Thomas Aquinas. Nonetheless, its permanence in power, its achievements, and its failures are consonant with the truth that the party, a servant of the state virtually indistinguishable from the government, went beyond the liberal and conservative tendencies at odds throughout Mexico's independent republican history and fashioned a superior synthesis of both, a liberal and conservative politics, Christian but secular, revolutionary though reformist, traditionalist because it was modernizing, interventionist but laissez-faire. Official Mexican political eclecticism was as contradictory, and as fascinating, as the images of the Virgin of Guadalupe that festooned the sombreros of Zapatista guerrillas who, with nothing sacred in mind, assaulted the rural churches of Morelos. But then, had not the Virgin of Guadalupe been depicted on revolutionary banners ever since Father Hidalgo rose against the Spanish in 1810, and had not Spanish regimental officers ordered the image of the Virgin shot by royal firing squads?

One thing the party and government of the Revolution did not denounce, in spite of its capacity for synthesis, was centralism, the domination of political life from the center and from the top.

The Institutional Revolutionary Party, or PRI, then, which Calles had first called the National Revolutionary Party, had as its purpose to overcome the military factionalism that divided Mexico and turned every election into what the novelist Martín Luis Guzmán called "a fiesta of bullets." Calles wanted, he said, to replace individuals with institutions. Yet, between 1928 and 1935, he remained the power behind the throne, the true ruler of Mexico, as his stand-ins in the National Palace—Pascual Ortiz Ribio, Abelardo Rodríguez, and finally Lázaro Cárdenas—followed their boss's instructions.

After the assassination of Obregón, Emilio Portes Gil became provisional president. An astute politician from the Gulf state of Tamaulipas, he had energy enough to be his own man—to an extent—and to solve, in two years, at least three thorny problems: the granting of autonomy to the National University; the suppression of the last full-fledged revolt by a dissident army general, Escobar; and the end of the Cristero war waged in western Mexico by armed Catholics against the anticlerical measures of the constitution. Pascual Ortiz Rubio came to power in 1930 as a result of the first superfraud of the government party, stealing the election from the philosopher-statesman Vasconcelos. Ineffectual and ridiculed, Ortiz Rubio resigned in 1932, and yet another Calles crony succeeded him, the Sonora general and businessman Abelardo Rodríguez, who was interested more in promoting his business interests in racing, real estate, gambling, and other, shadier enterprises than in running the country. Finally, in 1934, General Cárdenas of Michoacán became president. Though considered yet another faithful Calles puppet, he expelled Calles from Mexico in 1935 and began his own energetic presidency, taking the Revolution to its most dynamic phase.

Between 1936 and 1940, Cárdenas gave the system its true form and content. He organized all the forces that had contributed to the Revolution—peasants, workers, the middle class—into corporations within the party. This was not merely a gesture. Cárdenas made sure that these organizations carried through revolutionary policies that strengthened the alliances of the social classes with the state and party and, through them, with the nation—its goals, its independence, its well-being.

Under Cárdenas agrarian reform not only gave land back to the despoiled Indian and agrarian communities but initially boosted production and freed the field workers from their immemorial servitude to the hacienda, plunging them into a vortex that has yet to be stilled. Millions of uprooted peasants migrated to the cities and became cheap industrial labor, others became drifting subproletarians at the periphery of the larger cities, while millions more began migrating to the United States and Canada. Yet another important fact is that three million peasants a year, once chattel of the hacienda system, passed from subsistence agriculture to working on cash-crop exports.

President Cárdenas's nationalization of oil in 1938; the creation of a national infrastructure in health, education, communications, and public financing; the protection given to official trade unions; the growth of industry and an industrial proletariat (abundant and badly paid); favorable tax breaks; and a captive consumer market isolated from foreign competition—all these finally led, after World War II and the astute manipulation of export-substitution policies, to the birth of an entrepreneurial class that, criticize as it might the rhetoric of the Revolution, handsomely benefited from the policies of the Revolution. Were they very different from the capitalists in the United States who railed against Franklin D. Roosevelt when the New Deal saved U.S. capitalism from the self-inflicted wounds that had led to the stock-market crash and the Depression? Cárdenas and Roosevelt were the two greatest reformers of politics in North America; Cárdenas constructed the house of Mexican capitalism, while FDR cleaned out capitalism's Augean stable.

Yet as capitalists flourished in Mexico, thanks to the Cárdenas reforms, so did the other social strata. This was the big difference between Cárdenas and his successors: he set the foundations for the 6 percent annual growth the Mexican economy was to enjoy between 1940 and 1980. Along with GNP, real salaries and purchasing power throughout the society also grew. And even if the upper and middle classes were favored, the working and peasant classes also received larger slices of the national pie than they ever had before or ever have had since.

Growth with social justice: this ideal became real under Cárdenas. But the other leg of the Revolutionary troika was missing, that of political democracy. Cárdenas gave Mexico a unique political system whose central players were the president and the party, both serving a national state that would eventually strengthen Mexico—so it was hoped—and save it from internal anarchy and foreign pressure. Was this the formula needed to achieve our cherished ideal of an independent nation? Cárdenas believed that he had, first of all, to set certain goals for and certain limits on the Mexican presidency. When he expelled the Maximum Leader, Calles (who boarded a plane for Los Angeles clad in pajamas, with a copy of *Mein Kampf* under his arm), the courageous young president (thirty-eight years old at the time) established new rules: the chief executive was to have virtually untrammeled powers while in office, but only for a single six-year term; he could not succeed himself but had the right—just as Augustus had—to name his successor. The dauphin, thus chosen, would inevitably become the new Caesar, given the party's practically total control over the electoral system. He would then, once inaugurated, exercise full powers for six years, reverentially respecting the non-reelection rule and designating his own successor—and so on ad infinitum.

For five decades the system worked. The nation periodically gave vent to grumbles: these were dissident candidates for the presidency in the 1930s (José Vasconcelos), in the 1940s (Juan Andrew Almazán and Ezequiel Padilla), and in the 1950s (General Miguel Henríquez Guzmán). Yet fundamentally the party did not permit its mad Penelope's tapestry to be unraveled, adding successes even as its failures began to show and changing its name to suit the times (becoming the Party of the Mexican Revolution under Cárdenas, and then PRI, as it has been since Alemán in 1946).

The PRI's biggest success was, of course, to establish social peace and political stability. As Latin America zigzagged between dictatorship and anarchy and as transitory democracies were repeatedly overturned in military coups, Mexico, on the southern border of a hegemonic continental power, maintained its constitutional continuity and its economic development. It was hailed, with no cynicism at all, as a miracle.

What is your greatest desire as president of Argentina? I once asked Raúl Alfonsín in Buenos Aires, when he was still in office. To conclude my term on the date foreseen by the constitution, the president answered. When was the last time that happened in Argentina? I went on. I don't remember, Alfonsín said. Fifty, sixty years ago? In Mexico, I shot back with a hint of pride, we have had nine punctual presidential successions since 1934.

Alfonsín did not achieve his goal. He resigned the presidency weeks before his term was up. In a nation of heterogeneous composition—racial, cultural, geographic, economic—Mexico achieved what Argentina, for all its homogeneity, could not: political stability, constitutional succession. Perhaps the very variety and contradictions of the Mexican experience forced us to search for synthesis and find stability, even at the price of democracy. Perhaps this was what the country, after twenty years of civil war and a million dead, really wanted.

The fact remains that for a long time, and thanks to revolutionary transformations—those so well described by Florescano—Mexico was capable of sustained growth, of creating a modern infrastructure, of establishing communications for a vast, isolated country, of freeing social forces that had lain dormant or been chained for centuries, of making effective a vast transference of property, of motivating an enormous movement of population, of creating modern social classes with state initiatives, educating a mass of illiterates, and promoting a new and energetic republic of middle-class and working-class city dwellers.

But soon this success turned against the system, as time, the government's sleepy complacency, and the limitations inherent in the system itself began the decline of the Mexican miracle.

The End of the Compromise

Why did the revolutionary contract fail? Why the sudden, steep crisis in a system that had been so successful (in comparative Latin American terms), offering six decades of political stability and economic growth in exchange for practically unlimited political power?

Between 1920 and 1940, the three great presidents of the Mexican Revolution—Álvaro Obregón, Plutarco Elías Calles, and Lázaro Cárdenas—governed, with intelligence and energy, over the transition from the old rural country, illiterate, semicolonial, isolated, to the new developing nation, conflicted, liberated, and ever on the brink of modernity. As I have said, agrarian reform liberated millions of peasants traditionally tied to the hacienda and gave them freedom of movement. Many migrated to the cities to become workers in industries activated by state intervention, by the nationalization of oil, and by the creation of infrastructure. But above all, the revolutionary state educated millions of once illiterate men, women, and children, and it was they, the country's ever more alert human capital, that started to give Mexico its new character, critical, conscious of its history and of its culture.

Lázaro Cárdenas culminated this process with a magnificent attempt to ally economic development, individual freedom, and social justice. After 1940 his successors stressed development for development's sake, growth directed by the government and its party, with the happy association of a capitalist class born with and from the revolutionary changes taking place. A few reformist measures here and there, now and then, were not enough to keep the system from growing rigid; it was dividing the country in two—a modern or modernizing nation, relatively prosperous and satisfied with the Mexican miracle, and a poor, isolated second nation, whose only miracle, as the poet López Velarde wrote, was to stay alive and hope for a winning ticket in the lottery.

What was needed to enable the forgotten ones, those left behind, the system's social creditors, to join the system? The condition set by Mexico's paternalistic politics was simple, if expensive: the state and the party would control the levers of national politics in the name of the common good. But when a lack of checks and balances and a lack of accountability began to transform the system's benefits into losses, when once liberating forces exhausted themselves and became forces for injustice, the system went on as if nothing had happened, celebrating itself, insisting on tried and true formulas that were worn out and could not deal with the new situation: Mexico's very growth, thanks to the policies of the Revolution, had now surpassed the Revolution. New social actors were demanding new freedoms, a new justice for new realities that no longer coincided with those of 1910, 1920, 1930, or even 1968, when the system started to fall apart.

The cracks in the wall of the Mexican Revolution became more and more visible. The revolutionary alliance between the state and the peasants, workers, and entrepreneurs lost both floor and roof as the centralist system proved less and less able to satisfy the growing demands of those less favored by development. The proletarian front broke during the Ruiz Cortines administration (1952–58) as it faced an independent workers' movement headed by leaders of the electricians (Galván), teachers (Salazar), and railroad workers

(Vallejo). Unity with the working class deteriorated further when López Mateos (1958–64) broke strikes, jailed left-wing leaders, and condoned the murder of the agrarian leader Rubén Jaramillo (see chapter 5). The middle-class and youth fronts also crumbled during the disastrous presidency of Gustavo Díaz Ordaz (1964–90), when several hundred middle-class university students were massacred in a "clean-up" measure prior to the 1968 Olympics; this infamous event in Tlatelolco Square became the breaking point of Mexico's system as we had known it. The utter incapacity of the rulers to answer a political challenge in political terms proved that the government, having no political answers, had only force to suppress dissent.

Alvarez Echeverría's highly rhetorical, well-intentioned, but severely limited attempt (1970–76) to heal the wounds of 1968 provoked a further rupture, this time with the entrepreneurial class, which he attacked with gleeful Third World enthusiasm while making its members richer than ever. Finally, the very illusion of progress shattered after José López Portillo (1976–82) promised Mexico unbounded wealth based on oil exports and brought inflation, debt, despair, and disillusionment. Riding the crest of the oil boom, Mexico contracted gigantic debts that it could not pay when the oil glut, followed by a plunge in prices, left the country without liquidity. In 1982, Mexico went broke. The miracle had become a nightmare.

The paradox is that, as so often, the successes of yesterday create the problems of today. The success of Mexico's public-health programs, for example, led to an explosive demographic problem. We were 20 million Mexicans in 1920 and the capital city had only one million inhabitants. Today Mexico City has as many people as the whole country had in 1940, and the country has 100 million people. The success of commercial agriculture impoverished small landowners, confirming John Kenneth Galbraith's assertion that when the equilibrium of poverty persists, distribution of land is not enough to overcome it. Betterment tends to be reabsorbed by the forces working to reestablish an accommodation with poverty. The social dynamic of agrarian reform, as I have pointed out, flooded Mexico's cities with workers, which in turn destroyed the delicate balance between cheap labor, government-controlled unions, subsidized services, and stable prices on the one hand, and on the other, growing benefits and growing concentration of wealth in the upper classes. As the equilibrium broke down, the latter won, the former lost.

And the extension of education, though severely undermined by demographics, permitted the people to perceive ever more clearly that something was wrong, that there was a serious contradiction between what was taught in the schools—a philosophy of development with justice and democracy—and what happened in actual life—development without justice or democracy.

In spite of everything, we continued to be two nations.

Between both, born from the first, wounded by the second, a budding civil society, stronger, more critical, better educated, more diversified, began to manifest itself. It did so once and forever, surprisingly, spontaneously, and even chaotically, in 1968. The complacent and authoritarian Díaz Ordaz government did not understand what was going on. It answered the social challenge with armed force. The Night of Tlatelolco, 2 October 1968, is the deep trench that divides the contemporary conscience of Mexico.

Twenty years later, the nation's civil society had made rapid strides. Economic disasters—oil boom followed by debt bust—had taken it closer to the second nation. Inflation with unemployment, a steep fall in purchasing power, and, above all, disillusionment— a general decline in the standards of living—came as a result of the greatest economic expansion that Mexico had ever known; during López Portillo's six-year term more foreign hard currency entered the country than had during the previous 157 years of independence. The crisis of conscience rapidly became a crisis of wallets. And between conscience and wallet, a political crisis took shape in the electoral process of 1988, which revealed the existence of an unheralded country, for whom the previously consecrated formulas of the government and the party had become irrelevant.

When, in 1982, economic crisis had ended Mexico's economic expansion and the revolutionary compact was definitively broken, another, deeper impulse to change had appeared. Modern social forces were present on the national scene at all levels of society— among the middle class, among bureaucrats, technocrats, students, intellectuals, women, and even, perhaps, among new young leaders in the clergy and the army (not enough is known about these last two institutions in Mexico).

This new society was not determined from above. It came from below, the product of better education and rising economic conditions and social hopes, as well as of worsening conditions, growing contradictions, and dashed hopes. And it did not radiate out from the omnipotent center, Mexico City, and its supreme head, El Señor Presidente. It grew at local, state, and municipal levels, from the northern states of Mexico's liberal tradition and from the gulf states, where European radical influences have traditionally entered Mexico. And not only from the various centers of transformation in the north and west but also from Mexico's central and southern regions, where unbalanced development highly favorable to the alliance between the bureaucracy and an overprotected entrepreneurial class had failed to encourage economic growth and social justice. The Chiapas rebellion in January 1994 confirmed this.

All these factors came together during the years of the Miguel de la Madrid administration (1982–88), and they colored the disputed general election of 1988, which saw a spectacular rise of both the left and the right at the expense of the once monolithic PRI. From the right, the Partido de Acción Nacional (National Action Party, PAN) reaped the harvest of many decades of struggle for democratic procedures and managed to disguise the reactionary nature of its antigay, antiabortion, proclerical social agenda. On the left, a splinter group of the PRI, headed by its former president, Porfirio Múñoz Ledo, and the former governor of Michoacán, Cuauhtémoc Cárdenas (son of Lázaro), joined other divided and dogma-driven left-wing parties in a National Democratic Front, the group that brought Salgado and his sacks of ashes to the congress. The more sophisticated urban votes seemed to favor Cárdenas for the presidency; the PRI had to rely on more easily cowed, traditionally isolated rural votes, while the PAN drew from its provincial Catholic reserves to back its own candidate, Manuel Clouthier.

The PRI candidate, Carlos Salinas de Gortari, won this decisive election by the barest majority, if at all. The PRI in 1988 had reached the ripe old age of sixty—sixty years of continuous power without the loss of a single presidential or gubernatorial election. But the important thing was that the election clearly demonstrated that the PRI was now only a part, not the whole, of Mexican politics, a party among other parties and liable to defeat on a level playing field. The field was far from level, however. When the government failed to communicate election results promptly, lamely declaring that the system had broken down, the general public attributed the breakdown not to the computer system but to the political system as a whole. Salinas was inaugurated under a dark cloud. Was his election legitimate or the result of a gigantic fraud?

Salinas had to legitimize his election, and he did so swiftly, energetically, even spectacularly. He decapitated the oil workers' union by driving out its powerful but corrupt head, Joaquín Hernández Galicia, aka La Kina; and he went forward, at a quicker pace, with de la Madrid's macroeconomic reforms, stabilizing an economy that had hit rock bottom in 1982, taming inflation, opening up Mexico's closed economy to the world, and concluding the North American Free Trade Agreement (NAFTA) with the United States and Canada. Through his able Solidarity campaign Salinas, until then known only as a competent public administrator, managed to reach the country and the people, spreading hope, seducing the collective will, and alleviating the social effects of harsh fiscal policies. In fact, no president in recent years elevated the expectations of the Mexican people so highly and so quickly. He left the presidency in 1994 with a 75 percent public-approval rating. His fall into universal rejection cannot be separated from the expectations he raised.

Salinas's initial successes did not change certain hard facts, which refused to yield to triumphalist zeal. In spite of market reforms, the economy did not grow, as it did in Chile (where comparable reforms took place) and Brazil (where there was no reform but where, in addition to inflation, there was major export). Mexico's social debt increased; diminishing it continues to be imperative for any Mexican government that wishes, finally, to reconcile growth and justice. But privileging the fight against inflation over savings and investment left the administration with no appeal but the hope that foreign investment would make up for the growing deficit. It did, and then it flew out, leaving the much-decried peso crisis of December 1994 in its wake.

The privatization schemes of the Salinas government dismantled a large part of Mexico's economy and concentrated wealth and power in what the president considered to be big, competitive conglomerates for our entry into the world scene. The losers were small- and medium-size businesses, lacking credit, and Mexican society as a whole, lacking the public investments that had once had repercussions across the whole economic board, stimulating further investment, employment, production, and a healthier balance of payments. Putting anti-inflationary policies at the head of the cart, and balance of payments in the driver's seat led to excessive dependence on foreign financing, with the results that today have become dramatically evident.

Furthermore, President Salinas's privatization program had the political effect of weakening the government and the PRI (twins in this matter as in many others) as sources of patronage. If the state and the party were not forthcoming in their financial generosity, their former clients would have to look elsewhere in order to expand and even to survive. But party hacks (the dinosaurs of the PRI) are not so adventuresome. More and more, they entrenched themselves to protect their old habits and vested interests. The PRI began to crack down the middle as reformists and dinosaurs pulled apart. But the two major opposition parties also showed signs of division. The Partido de la Revolución Democrática (Party of Democratic Revolution, PRD) succeeded the left's National Democratic Front as a legitimate socialist grouping. But instead of negotiating from the strength of its 1988 electoral showing, it wasted its fire in denunciations of the system, refusals to speak with the government, and a lot of preaching to the converted. The more modern, social-democratic wing of the party was often left high and dry by the intransigence of Cuauhtémoc Cárdenes, the party's leader, a man many saw as fit more to occupy a niche as a saint than to stand on a soapbox as a pol. The right-wing PAN was also divided between purists who demanded allegiance to the party's longstanding independence and those who saw their principles vindicated by Salinas's market reforms. How could one oppose a government that was doing what one had proposed for half a century? But the PAN was wiser than the PRD: it did not exhibit its wounds in public and began adding up notable electoral triumphs, including the first state governorship to be wrested from the PRI, that of Baja California.

President Salinas responded rather Solomonically, overturning PRI victories when opposition to them became too vocal and ending up with seventeen interim state governors: in 1994, more than half the country was governed by people who had not been elected. Known as *concertacesiones*, or concerted concessions, these measures might have been the basis for a more democratic politics of negotiation and consensus. They were not. A cloud hung over each *concertacesión*, causing ever more division and ill feeling among the PRI stalwarts; ever more smugness among the PAN's leaders, repeatedly favored by Salinas's concessions; and ever more bitterness in the PRD, signally scorned by Salinas but, even more dramatically, physically victimized by the government's security and repressive forces. More than three hundred PRD militants had been killed in confrontations with the army and the police by the end of the Salinas administration.

Salinas's reforms will be long and hotly debated. Measures such as privatization, the return of the Catholic Church to the political scene, and revision of article 27 of the constitution, dealing with agrarian reform and the culture of the *ejido*, or communal property, in Mexico were, and will continue to be, the subject of much disagreement.

All and all, Salinas remained well satisfied with himself up to the final days of 1993. The political commentator Jorge Castañeda and I had a long lunch with him on 22 December of that year. Salinas was, as always, full of energy, witty, nimble, amenable to dialogue, and supremely self-confident. Then, on 1 January 1994, all hell broke loose. The Chiapas rebellion was but the prologue to our year of living dangerously. (I devote a month-by-month diary to that year in chapter 7.)

Remembering the Future

Behind these events, other persistent realities survived in Mexico.

The crisis that began in 1994 showed that in Mexico authoritarian traditions, whether of Aztec or Spanish origin, die hard, as do populist legitimations and Scholastic rationalizations that go with them. Salinas stabilized the economy, building on the years of monastic discipline of de la Madrid. But democratic reform did not keep pace with economic reform. By the time the clock struck midnight, other factors—hidden, barbaric, born of the worst of modernization and the worst of tradition—had exhibited their corrupt and criminal symbiosis: terrorism and drug traffic, drug traffic and government, government and assassination.

There remains nevertheless a profound central reality in all this, and it is the reality of a new Mexican society yearning for democracy, besieged by ill fortune, but the beneficiary of the Mexican people's incredible capacity for resistance. Mexico seems to be able to survive it all—earthquakes and hurricanes, wars and revolutions, territorial mutilation, crime, and corruption. A marvelous country of tender and hardworking people, intelligent, modest, hospitable, and secret people, although at times, too, an enraged and sentimental people, prideful and resentful as well.

The writer Carlos Monsiváis asks that we not trust unduly in civil society but that we not minimize it either. Perhaps we can go beyond the traumas of 1994 and 1995 (foreseen, by the way, in my novel *Christopher Unborn* of 1987: literary fantasy in Latin America becomes realistic literature in a matter of years). We can turn to the society itself, the society whose future actions are incomprehensible without the integrity of an agenda of political democracy with social justice and economic growth. A living past is the best guarantee of a living future.

Can we postpone indefinitely the demands of the rural communities, the industrial workers, the urban middle class? Fear of change will pass, as will the identification of change with violence and of violence with a vacuum of power. What will remain are the social realities of Mexico, the legitimacy of the people's demands, the right to have democracy in the polling booth, justice in the courts, security in the streets, truth in the media.

There is nothing intrinsically wrong in having a new entrepreneurial class that can compete internationally and work in an interdependent world economy. But modernization will be as crippled as our picturesque one-legged dictator Santa Anna, and will give up as much as he did, if it disregards the situation of thousands of small communities and small businesses that still form the backbone of Mexico. Mexico is not a poor country. It is an *unjust* country. There is much leeway for greater fiscal reform. The upper 4 percent, who control almost half the nation's wealth, can pay much more than they do now. A tax reform in Mexico would do wonders for the basic purposes of achieving greater savings, employment, production, and higher salaries.

Modern rural Mexico struggles to increase democracy as well as production. At times invisible, always fighting an uphill battle, at times repressed, at others depressed, Mexico's rural classes have a history rooted in violence but also in traditions of self-government. Our town halls, whenever given a chance, have proved that Mexicans can rule themselves. The central state invariably intervenes to wipe out these democratic movements. But the Mexican village must now move beyond Zapata and proclaim loud and clear that there will be no good weather in the skies of Mexico if there is not first good weather in the soil of Mexico.

Indigenous movements, rural credit unions, collective-interest associations, leagues of communal production are all forms of action in the Mexican agrarian world that, united in the effective exercise of municipal freedoms, could prevent rebellions like the one in Chiapas. Perhaps the stage of redistribution of land is now over (the peasants of Chiapas would deny this), but what has certainly arrived is the age of decentralized organization of production, with legal guarantees.

The more successful collective farms in the north of Mexico have used credit and organized production wisely, permitting the workers to negotiate, both with the state and with commercial competitors, without being loaded down by corporate deadweight. They have a secret: they keep their earnings and use them effectively. Besides, rural associations share a goodly number of values. They are cohesive, they know how to discuss democratically, they are willing to resist state authoritarianism and local political bosses, they have good legal counsel. Their oxygen flow is greater, of course, in zones with richer production, not in the poorer regions. But the latter, unfortunately, continue to be the majority.

Furthermore, experience throughout the developing world has demonstrated that the rural poor, especially women, are good credit risks. Microlending to poor women in India, for example, shows that, for every hundred rupees a poor woman receives, she invests ninety-two rupees in children, health, and education; repayment rates are as high as 95 percent and defaults are never higher than 2 percent. Microlending to poor women in rural localities, which in 1985 had 1 million clients worldwide, today reaches 10 million clients. But the potential clientele is 600 million women, and all they need is an average loan of five hundred dollars to get moving, produce, and repay.

Can we hope that all these imaginative, decentralized, self-governing rural movements will take hold in industry, among unionized and nonunionized workers, the masses of the urban marginalized, and also among entrepreneurial, intellectual, and bureaucratic groups? Mexican civil society will have to move between two extremes: on the one hand, domestic frugality, reconciliation of change and tradition, increases in productivity, savings, and employment, with democracy from the bottom up, and on the other hand, international competitiveness encouraged from above, since to live isolated from the world has become, if not a defect, then certainly an impossibility. Of both realities, internal and international, we should make not only a necessity but a virtue and a responsibility.

At one point in the Salinas administration, the acute social commentator Gabriel Zaíd could state that the cashier's problems seemed to have been solved. Inflation was under control, foreign-currency reserves were large, parity with the U.S. dollar was controllable. But even then, as the 1990s dawned, the overall picture was not good. Apart from the extremes of wealth distribution, population continued to grow more than production, and production in 1993–94 did not grow at all. That same year, manufacturing declined 1.5 percent, textiles 7.4 percent, publishing 6.4 percent, and the timber industry 10 percent. The growth of the agricultural and service sectors was minimal, less than 1.8 percent.* And the cost of modernizing the infrastructure and establishing uniform norms for competition within NAFTA was forecast, in 1994, as a mere $23 million over the following five years. In any case, though, the financial crisis of December 1994 put an end to either possibility. This partial but ominous picture was further blackened by the appearance of narco-terrorism as a factor in Mexican politics.

Are we going straight back to our unending dilemma, that of being two nations? Are we practicing an archaic, savage capitalism, concentrating wealth in a minority and waiting for the impossible

---

* The figures are from the World Bank.

miracle of trickle-down from the first to the second nation, the cruelly excluded, sometimes patient, sometimes frightened, but sometimes rebellious nation?

Democratic action from below and economic justice from above can yet become the sources of a Mexican social democracy in which the state, the indispensable state created with so many sacrifices and against such odds in the nineteenth and twentieth centuries, can be limited by checks and balances, separation of powers, and efficient justice while retaining initiatives that, democratically controlled, strengthen rather than weaken it. The weakness of the Latin American state, the Spanish critic Ludolfo Paramio explains, is due to a hyperextension created by demands—on the part of workers, peasants, businessmen, the army, the bureaucracy, foreign creditors—that the state, finally, cannot satisfy. That is why the Southern Cone succumbed to military rule. Pinochet and the Argentine generals sacrificed social demands to the twin demands of political order and economic privilege. Mexico, besieged by external debt, had to make concessions to creditors yet managed to maintain important zones for her sovereignty. Will she be able to maintain these, not by administrating bankrupt enterprises but by finding a balance between the public, the private, and the social sectors? The obligations of the public sector—infrastructure, human resources, education, defense, foreign policy, monetary and fiscal policies—can be balanced with those of the private sector—investment, employment, productivity, commercialization—only by devcloping the social sector, the third, or intermediary, sector, made up of nongovernmental organizations: feminist and youth movements, gays and grays, rural co-ops, unions, neighborhood associations, religious groups, and volunteers. As the Mexican entrepreneur Manuel Arango puts it, voluntarism provides "private administration with public ends," tracing routes for both the market economy and the welfare state that complement each other. In the United States, 90 million volunteers invest an average of three hours a week without pay to attend to the third sector. How many people do the same in Mexico?

Héctor Aguilar Camín, the noted Mexican novelist and political commentator, is right when he says that whoever is capable of organizing the new relationship between the Mexican state and

Mexican society on democratic grounds will have found the key to governing the country in the twenty-first century.

The nation, as with Juárez in 1857, as with Obregón, Calles, and Cárdenas between 1920 and 1940, will have to reach a major new contract with itself, a contract that builds up strengths, extends benefits, identifies aspirations, and provokes enthusiasm. This will not be achieved by merely technocratic governments, narrow and lacking in vision. Rarely has Mexico demanded more greatness from those who govern it. Rarely, as well, has Mexico had fewer illusions that these men and women will be of the stature that the country hopes they will be.

7 : THE YEAR OF LIVING DANGEROUSLY

. . . .

A Diary of 1994

January: Chiapas, Where Even the Stones Cry Out

Before now, there have been two great uprisings in Chiapas, Mexico's poorest and southernmost state. In 1712, a girl named María Candelaria said she had seen the Virgin. Thousands of campesinos thronged to the site of the apparition. The church refused to legitimize the miracle and tried to destroy her altar. A revolt led by Sebastián Gómez de la Gloria and eventually joined by six thousand Indians flared up into a war of extermination against the Spaniards.

In 1868, another young girl, Agustina Gómez Checheo, reported that the stones of Chiapas were speaking to her in God's voice. The talking stones attracted many pilgrims, and the cult became a center of social protest. Agustina was jailed but Ignacio Fernández Galindo, a non-Indian from Mexico City, became head of the movement; he promised the Indians that he would lead them to a "golden age" in which their land would be returned to them.

The Tzeltal rebellion of 1712 and that of the Chamulas in 1868 could have been invented by a grandfather of Juan Rulfo or Gabriel García Márquez. Both revolts were crushed and their leaders executed—by the army of the viceroy in the first instance and by that of the republic in the second. The current uprising in Chiapas may also be short-lived.

What has lasted a long time is the dire poverty, injustice, plunder, and rape that since the sixteenth century have been the lot of those Indians who are campesinos and those campesinos who are Indians—that is, most of the people of Chiapas.

"The revolution did not succeed in Chiapas," states an open letter signed by the principal writers of this state so rich in literary and artistic talent. The revolutionary movement begun in 1910, which radically transformed Mexico's social and economic structures (less, the political ones), passed Chiapas by. Not only did the oligarchy not return the land to the campesinos, but it was further taken away from them, inch by inch, to benefit the cattle ranchers, landowners, and loggers who exploit Chiapas as if it were a colonial preserve.

And political authority? That is the issue. A state that could be prosperous, with fertile land aplenty for most of its men and women, is not—because the local authorities, thanks to the complicity or indifference of the federal government, are in league with the overlords of economic exploitation. Cocoa, coffee, wheat, corn, virgin forests, and abundant pastures: only a minority reaps their benefits. And the local government allows that provincial minority, with no national ties or identity, to do whatever it pleases. When someone protests, the government acts on behalf of the oligarchy —it represses, jails, kills, and rapes—so things will stay the same.

There could hardly be a more predictable recipe for a social explosion. The only strange thing is that it didn't happen earlier. That the authorities knew about the situation is proved by the fact that in recent years Carlos Salinas's Solidarity program has channeled substantial funds—more than $50 million—into the state of Chiapas. More than any other state in Mexico, Chiapas needs help: 60 percent of its people are still employed in the primary sector (compared to a national average of 22 percent), a third of its homes lack electric power and 40 percent have no drinking water, the illiteracy rate is very high and per-capita income very low.

The aim of Solidarity has been to alleviate the social effects of supply-side medicine and to promote local projects and a sense of dignity. But the Chiapas uprising has confirmed what many in Mexico already suspected: economic reform is fragile and even deceptive if it is not accompanied by political reform. If the flow of Solidarity funds into Chiapas had been accompanied by a political renewal, the current violence might have been avoided. As things stand, however, the good intentions of Solidarity were like water sprinkled on a beach: they merely vanished into the sand. A program like Solidarity requires a solid democratic context to be truly effective.

Democracy in Chiapas? How does one go about preparing such a dish? In my opinion, it should be served up with trust in the people, beginning in the smallest villages, where people know one another and know how to choose the best among themselves. Any democracy must begin locally. The centralized authoritarian system embodied by the PRI prevents real people, in their real localities, from organizing politically and electing their best representatives. In contrast, those at the center almost infallibly impose the worst. And no wonder: only they can work in tandem with the Chiapas oligarchy. Mexico's antidemocratic and unfair political and economic system must share the blame for the Chiapas explosion.

This system, if it wishes to renew itself, to persuade Mexicans that their individual votes count, and to prevent future explosions, must embark on an urgent process of reform. It cannot impose reform from above. It must learn to respect it from below. Federalism, limits on the executive branch, strengthening of the legislature and especially the judiciary, elections that are both clean and credible—only these will prevent recurrences of the Chiapas drama.

But there is worse. The great conservative reformer Benjamin Disraeli spoke of "two nations" in describing an England divided by the injustices of the first industrial revolution. Today, as the world faces the knowledge and technology revolution of the twenty-first century, Chiapas rises to show us the wounds of a preindustrial, in some ways prehistoric, situation, brutish and miserable. No, Chiapas is not all of Mexico. Despite flagrant injustices, both vertical and horizontal, Mexico has gone in sixty years from being an agrarian, illiterate country of submerged cultures to being a modern nation with a sense of its identity and possible unity, the thirteenth largest economy in the world—a country determined to achieve growth and justice.

The drama of Chiapas, however, casts a long and ominous shadow over Mexico's future. The stones of Chiapas still cry out, bespeaking the prospect of a country divided between a relatively modern, prosperous north, integrated into the world economy, and a ragged, oppressed, backward south. There is no Balkanization in Mexico; we have escaped that evil of the waning century. But events in Chiapas reflect situations of poverty and injustice that can also be found in other areas of southern Mexico, especially Guerrero and Oaxaca. Recognizing the drama of Chiapas, allowing political democracy to express itself there, and guaranteeing that social progress is not lost in the sands of economic oppression or swept away by the tides of political repression—these are important steps in ensuring that Mexico is not someday divided geographically and that it is less divided economically today.

There is a war in Chiapas. The entire country condemns the violence. First of all, that of the guerrillas. Their despair is understandable—but not their methods. Were there others? They say there were none. It is up to us, government and citizens, to prove to the rebels that there are. A political solution will be much more difficult, however, if the army is overly zealous and, mistaking Chiapas for Vietnam, defoliates the Chiapas jungle with high-powered bombs. There's no better way to terrify a population into submission, of course. The people in an indigenous village see the first shells fall as their forefathers saw the first horses appear; filled with fear, they surrender, preferring peace, even if it comes with poverty. But to accept fear as a basis for peace is to ensure that new uprisings will occur. Moreover, the army's image has been tarnished since the October 1968 massacre of hundreds of innocent students in Tlatelolco, and the army would do well not to harm itself further with an excessive use of force in Chiapas.

There can and should be dialogue, there can and should be political solutions in Chiapas, no matter how difficult in that cauldron of racism, liberation theology, Protestant sectarianism, economic and ideological exploitation, archaic guerrilla action. But the authorities now in place make a political solution hard. The current interim governor has demonstrated his incompetence. His boss, the previous governor, on a leave of absence, is the virtual head of the Mexican cabinet. They must both make way for a governor truly representative of the people of Chiapas, a governor who inspires trust and concord. Let the citizens speak in Chiapas, not the stones.

Only a renewed local government, supporting dialogue and conciliation but also determined to achieve justice and democracy, can convert the tragedy of Chiapas into the epic of Chiapas, the first step toward a parallel economic, political, and cultural transformation that might deliver Mexico—but not into that illusory First World meant to be ours instantly (like Nescafé) thanks to NAFTA, in force since 1 January along our northern border, or into backward and turbulent Central America, toward which we are dragged at the southern border like speechless stones. Chiapas must be a part, henceforth a representative part, an indispensable yardstick, of national development.

We should see Chiapas in Mexico, but we should also see Mexico in Chiapas; there should no longer be a separation between our economy and our politics, between development and democracy. The Chiapas uprising will at least serve to awaken Mexico from its First World complacency and self-satisfaction, while saving us from Third World poverty and self-flagellation. This will be decisive in the present election year. It is less important that Mexico's "international image" may suffer than that millions of Mexicans continue to suffer without homes, land, or water. It is for them that the stones of Chiapas have so emphatically spoken.

February: The Two Democracies Are But One

One of the most dramatic moments of the Chiapas uprising occurred in January, when representatives from the region's farming and indigenous communities met with President Carlos Salinas de Gortari in Tuxtla Gutiérrez to describe the injustice of their situation.

Alfonso Reyes recounts a trip to Andalusia with a Spanish philosopher who, after listening to the peasants, exclaimed, "These illiterates are so cultivated!" We might say the same of the Chiapas campesino Luis Herrera, who said to the president in halting Spanish, "You said you change society in Chiapas to make new, Mr. President. But nothing happened. Only stayed in words."

What is it that these profoundly intelligent men hope will change? Another peasant, Hernán Cortés Méndez, spoke of "the large-scale persecution of campesinos, the jailings and murders that have never been punished or solved." "Today, under current law," said Jácobo Nazar Morales, another worker, "all of us campesinos are potential delinquents."

Protests against these abuses have fallen on deaf ears. "I sent you a letter and have received no answer," says the Chamula Indian Domingo López Ángel to the president before describing in detail how the governments of Chiapas have protected the local *caciques*, the political bosses. In Chiapas we must reform laws, attitudes, behavior, and the mechanisms by which institutions relate to our people," adds Nazar Morales. "There must be respect for our ways of working and the structure of our organizations."

Alfonso de León, a campesino of rare wisdom from La Pijal Yacaltic, sums it up when he explains that he and the others do not aspire to egalitarianism but that "there must be room for all of us in society."

Room for all of us in society: this almost perfect definition of democracy has its origin in the profound ancient culture rooted in self-government that the extraordinary anthropologist Ricardo Pozas describes in his *Juan Pérez Jolote*.

That's the problem. The Indians and campesinos who spoke to President Salinas do not need the guardianship of the PRI; they know how to govern themselves. Their words destroy the myth cultivated throughout our history that they are illiterate and pre-modern children. Yes: these illiterates are cultivated indeed; with only a few words, they have shown themselves to be true "people of reason," as opposed to the putative monopolizers of reason— the ladinos, whites, and mestizos who are entitled to the sidewalk while Indians must walk in the gutter.

For centuries, they have exploited the working population of Chiapas and tried to subdue its millennial culture. Today that culture is expressing itself anew and speaks to us all with an inclusive understanding of modernity. There is no such thing as an exclusionary modernity. It must be inclusive. Chiapas has reminded us that we can continue to be only if we do not forget all that we are and have been.

Chiapas, however, has also revived or revealed the deep-rooted racism and intolerance of many Mexicans. I have heard many people of Mexican high society—bankers, media magnates and their wives—call for the liquidation, the silencing, of Chiapas's workers. How dare they wreck our peace of mind, this bunch of Indians who don't even own stock in Banamex or chalets in Vail, who don't even watch and appreciate Televisa. They're nobodies.

Now those nobodies who live in the shadow of Mexico have stepped out into the sun. And they have put their fingers in the wound: democracy is possible in Chiapas only if there is democracy in Mexico. And democracy is possible in Mexico only if there is democracy in Chiapas.

Democracy in Chiapas? The causes of the first post-Communist revolution, which began in Mexico this year on 1 January, are local and profound; they have to do with a situation of unresolved injustice, revealed worldwide by the fall of Communism. These causes continue to grow day by day.

They are ancient indeed, as we have all insisted. Some date back to the Spanish colony. Others are more recent: the end of the public-works programs in Chiapas; the fall of coffee prices, without the old subsidies to lessen the effect of fluctuations; declining incomes and living standards for not only campesinos but also the middle class and the bureaucracy; consequent radicalization; evangelization and liberation theology; the translation of Mexico's constitution into indigenous tongues; the revision of article 27 of that constitution, which, while trying to recognize failings and promote modernity in the countryside, completely sidestepped the existence of latifundios and eliminated hope for the many landless campesinos still grounded in the culture of the communal lands, the *ejido*. Zhou En-lai, the Chinese Premier—sounding like a composite of Confucius, James Bond, and Charlie Chan—once remarked that agrarian reforms never happen twice. Even when the reform fails, if it keeps alive the hopes of the peasantry it has been a true success.

In Chiapas, an entire campesino culture felt threatened. This dignified and intelligent people, increasingly aware of its rights, can and should elect its local leaders freely, for they alone can be held accountable. The problems cannot be resolved without democracy there, but it is true, too, that democracy in Chiapas cannot be effective without a national democracy it can join.

How? Through two great reforms of the Mexican political system.

The first consists in an effective federalism that, in Madisonian terms, extends the republic—that embraces everyone, makes room for everyone, as urged by the campesino Alfonso de León. How? Madison again: through a strong government subject to checks and balances, a separation of powers, and decentralization that allows local initiatives. Thus, federal reform is inseparable from reform of the executive branch and an updating of the balance between the branches of government. In this election year, it is impossible for the drama of Chiapas and its democratic solution not to affect the drama of Mexico and the entire country's democratic solution. The basic agreement reached by all political forces (similar to the Moncloa Pact that allowed the transition from dictatorship to democracy in Spain), the Twenty Proposals for Democracy signed by a group of citizens, and the six proposals for a credible election set forth by the PRI candidate, Luis Donaldo Colosio—these complement and reinforce one another.

All agree on the need for impartial electoral authorities, trustworthy electoral rolls, access to the media, spending limits, a ban on the use of government resources for partisan purposes, and prosecution of electoral offenses.

Colosio insists on an audit of the electoral rolls as well as on an agreement prohibiting penalties for the exercise of political rights. But the essential commitment is to be found in the parties' overall agreement. It must now be updated.

What cannot be done is to separate the Chiapas negotiations from the agreement on democracy. In the final analysis, if the problems of democracy are not resolved in Chiapas, they will not be resolved in Mexico; if they are not resolved in Mexico, there will soon be one, two, three Chiapas in Hidalgo, Oaxaca, Michoacán, Guerrero. But here I use the outdated vocabulary of Che Guevara, and the Chiapas revolution, among its other virtues, speaks a language that is fresh, direct, post-Communist. I would say that Subcommander Marcos, the Zapatista leader, has read more Carlos Monsiváis than he has Carlos Marx.

March: Mexico at Point Zero

The PRI has lasted longer than the Communist Party of the Soviet Union or the Spanish dictatorship of Francisco Franco. Like them when they disappeared, it has no valid answers to the nation's central problem: the gap between the country's economic, social, and cultural substance and its political institutions.

As the novelist Héctor Aguilar Camín observes, Mexico has lived through two periods since the Revolution of 1910: the phase of the caudillos lasted until 1929; the so-called Maximum Leader, Plutarco Elías Calles, launched the next phase when he founded the PRI. Now, says Aguilar Camín, it is time for us to embark on a period of *democratic* institutions as Spain did, beginning in 1977, with its Moncloa accords.

Four factors will determine the nature of Mexico's transition:

the rebellion in Chiapas, political agreements about electoral issues, the guarantee of democracy held out by President Salinas, and, of course, the fact that all this is taking place in a general-election year.

On 21 August, we Mexicans will go to the polls to elect a new president, a new congress, and many governors. But the fly in the ointment is that all our elections are burdened by a history of fraud and mistrust. Like all good brothels, the PRI has lived off the pleasure it provides—stability, in this case—and despite its reputation for constant fraud. But nobody any longer believes in its virtues, while its vices have become more obvious.

If the PRI long sustained itself through the double promise of internal stability and economic development, the Chiapas rebellion has shattered that promise. Mexico is on edge, dissatisfied; too many Mexicans have been left behind, and the successes of the macroeconomy can no longer conceal or resolve the harsh realities of the microeconomy. As Manfred Max Neff, the unorthodox candidate for the Chilean presidency, said to me last December in Santiago, "Nobody lives in the macroeconomy."

This is not to deny the achievements of President Salinas's economic reforms. Salinas stabilized an economy that had hit bottom; he curbed inflation, freed the state of deadweight, secured consecutive budget surpluses, and opened a closed, overprotected economy to free trade and global integration. All of this naturally created new challenges, new problems.

But the Salinas government was also convinced that economic reform from the top down would eventually improve living standards from the bottom up and would be enough at least to postpone demands for democratic reform. This belief was a fatal mistake. People in the government constantly pointed to the Soviet experience: one cannot, we were told, have perestroika *and* glasnost, economic reform *and* political freedom, at the same time.

Obviously, many Mexicans did not agree. Each election since 1988 has been tainted by fraud, postelectoral conflict, and the death of opposition activists, and each has invariably led to the designation of interim governors by the president. Of Mexico's thirty-two states, seventeen are currently headed by interim governors. This means that half the country's nearly 100 million inhabitants are governed by officials they did not elect.

We need a federalism that works, not the counterfeit paraded before us. But creating an effective federal system requires a true separation of the branches of government—a freely elected congress and an independent judiciary. This, in turn, requires accountability, checks and balances for the executive branch, and clean elections. A lengthy list indeed, a true challenge for a country steeped in authoritarian tradition.

Electoral reforms during Salinas's term gave the PRI automatic majorities* and left electoral institutions in the hands of the government and its militant operatives in the PRI. Demands for electoral reform began in 1993 but did not make headway until the Chiapas rebellion forced everyone to sit down and negotiate.

So Chiapas has been the catalyst. Even the rebels' wooden rifles were on target: Mexico's inequality is too extreme, the collusion between local authorities and local exploiters is obscene, and the ills of Chiapas cannot be solved without democracy.

Whether they like it or not, the government and its negotiator in Chiapas (Manuel Camacho Solís, the former mayor of Mexico City) must accept that the local problems of Chiapas and the national problems of Mexico are intimately linked. The people of Chiapas have recognized the imminence of a horrifying change: for centuries, they were exploited, but in the coming millennium they may simply be marginalized. I believe they would rather be exploited than marginalized, forgotten, abandoned to chance and to death, under the technocratic horizons of an integrated global village.

There are millions like them in other Mexican states, in Guerrero, Michoacán, Oaxaca, Hidalgo, Puebla, and Chihuahua, which I visited in late February. There I saw for myself the distress of the Tarahumara Indians and of the campesinos edging toward civil resistance. A sign from Subcommander Marcos could ignite many rebellions like that of Chiapas. How would the United States react to something it perceived as a security problem? The Mexican

---

* The argument was that if no party had at least 51 percent of the parliamentary seats, the country would be ungovernable; therefore any party that had at least 35 percent of the vote would automatically receive 51 percent of the seats. At the time only the PRI could even aspire to 35 percent, but today the rise of the PAN may make the PRI think twice about the wisdom of this ruling.

army does not have the resources to put out more than one fire at a time. Marcos knows that. So does Camacho. There must be a settlement in Chiapas. And that cannot but affect the national situation in an election year.

President Salinas, who in the first hours of the rebellion reacted classically by suppressing it with force, changed course the next week and—to his credit—rearranged his cabinet, named Camacho peace commissioner for Chiapas, decreed an amnesty, and laid the groundwork for national political negotiations. They are being conducted in Mexico City by the new minister of the interior, Jorge Carpizo, the independent and combative creator of the National Human Rights Commission. He replaces the discredited Patrocinio González, who—God help us—was previously governor of Chiapas. Salinas said he wanted to rectify past mistakes. No Mexican president had ever admitted to making any errors at all.

But now this young, energetic, and very intelligent president faces the greatest challenge of his career. Mexican presidents are always known for one single thing they did: Lázaro Cárdenas means oil, Miguel Alemán industrialization, Gustavo Díaz Ordaz the massacre of Tlatelolco, José López Portillo foreign debt. The labels categorize them once and for all. Until 31 December, 1993, Carlos Salinas would have gone down in history under the label of NAFTA. Since 1 January, his legacy bears the stamp of one word: Chiapas. But before leaving office in December, Salinas should take up democracy as his singular historical banner.

The negotiations led by Carpizo have a clear agenda. The electoral law must be reformed in a special session of the congress, to ensure that electoral authorities are independent of the government and the PRI. As the distinguished political analyst José A. Ortiz Pinchetti writes, "If the 1994 electoral processes were organized, administered, and ratified by autonomous agencies, the other innovative rules would become effective."

The rules mentioned by Ortiz Pinchetti would guarantee clean, fully audited, and current electoral rolls. The dead souls of Nikolai Gogol must not vote instead of the living souls of Cuauhtémoc Cárdenas. Limits must be placed on the parties' financial backing, and government resources should not be used for partisan purposes. Electoral fraud must be penalized. Access to the media must be guaranteed and equitable. Results must be made public in a timely and effective way.

The greatest problem facing Mexico's electoral system is that it lacks credibility. Indeed, many people consider there is no fraud only if the PRI candidate loses. Electoral reform must make the system credible enough so that people will believe it even when the PRI candidate wins.

A definitive step would be the presence of Mexican and foreign election observers. The former have always been accepted, but the government has traditionally rejected the idea of the latter. Accepting them would mean that the election could be monitored and corroborated by men like Adolfo Suárez, the former president of Spain, who oversaw the transition in his own country. Pierre Trudeau of Canada, Pierre Schori of Sweden, former presidents Raúl Alfonsín of Argentina, Oscar Arias of Costa Rica, Patricio Aylwin of Chile, and Julio María Sanguinetti of Uruguay—any of these would make even the incredible credible. (For historical reasons, Mexico does not accept observers from the United States, especially if they are former presidents. But the United States will be present through its ubiquitous news media.)

Negotiations in Chiapas and Mexico City. Reform of the electoral laws. The fourth card in this Mexican game of poker is President Salinas himself, who must now serve as guarantor of a democratic process. But a passive guarantee is not enough. I think the president has to take up the banner of democratic reform himself and campaign for democracy in Mexico with the same energy he invested in NAFTA. Will he? Can he?

This political year will be complicated and dangerous, though it is gratifying that the first part of the agreement between the government and the Zapatistas has been fulfilled. That which took years in Central America required but a few weeks in Mexico. But we must also recognize that Salinas made a mistake when he triumphantly vaulted over his own party members and named one of the three precandidates (Luis Donaldo Colosio, Pedro Aspe, and Manuel Camacho) presidential candidate by fiat. Both the PRI and Mexico as a whole would have benefited from a nomination process or precampaign. We citizens would have learned more about these three men and their programs.

Colosio was named not just candidate, but heir. Now, after Chiapas, he must establish his own credibility, independence, and commitment to democracy. He faces not only the traditional opposition forces of the right (the National Action Party, PAN) and the left (the Party for Democratic Revolution, PRD) but also a unique—not to say unnatural—challenge from within his own ranks. Camacho, condemned to political death after the president chose Colosia in November, rose from his grave when the president named him peace commissioner for Chiapas on the very day Colosio launched his campaign.

The country is abuzz with rumors. Will Camacho run for president or not? The issue is not whether he will replace Colosio as the PRI candidate—both are honorable men, and that course of action would be less than honorable—but can he be a viable *independent* candidate? Even without announcing his candidacy, he already has 21 percent of the intended vote, according to the polls of Miguel Basáñez, compared with 26 percent for Colosio, 21 percent for Cárdenas, and 14 percent for PAN candidate Cevallos.

In any case, Camacho's presence in the ring would make this the most hotly contested election in the history of modern Mexico. Camacho will not have another chance this year to advance his presidential ambitions. But Colosio could not ask for a better rival to make his own victory credible. Mexican democracy will hinge, however, not on these few men or even on clean elections but on a whole new culture of civil society, of nongovernmental organizations, cooperatives, and labor unions, of media and associations—of participatory elements in society come from below and from the periphery. This takes time. The year 1994 will tell us just how much—a lot, a little, or none at all.

April: A Vale of Shadows

The poet David Huerta sends me a beautiful line by his father, Efraín Huerta: "This fearful, vibrant vale of shadows that is our country." There could be no better description of Mexico at this time. The death of Luis Donaldo Colosio touched chords we did not even know we had. This good and decent man was moving rapidly toward a democratic transition. Colosio knew that clean elections in August were the only guarantee that he could govern effectively and carry out the political reform that lags far behind our economic reform, as we now see. His assassination enshrouds us, grieves us, diminishes us.

His death should have led his party to render him democratic homage. According to article 159 of the PRI statutes, "In cases of force majeure that necessitate the replacement of party candidates . . . the National Executive Committee may call for or authorize the holding of a special convention; if political conditions or an approaching deadline for legal registration makes this impossible, said committee may designate the new candidates." There was no room for exceptions. The rule should have been followed. The times required not precipitate action but reflection. This was a chance for other personalities to express themselves and for other themes to be heard in a party that cannot be reduced to two men and a ghost. The PRI does not lack for leaders better suited to the huge task of democratic transition than the chosen—or named— candidate, Ernesto Zedillo.

It will be argued that Colosio, too, had been "tapped," having been appointed by the president. But many Mexicans thought that was happening for the last time; they thought that democracy, like charity, would begin at home, emerging within the PRI the next time around. Two special tappings by the president in less than four months is too much for most citizens and certainly for PRI militants, treated once again like sheep. If this is the treatment accorded PRI members, what are the implications for the citizenry at large? What guarantees can there be that the worst PRI vices will not extend again to the political process as a whole?

In any case, Luis Donaldo Colosio had fully committed himself to democratic reform. Will his successor as candidate do the same? Many people have their doubts. His critics describe Zedillo as a chilling technocrat, devoid of political imagination or human warmth. He has the "lean and hungry look" of Cassius in *Julius Caesar*; "such men," says Shakespeare, "are dangerous." He himself confesses that speeches do not come easily. He lacks an easy charm.

But it's much more important that we know, first, Zedillo's commitment to democratic reform; second, his capacity for political tug-of-war in a presidential administration whose top priority will be politics, not the economy; and third, how credible his election can be in the "fearful, vibrant vale of shadows" that is Mexico today. In other words, will Zedillo's candidacy give the opposition a chance to win? There's no guarantee. The PAN has lost many of its mottoes, taken over and implemented by the Salinas government, but it still holds the card that first gave it popularity: democracy. The PRD is a heroic party: it lost hundreds of activists, killed in avoidable postelectoral battles during the Salinas administration. But its candidate, Cuauhtémoc Cárdenas, a not very charismatic man though decent, has a strange tendency to undermine his political successes and to rely on the opinion of his most extreme advisers.

Zedillo is a bad speaker, but he holds an ace. I fear that this time the elections will be won not in rallies or rhetorical contests but rather in a forum new to Mexico (though common enough around the world): the televised debate. And while Cárdenas and the PAN candidate, Fernández de Cevallos, mix better with people and make better speeches than Zedillo does, Zedillo has the weapons of mental detachment, an abundance of arguments, and access to the computerized data and statistics you need to win a cold debate in a hot medium. I don't sympathize with the ideas I know he holds—his extreme neoliberalism, his monetarist and utilitarian criteria, his lack of interest in universal public education. It's no coincidence that his candidacy was first backed, two years ago, by a Mexican magnate who saw in him the heir to Mexico's first conservative champion, Lucas Alamán.

But Zedillo does have the trenchant consistency of the Anglo-American conservatives who imposed their militant philosophies in England and the United States with such crusading zeal. Ronald Reagan routed Jimmy Carter, and Margaret Thatcher the Labourites; Zedillo, in Mexico, could well win a debate against his opponents and impress a mostly urban audience hungry more for security than for anything else.

The opposition has a chance to forge an alliance, however, with or without the PAN, by running a candidate who can attack the PRI on all fronts—in the streets, the countryside, and the television studio. This would require an abler politician than Zedillo, someone more informed, stronger in debate, more cunning in the use of the media.

The two best successors to Colosio, Manuel Camacho Solís and

Jesús Silva Herzog, took themselves out of the game because they played their cards poorly. They could have run successful campaigns not only for the PRI but, if needed, for the opposition, the nation, and its future. It's a pity. In contrast, a common opposition candidacy centered on Senator Porfirio Muñoz Ledo or any of the PRI's other attractive figures—if they left the party—would elevate the campaign, would give it a resonance and a credibility that would deliver us from our "vale of shadows."

May: Fatal Collision or Democratic Imagination?

We are indebted to Demetrio Sodi for his apt metaphor: two locomotives are headed for a tragic collision on 21 August; one is the PRI, determined not to lose power in Mexico after sixty-five years of national leadership; the other is the PRD, ready to denounce a PRI victory as one more fraud, albeit the most brazen, in a long history of electoral irregularities.

Once again, the matter of credibility is at center stage. Are the electoral reforms, under way or already implemented, compelling enough to eliminate doubt and make each side recognize both victories and defeats, including the PRI's loss of the presidency or the PRD's acceptance of a PRI victory? It is insane that a political system should be deemed democratic only if the party in power loses. The point is for everyone to believe in the democratic system, even if the party in power does win.

The defenders of reform say the Mexican electoral rolls are among the best in the world today. Will there be enough time before election day to finish the external audit proving it? The electoral reforms include limits on campaign spending. Does anybody really believe that Zedillo's resources are as modest as those of Cárdenas or Cevallos? The reforms also posit equal access to the news media. Will Televisa, the pseudomonopolistic giant of Mexican television, give proof of its democratic contrition between now and August and really open the door to news and debate from the opposition?

The law defines electoral offenses—including the use of government resources in support of a candidate—and their penalties. However, the PAN's accusation against Secretary of Agriculture Carlos Hank González—our *Tyrannosaurus rex*, the finest specimen in our Jurassic Park—did not stick. The PAN charged him with using ministry funds and official stationery for an open letter supporting Zedillo, signed by former ministers of state and reproduced in our leading newspapers. These allegations cast a long shadow on an electoral process that, to be credible, must adhere strictly to the law. But the rule of law is in no way abetted by hurried decrees that seek to fill long-neglected security gaps.

The year began, if not with a failure in security, at least with a minuet of mutual courtesies, as Gabriel Zaíd has described it. Did the government know about guerrilla activity in Chiapas and choose to do nothing, so as not to jeopardize the passage of NAFTA in the U.S. Congress? Did the guerrillas bide their time until NAFTA's enforcement on 1 January, so as not to let Ross Perot and other U.S. opponents of NAFTA hurl accusations of manipulation at them?

Whatever the answers, Carlos Salinas acted with common sense and democratic vision when he renounced bloody repression in Chiapas and chose instead the path of negotiation. Luis Villoro urged him to do so in a memorable article in *La Jornada*. We must remember this example—not the only one—of courage and responsibility in an intellectual of unique stature.

The peace process has conferred dignity on the indigenous communities and campesinos of Chiapas, has restated the issue of agrarian reform as a matter not only of land distribution but of productivity, employment, and justice, and has given Mexican democracy its broadest definition: for all and from below. The negotiations headed by Manuel Camacho Solís have reached an admirable, if critical, point: he who fires the first shot in Chiapas will have lost the war. It is incumbent on all of us in Mexico to ask ourselves seriously what we must do to avoid more Chiapas, so that resorting to violence is never a necessity for Mexicans living in despair.

The answer is obviously not to be found in the *capitis diminutio* of those institutions legally empowered to enforce the law. But the assassination of Luis Donaldo Colosio and the shadowy labyrinths into which its investigation has fallen have awakened in the government a paranoia by decree that takes away from the credibility of law enforcement. The appearance of that unconstitutional mastodon the Joint Security Agency undermines the attorney general's office, the Ministry of the Interior, and even the ministries of Defense and the Navy, stripping them of their lawful capacity to coordinate their efforts and imposing an illegal link in the chain of command, an intermediate power between the president and his ministers of state.

These factors, though encouraging in the case of Chiapas, in other areas can only arouse pessimism barely mitigated by the illusion that the heavy-handedness will eventually satisfy a hypothetical majority party, that of stability. How can there be stability in Mexico if the laws are not respected, if the promise of democracy is not fulfilled, if the desperate search for security leads only to greater insecurity?

The two trains are heading for each other at tremendous speed. To prevent a crash, to prevent postelectoral violence on 22 August, requires the commitment of all Mexicans of goodwill. The government has no better path to follow than strict adherence to the law, punishment for those who violate it, and respect for the pluralistic expressions of civil society. The society, for its part, has a chance to organize itself, to position itself at the center of the railroad track and demand of the trains' engineers: Don't run us over. Coalitions, strategic alliances, delegations able to make themselves heard by the three main candidates and the president—voices of concord, reason, and resolve—these are needed now more than ever to keep the trains from colliding, to keep us from even more unprecedented turbulence. Coalitions, alliances, movements helping to ground our options within the law, within an electoral process monitored by citizens, within a democratic debate among candidates.

Imagination. Luis Donaldo Colosio had it; that is why, in the days before his death, he concluded a strategic alliance with Manuel Camacho Solís for a democratic transition. The outcry against the former mayor on the day of Colosio's funeral does little credit to the democratic politics of the slain candidate from Sonora.

Imagination. Carlos Salinas de Gortari had it, also, when he responded to the challenge of Chiapas with instruments for peace and negotiation. He must prove it again in this acute phase of democratic transition. Salinas, and he alone, is president of Mexico until 1 December 1994. During that time he must act as president of all Mexicans—not as head of a party, faction, or generation.

He still has time—one hundred days—to go down in history as president of a democratic transition.

Imagination. The three candidates need more of it in their public debates. So far, they have stood out more for their dullness than for their brilliance. Debate gives them a chance to offer Mexicans what we all crave in this time of crisis and transition: a national vision that excludes no one, a nation that embraces everyone. Imagination is especially needed in a civil society, in its plural organizations, emerging bodies, representative individuals, and indomitable hope. If all this can be accomplished, we shall be able to ensure that the trains do not crash on election day; the locomotives will brake and stop, and at the station we shall all be able to climb aboard the convoy of democracy.

June: An Intermission and a Self-Interview

1. *Where are we?* I agree with Héctor Aguilar Camín's observation that Mexico has lived through two historical periods in this century, that of the armed revolution and that of revolutionary institutions. We must now go on to a third phase: that of democratic institutions. Of course, these three phases are not clear-cut; as in any other historical process, the past persists in the present and the present prefigures the future. The will to radical reform was already inherent in the first agrarian laws; the will to democracy was already a fact in Zapatista communities—all this in an armed phase that still persisted, even within the institutional period, with the Cristero wars and the uprisings of Escobar and Cedillo. Yet in the institutional phase, too, the will to democracy was expressed in Obregón's legislation, the Vasconcelos campaign, the continuity of labor union and agrarian struggles, and the watershed of 1968. That year marks the breakdown of the institutional revolution. It's a striking paradox: the offspring of the revolution demand from the government of the revolution what it had taught them to venerate: revolution, democracy, justice. Since 1968, governments have aimed more at saving the system than at reforming it democratically. Actually, our presidents have flirted with three alternatives: saving the country, saving the system, or saving themselves. They have mostly opted for the second alternative—and, in the worst cases, the third. In the best cases they have opted to deceive

themselves, believing that to save the system meant to save the country. Today, I believe, Mexico has decided to save itself.

2. *Are we being Latin Americanized?* Mexico had a radical revolution. This is what sets it apart from the rest of Latin America. We went to the very roots of the problems that have prevented a more just human development throughout our continent, problems of land ownership, education, health, communications, the creation of infrastructure by a dynamic public sector. Until the presidency of Cárdenas, a relatively fair distribution of income allowed all sectors of society to move ahead. Then the accumulation of wealth propelled us down paths we thought we had left behind. The argument that wealth could accumulate at the top and sooner or later would trickle down to the bottom has been our Latin American (if not Asian) model. This economic theory bolstered the structures of injustice and sweetened the pill with tidbits of well-being: import substitution, closely watched markets, highly protected businessmen, captive consumers, plus appropriate doses of education, communications, health. In the long run, the ECLA* model (to give it a name) was not sustainable. The state grew disproportionately to satisfy its voracious customers: businessmen, workers, campesinos, the armed forces, foreign banks. We became Latin Americanized inasmuch as the state became weaker even as it grew, incapable of satisfying all the demands of the various sectors. The most dissatisfied among them were the weakest; their aspirations were postponed. But successive shocks in the international economy—Vietnam and the breakdown of U.S. economic balance (guns and butter), Nixon and the departure from solid parities, the international banking system's shift from development to debt, the emergence of OPEC—kept us from satisfying not only the workers and even the middle class but our international creditors. We entered on a critical phase of shared collapse and decline. From Mexico to the Southern Cone, we were brothers in misfortune. Then we met again in yet another reprise of extralogical imitation: cactus Reagonomics, tango Thatcherism, a lack of imagination in achieving capitalism with a social chapter or a

---

* ECLA: The United Nations Economic Commission for Latin America, directed in its heyday by the Argentine economist Raúl Prebisch, the principal proponent of the theory I have just described.

healthy balance between public and private sectors. We know the failings of statism and neoliberalism. Why persist in them? We need a balance between the public and private sectors. How? Through development of the social sector, which is where Latin America is most dynamic today and which is the only solid basis for the development of democratic institutions. Mexico is no longer exceptional in this regard. It is unique today only insofar as its political institutions hinder the development of civil society. All of us in Latin America must find a greater affinity between cultural continuity, social dynamics, and political institutions.

3. *Chiapas?* Chiapas awakened us from our complacency. It reminded us of all we had forgotten. It forced us to rethink modernity—no longer in exclusive but in inclusive terms. It revealed unsuspected strata of racism in Mexico. It exposed the infinite bad faith of television's quasi monopoly—Televisa and its misanthropic ogre, "Tiger" Azcárraga—dedicated to deluding the "country of the screwed," as the said Feline calls us. It proved, once and for all, that democracy is always local: it begins in villages and towns and does not need orders from above or from the center.

The local uprising in Chiapas is but a part of three larger revolutions: the democratic revolution in Mexico; the labor revolution throughout the world, a revolt by millions of workers against their marginalization; and the political revolution following the cold war. This last now prevents us from labeling any movement for justice in Latin America as "Communist" and requires that we call it by its real name, as a genuine problem that we must resolve ourselves, without any terrified invocations of Soviet interventionism or continental security. This time, even Henry Kissinger has understood Chiapas!

4. *Free Elections in Mexico?* I hope there will be clean, democratic, open, and credible elections in Mexico on 21 August. We have many people to thank for this real possibility: Marcos and his followers in Chiapas, for having awakened us; President Salinas, for having responded to events there with dialogue instead of repression; Luis Donaldo Colosio, for his sacrifice; Jorge Carpizo, for his efforts as minister of the interior; the many sectors within the parties that have shown sufficient good faith to reach basic accord on organizing and verifying the election. In contrast, others have militated against the democratic electoral movement: Tele-

visa, with its scandalously biased coverage; reactionary and impolitic party sectors, especially within the PRI and PRD. If the PRI commits fraud or if the PRD insists there has been fraud even if the PRI wins fairly, we shall be playing out another scenario, that of postelectoral violence and, perhaps, a suspension of the results and designation of a provisional president, to assume office on 1 December. These are dark paths indeed, and I hope we won't be obliged to take them. Most probably, a new president will be elected with at most 40 percent of the vote, will have an even more divided congress, will have to negotiate with the congressional opposition, and will have to install a government for national unity.

The governing circle has been getting smaller and smaller. It must be broadened. The San Ángel Group gives some indication of the breadth and resources to be found among the country's thining political classes.*

5. *Democracy in Mexico?* Democracy is not limited to elections. Democracy in Mexico also means checks and balances for the executive branch, separation of the branches of government, federalism, law enforcement, education, tax reform, and respect for labor union, agrarian, and civil-society organizations.

July: Soccer Metaphors

The day before the Mexico–Italy World Cup soccer match in Washington, I was interviewed by the Rome daily *La Repubblica* and asked for a prediction. I predicted what I said would be the best outcome: a tie between these two battered countries, Italy torn by scandals, Mexico engulfed in a cascade of surprises. I was right.

By contrast, in the last forty years I have always been terrible at guessing who'd be the next president of Mexico. During my adult life, this has merely meant guessing which PRI candidate would be

---

* The San Ángel Group, formed in the spring of 1994, brought together many distinguished men and women, both the politically aligned and those without party affiliation, for the purpose of clarifying the issues and personalities of the campaign; it was an unusual venture in the politics of respect for the opponent. All three major candidates—Cárdenas of the PRD, Cevallos of the PAN, and Zedillo of the PRI—as well as President Salinas, came to its highly publicized luncheons. The result was a more civilized atmosphere during the campaign. The San Ángel group played an important part in avoiding the clash of trains I foresaw in May.

chosen by the president in office, assured as he was of a landslide victory whatever happened. Just listing some of the precandidates I presumed to support shows how pathetic my track record has been: Javier Barrios Sierra or Raúl Salinas Lozano in 1964, Mario Moya Palencia in 1976, Alfredo del Mazo in 1988. I fervently opposed one designation, however, that of Gustavo Díaz Ordaz. I had met him at a turbulent lunch at the home of the journalist Elvira Vargas and had immediately seen through him: his intolerance was born of basic insecurity, and he compensated for his lack of internal fortitude with defiance, drawing on the strength of others to bolster him. As is now said of him with dangerous admiration, he stopped at nothing.

Last year, depressed by my failures at divination and these tedious exercises in guesswork, I abstained from prognosis. But there was something else: I felt for the first time that we could no longer equate "PRI candidate" and "president of Mexico." In this regard, at least, my crystal ball was in working order.

The difference hinges not on guessing skills or even on superior will acting from on high. The change has come from below. What now keeps us from equating "PRI candidate" and "president of Mexico" is Mexico's civil society and its ability to act, exert influence, make itself heard. No more imposture, fraud, *tapados*—secret successors—and no more massacres like Tlatelolco. If in most countries of America, Europe, and Asia, even in the South Africa of apartheid, citizens can express their cultural, social, and economic substance and translate it into civic forms, why must we Mexicans be the eternal, oppressive, singular exception? Is there indeed, and unfortunately, no place like Mexico? Divination in Mexico, democracy in the rest of the world?

I watch our excellent soccer players on my television screen in Europe. They are doubtless an image of what is best in our country: they are young, dynamic, imaginative; they have ambition and determination. But the same could be said of Mexico as a whole. Whether with the Nobel Prize in literature awarded Octavio Paz, or the unprecedented success of the book and the film *Like Water for Chocolate*, or the music of Eduardo Mata and Carlos Prieto, the architecture of Ricardo Legorreta and Diego Villaseñor, the paintings of Cuevas and Toledo, the films of Hermosillo, Ripstein, and María Novaro, Mexico has a culture of universal scope that faithfully reflects the country's extraordinary social and economic development.

Our politics, though, do not reflect it. Our politics are separated from society. They are a succession of bets, rituals, fronts, blusters, and lotteries that feed on themselves and end up representing nothing and nobody. Zedillo can continue to polish his fellow Mexicans' shoes, as he did during the campaign as proof of his modest origins (omitting, of course, Indian sandals and bare feet); he can polish all the shoes in the nation, and Fernández de Cevallos can buy beers for all the bullfight fans in Mexico. These populist vaudevilles do not bring them any closer to the central drama: How can civil society and its representative institutions finally be brought together?

This was the dilemma of Spain after the death of Francisco Franco. Politics was one thing and society quite another; society was alive, politics was dead. Spain's political players—the Communist Santiago Carrillo, the rightist Fraga Iribarne, the Socialist Felipe González, and King Juan Carlos, holding the scales—all thought of Spain, not of their partisan interests; they forged the Moncloa accords and ensured a democratic transition for a country rooted in authoritarian tradition. Rather than fight the Spaniards, as we did in 1810, we Mexicans would do well, this time around, to imitate them.

Bernardo Sepúlveda, the minister of foreign relations in the de la Madrid government, eloquently recalled this Spanish transition at the first meeting of the San Ángel Group. This group presents itself simply as a part of civil society—not as a totality intent on becoming the supreme arbiter of the citizens' aspirations, which is how Zedillo characterizes any active pluralistic gathering. Will the PRI insist on seeing Mexico only through the lens of monopolitical unity, as it has since 1929? This is now impossible and undesirable, and it could be fatal if imposed by force. The country will not survive another fraud or suspicion thereof or any further deception.

The pluralistic groups that have formed and will form in Mexico are a positive force. They express concerns and wishes in civil society that for various reasons the political parties are unable to interpret. But they also testify to the fact that civil society, with its energy, sense of nationhood, culture, economy, and justice, is far ahead of both government and political parties.

This is a universal phenomenon. European citizens no longer fit into their parties; they have outgrown them and even burst them at the seams—notably in Italy. The contests have been even fiercer in the totalitarian regimes. The chained energy of Cuba or China will be released sooner or later—not from outside with Mascanosa's intrigues in Miami or Torricelli's capers in Washington—but as it should be, from inside.

The other Latin American countries, more flexible than we, watch Mexico's political situation with concern and alarm. They also, in varying degrees, are in transition. Wherever there are democratic institutions, the excesses of neoliberal policies can lead, by many paths, either to popular uprisings or to military coups. From the Caribbean to the Southern Cone, the question is, How much poverty can democracy sustain? The macroeconomic reforms of recent years must be translated into positive realities of growth with justice, productivity, employment, salaries, housing, education, and health. That is the Latin American challenge at this turn of the century, as Patricio Aylwin has long said in Chile and as Ernesto Samper in Colombia is now also saying.

Governments can no longer respond with authoritarian, centralist measures. And there can no longer be coherent policies based on the incoherence of electoral fraud. As it has in its culture, Mexico must now bring together its society and politics. Otherwise, like Maradona, we shall be booted out of the game.

August: Mexican Temptations

A postmortem of the Mexican elections tempts one, first of all, to indulge in psychosociological analysis. A country in which family counts more than society, Mexico voted for its father and mother: the PRI, an almost parthenogenetic sum of our need for parental protection. Never mind that our father beats us or that our mother has fallen by the wayside. What the hell, they're still our father and mother, defects and all. They keep us from being orphans. For sixty-five years they have limned our horizon.

If only they were better, less deceitful, less violent, more democratic. What they apparently cannot help being is "family," handing out positions, goodies, sinecures, rewards, reproaches, scoldings, and punishments. Wouldn't it be ungrateful of a campesino or villager to vote for the opposition when he's just gotten a grant from Pronasol or Procampo, President Salinas's welfare organizations?

Are we a country disposed to dynastic rule? We were governed by an Aztec monarchy until the fourteenth century; then, from 1521 to 1700, the Habsburgs had us eat at their table (leaving the small dessert offered by Maximilian, another member of the family, from 1862 to 1867). The Bourbons took up the dynastic mantle from 1700 to 1821; later, Porfirio Díaz gave Mexicans a home built so solidly that it felt more like a prison, and it weathered the next thirty years.

The PRI, with its hereditary republic, is about to enter the year 2000. It embraces us and leaves everyone an inheritance. Héctor Aguilar Camín has written eloquently of a forsaken people's need for shelter, and Octavio Paz of the Mexicans' infinite patience. Why, then, the sudden lightning bolt, the unforeseen eruption of Madero's revolution just two months before Porfirio's grand celebration of the Independence Centennial in 1910? Is it due, as Aguilar Camín suggests, to that sense of abandonment one feels when the roof disappears, the foundations sink, and one is exposed, shivering, to the elements? Revolutions in Mexico are a desperate craving for order and protection: the old roof has caved in, we want a new one. But "patient people" define the moment of abandonment. Two centuries of Aztec roofing, three of Spanish roofing, and sixty-five years of revolutionary institutional roofing.

A vote based on fear? In this, our year of living dangerously, the Chiapas uprising, Colosio's assassination, drug wars, growing personal insecurity, a stagnant economy, the deferred miracles of NAFTA—all of these, instead of favoring the opposition, have bolstered the PRI, our family and shelter. Is this a good enough reason to consolidate an old, a new, a final PRI government as we enter the new millennium?

Of course not. Almost half the country voted against the PRI and for the opposition. This fact illustrates the division in Mexico between its conservative, patriarchal, dynastic leanings (better an evil we know than one we do not) and its exhausted patience, its fighting instinct, its political ideal: democracy is the Mexicans' Tantalus; we are always hungering for the fruit that, seemingly just within our grasp, ever eludes us.

Two further temptations derive from this. One is the temptation to triumphalism of the PRI and its candidate; the other is the temptation to violence of the PRD and its own. Triumphalism and violence complement each other, but they both neglect the true postelectoral lesson for Mexico, which is that only setting forth and strengthening an agenda for political and social reform will save us from the unrepeatable traumas of this year. Elections should never again be a source of conflict in Mexico; if they are, the country may explode and identify those responsible for the explosion.

Groups within civil society like the San Ángel Group, which must emerge in other Mexican cities (now more than ever), are responsible for stating an agenda clearly and struggling for it—in order to banish the double temptation of Caesar's triumph and Antony's violence. Democracy is a process, not a single electoral event. But democracy begins at home, and nobody is more responsible for making it viable than the government and party in power. Of course, they have been its greatest enemies. Can one ask oranges of an apple tree? Yet there can be no democracy in Mexico if there is none within the PRI. The practice of *dedazo*, that tapping, that designation by big or small fingers, can no longer be endured. To make room for its best men and women, the PRI must elect its candidates internally and freely. This means it must fulfill a promise it has mocked as often as it has repeated it: a separation between party and government, an end to the state party. Not fulfilling this promise will cost the government and party dearly in years less traumatic than this.

Something more is required. The effort to organize 21 August and make it clean, an effort that reflected the demands of broad sectors within society, was marred by inertia within the official apparatus, as well as by attempted fraud at many other levels. Electoral authorities must multiply their efforts to expose and castigate these violations. And if there are governors who did not obey the president's order to abide by the law, they should receive exemplary punishment.

The persistent temptation of violence poses another problem: the fate of the opposition in Mexico. Outbreaks of violence will only strengthen the conservative leanings of the current majority; if almost half the country voted for the opposition, almost four-fifths of it voted for the PRI-PAN center-right, with the PAN tripling its 1988 vote and becoming Mexico's second-largest party.

But majorities are fluid and can move to the left—but only if the left moves toward the center. Although this might offend the left's theoretical sensibilities, there is no way to play politics other than to lure voters away from the PRI and the PAN. Doing so will require patience, but less patience without violence than with it.

The PRD should re-create itself so as to pursue its struggle from positions closer to the electorate and thereby weaken the PRI government and, most important, garner votes for a reformist platform, which the PRI government will not implement without such political opposition on the left—opposition that is not dogmatic, personalized, resentful. There can be no democracy in Mexico without an intelligent, modern, post-Communist political left. Social democracy? So be it. The PRI doesn't even get that far.

At the peak of its electoral power in 1988, the PRD didn't know how to negotiate politically and carry its strength into the crises of today. One can't shape politics with tantrums: Cárdenas couldn't in 1988; nor could Camacho in 1993. Politics is dialogue, negotiation, and one need not lose an iota of conviction or resolve.

If the PRI does not reform itself, this will be its last government. If the PRD does not reform itself, it will never reach the government.

I voted for Cuauhtémoc Cárdenas on 21 August. A highly respectable moral figure, this engineer has sufficiently proved his integrity and his courage to see reality and further the advance of the left he so fervently believes in. This advance implies a rejection of violence and a resolve to demand that the legal institutions fulfill their postelectoral role; it implies civic resistance against the abuse of power, reassertion of the national agenda from now until the year 2000, rejection of factional dogmatism (now, let us hope, on its way out), an opening and reorganization of the party, based on rational, balanced, and constructive elements. As the PRD's brilliant president, Porforio Múñoz Ledo, puts it, his party knows how to fill the streets; now it must learn how to fill the ballot boxes.

The temptation for all of us today consists in conducting politics against the fatality, fear, arrogance, triumphalism, inertia, and violence of our tradition. We believe in a new modern tradition that is inclusive and exacting—first of all, with respect to ourselves.

September: Who's Next?

The heinous assassination on 28 September of Francisco Ruiz Massieu, the PRI's secretary-general, has had a powerful retroactive effect: it keeps us from believing that the murder of Luis Donaldo Colosio was the isolated act of a madman. I have always been skeptical of conspiracy theories. I would rather not believe in them unless there is proof to the contrary. Now, though, I must subscribe to the hypothesis put forth by my friend Agustín Basave Benítez: we should believe in conspiracy unless there is proof to the contrary.

Last April, at a meeting at Brown University in Rhode Island, Federico Reyes Heroles gave us good reasons to attribute Colosio's death to a drug syndicate—ominous, masked, and symbiotically joined to the structures of Mexico's government and the PRI. The death of Ruiz Massieu seems to confirm this. Day by day, more sewage, more criminal associations, more sinister schemes and complicities are being revealed. They point toward something the Colombians already know all too well: anyone who effectively opposes the hegemony of the narco-structure will be cut down.

Many have fallen in Colombia since 1984 alone: Rodrigo Lara Bonilla, the minister of justice; Jaime Pardo Leal, the leader of the Patriotic Union (UP); Carlos Mauro Hoyo, the attorney general; Bernardo Jaramillo, Luis Carlos Galán, and Carlos Pizarro Leongómez, presidential candidates; Álvaro Medina and María Díaz Pérez, judges in the Escobar case; Antonio Roldán Betancur, the governor of Antioquia; and Guillermo Cano, the director of the daily *El Espectador*. These are brutal examples. The reader can draw up his own cast of characters for Mexico. Who's next?

I will be indiscreet. During a dinner with President Bill Clinton that I attended last August on Martha's Vineyard, Gabriel García Márquez forcefully presented his Colombian homeland's argument. Why is drug supply prosecuted so vigorously and demand so leniently? Who in the United States is receiving drugs from Colombia, laundering the money, marketing drugs every day to 30 million U.S. citizens, bribing lawyers, the police, and politicians? There must be U.S. drug barons far more powerful than any Colombian trafficker. But the people who are dying are those fighting them in Colombia, not in the United States.

Clinton replied that the anticrime bill he had sent to Congress, which finally passed after a difficult debate, was the surest weapon for reinforcing the struggle against the criminals García Márquez cited. We all knew with what integrity Clinton had defended his anticrime legislation; he is the first U.S. president to take a stand against the powerful and fearsome National Rifle Association, which defends its agenda on a perverted interpretation of the constitutional right to bear arms. The end result is that in the United States, teenage street gangs are better armed than the police.

Is it a coincidence that the PRI's secretary-general should have been murdered three days after his brother, Deputy Attorney General Mario Ruiz Massieu, announced a vigorous campaign against drug trafficking? Is it a coincidence that just a few days earlier the Treasury secretaries of Mexico and the United States, Pedro Aspe and Lloyd Bentsen, launched Operation Cobra to curtail the money laundering associated with drug trafficking?

A few months ago I signed a proposal drafted by García Márquez to decriminalize the use of drugs and thus to leave the drug barons declawed—as U.S. bootleggers had been left by the repeal of the Volstead Act, which in the 1920s banned alcohol consumption with such unfortunate results. No government today can, or is yet willing to, hear reason on this. But society does have an interest in emphasizing motive, so as to neutralize this poisonous threat posed by the cobras of the world.

In the meantime, the death of Ruiz Massieu has interrupted Mexico's postelectoral process, the testing of legal channels to uncover, and provide punishment for, voting irregularities, the beginnings of dialogue, the ratification of the elections—and it weakens both the outgoing and the incoming governments. It also reveals a huge gap at the very heart of Mexico's intelligence and security systems. But security requirements should never, under any circumstance, affect the requirements of freedom. We must now add to the long agenda for democratic reform in Mexico this priority: security with liberty.

And with justice. These events, so upsetting to us all, are also the responsibility of a notoriously ineffective, slow, and corrupt judicial apparatus. Nothing harms the implementation of NAFTA more than foreign investors' lack of confidence in the bedeviled Mexican judicial system. No wonder the World Bank, in a report on Mexico's prospects for the late 1990s, emphasized and criticized "shortcomings in the commercial juridical framework and dispute-settlement mechanisms, which constitute important limitations to the development of the private sector." The bank added that Mexican legal procedures are "lengthy, costly, and unpredictable," partly because of "an unacceptably low level of competence and integrity among judges."

Confronted by such serious events, our country will need all its political, intellectual, moral, and juridical capacity to recover—to save—the national project. If we can defeat the enemies of Luis Donaldo Colosio and Francisco Ruiz Massieu, the sacrifices of these two men will not have been in vain.

October: The Unfinished Time

The year of living dangerously is still not over and no one in Mexico can guess what surprises await us between now and 1 January. One date stands out from all the rest: on 1 December, Ernesto Zedillo Ponce de León will presumably take over the presidency from his predecessor, Carlos Salinas de Gortari. But even this assumption, a fact of life in Mexico since Lázaro Cárdenas received the presidential sash from Abelardo Rodríguez in 1934, is now uncertain. From now until 1 December, too many dangers loom.

The increasingly open alliance between drug traffickers and political power groups is the most serious and visible one; internal disputes within the PRI complicate and exacerbate it. Despite all the declarations of unity proffered by Ignacio Pichardo Pagaza, the PRI's president, the country can now see the intraparty struggle with its own eyes. Reformist groups are pitted against inveterate dinosaurs, fearful of losing their mountain ranges of power replete with gold mines, tunnels of corruption, caves of impunity, and peaks of pristine and prosperous respectability. Like an antiquated zoo, the Jurassic Park of Mexican politics should be shut down; its headquarters is the PRI. And if the PRI itself does not want to be shut down, it must reform itself. The dinosaurs and drugosaurs will have accomplished what neither the citizenry nor the opposition parties have succeeded in doing: bringing the PRI to an end.

Before internal warfare brings total collapse, Mexico might decide that what it needs is a democratic and reformed PRI. The country will support reformist PRI politicians. They must act quickly, before the reactionary elements in the PRI eliminate them either metaphorically or physically. The inhabitants of Jurassic Park act as if they were invested with divine right.

Cross-eyed Gorgons with crooked mouths, whose ugliness is even more frightening than their ferocity, guard the entrance to the Jurassic caves and try to discredit the many groups that have arisen in civil society to fill the political vacuum and, with the citizens' willingness, to limit the vices of a sclerotic regime that was expert in corruption but not in the science of government.

There is no greater danger to the republic than the continuity of those self-declared defenders of a certain style of politicking, which increasingly separates Mexico's institutions from its social, economic, and cultural realities. Unless the PRI reforms itself, it will go on being an obstacle to our democratization, as was recently noted by Juan Sánchez Navarro, the father figure of Mexico's private sector. And our democratization consists, precisely, of a growing convergence between institutions and society.

But when PRI members assassinate other PRI members we must ask ourselves, Whom does either side represent? What motivated Colosio and Ruiz Massieu, and what drove their assassins? Was Colosio's speech of 6 March—the most reformist and democratic ever made by a PRI presidential candidate—enough to bring about his elimination on 23 March? Was Ruiz Massieu's willingness to negotiate, as head of the PRI's ranks in the Chamber of Deputies, enough to seal his fate?

Alongside the government's responsibility to investigate these infamous crimes fully, there is a parallel national responsibility that no citizen can avoid: full adherence to legal order. Our second duty—which derives from the first—is to demand security with no infringements on our liberty. Third, we must lay the groundwork for a broad dialogue among all our political and social forces, from parties to citizens' associations, including labor unions, cooperatives, business organizations, the media, and universities, to proclaim aloud what unites us and what distinguishes us and to establish on that minimal but clear basis a list of national priorities and our common determination to overcome the challenges of crime, corruption, and impunity. The country must represent itself open and clearly, as the great poet Jaime Sabines has urged, in contrast to the powers of darkness, the moles, narcos, and oligo-saurs.

Internal division is useful within parties when, like the PAN and PRD, they seek to renew themselves in order to compete better and contribute more. In the case of the PRI, those who aspire to change are targets for physical elimination. What an advanced and dangerous degree of decomposition—yet so easy to neutralize!

How? Through open, public, nonauthoritarian negotiations among the forces seeking real democracy for Mexico—including the PRI's reformist and progressive elements, now legitimized by its martyrs. The best in the PRI can and should work with the best in the PAN and PRD. Mexico cries out for identification of its priorities and the association of them with both the life of its citizens and the new government's program.

November: The Terrible Year

The torrent of unforeseen events in 1994, a terrible year, has confirmed Miguel Basáñez's alarming thesis that since 1968 there has not been a single happy ending to a presidential term. Díaz Ordaz—the sequels of Tlatelolco; Echeverría—kidnappings, guerrillas, devaluation, the avoidable and mismanaged Excélsior affair; López Portillo—debt, frivolity; de la Madrid—the ongoing economic crisis, the PRI renegades, questionable elections. They all confirm the rule.

Carlos Salinas de Gortari seemed to be the exception: everything had gone well for him. But on 1 January 1994, the Chiapas rebellion triggered a chain reaction of shocking events: political assassinations of a magnitude unseen in Mexico since the death of Álvaro Obregón in 1928 (the year of my birth), kidnappings, criminal associations, a symbiosis between drug trafficking and politics, judicial corruption and incompetence, rumors, complicitous involvements, personal attacks, gaps in security.

That Mexico was able to hold peaceful elections—credible if not perfect, with greater independence for electoral agencies, exemplary citizen advisers, numerous impartial observers (though not as many or as qualified as we could have wished), massive citizen participation—is due above all to the determined, many-faceted action of Civic Alliance, the San Ángel Group, and other civic groups. It was also due to President Salinas's will, belated but welcome nonetheless.

We cannot yet claim victory. So far, each political advance has been accompanied by a persistent defect. The successes have mostly been the result of political negotiations after unforeseen events—the Chiapas rebellion or Colosio's assassination—not a genuine electoral reform, which is still pending. The agreements among parties, the Twenty Proposals for Democracy, the candidates' word to the San Ángel Group do not add up to a new law. And the elections of 21 August may have been as dubious as Cuauhtémoc Cárdenas, supposedly with proof in hand, claims they were; as flawed at their very root, with fixed electoral rolls, according to Fernando Bazúa; and as unfair as Santiago Creel Miranda, the rising star of a new politics based on good faith, decency, and the law, alleges.

I write these final lines of my 1994 diary before the ratification of the increasingly disputed election. I agree with the arguments pointing to an unfair election. Santiago Creel is right: some advances were made, but they were the product of "informal political agreements, reached under emergency conditions," and they could not sanitize basically unfair elections in which "irregularities persisted."

These are the powerful reasons Creel puts forth to posit the urgent need for new electoral reform consolidating the progress made thus far and preventing these continual postelectoral disputes that have made grist for so many political mills and, worse, have left a margin for uncertainty, recklessness, ambition, and crime—as the assassinations of Ruiz Massieu and of several hundred PRD militants show. Creel notes that the electoral process requires broad improvement since "the case is not yet closed in this matter; and as long as it remains open, it will be very difficult to process it and obtain the consensus needed to carry out in-depth political reform." Lacking a consensus translated into law, we shall suffer interminable postelectoral conflicts, which only benefit the reactionaries of all parties, cause disagreements to be settled through crime and revenge, and create political vacuums that are never empty for long but soon are filled by dinos and narcos, economic interest groups and armed force.

Under these circumstances, the new president must propose a government as broad as the democratic program of the entire nation. The ever-smaller groups that have governed Mexico in the last twelve years have, arguably, achieved relative efficiency and even macroeconomic success. But the political price has been enormous, as we have seen. Many voices, tendencies, contributions that might have prevented disaster were demonized by the priests of pure macroeconomic efficiency, the boys at the blackboard—the technocracy from which Ernesto Zedillo himself has emerged.

Mexico is a generous country; it has never denied an incoming president the benefit of the doubt. An oft-cited example is that of Manuel Ávila Camacho. The dour general ridiculed as "the unknown soldier," assumed the presidency in 1940, weakened by questionable elections and a lackluster personality. He was succeeding Lázaro Cárdenas, one of Mexico's strongest heads of state, perhaps the only one endowed with true greatness in this century. Ávila Camacho made up for these liabilities by installing a cabinet as broadly based as it was effective, with representatives of the business right (Francisco Xavier Gaxiola) and the agrarian left (Javier Rojo Gómez); a great technician of public finance (Eduardo Suárez), an unsurpassed technician of political negotiation (Miguel Alemán), and a respected professional experienced in public assistance (Gustavo Baz); a former Callista prosecutor (Ezequiel Padilla), a veteran Obregonista military figure (Pablo Macías), and one of Cárdenas's close collaborators (Ignacio García Téllez); the leftist Isidro Candia, the centrist Marte R. Gómez, the rightist Víctor Fernández Manero, and the eminent educator Jaime Torres Bodet.

Ernesto Zedillo has no reason to form a cabinet with party quotas, but he can form a government in which merit and representativeness assure Mexicans that their plurality has been embraced and that their business will be handled seriously, professionally, and patriotically. Mexican democracy will come from below and will be defined daily by municipalities, civic organizations, and a social sector that arbitrates between the public and private sectors. An agenda of undeferrable national priorities must be established. The new government's composition will speak volumes for its capacity to join in the great task facing the nation—or to hinder that task.

No new government enters office without prior commitments. It is better to assume them consciously than to suffer them blindly. "When I woke up, the dinosaur was still there," writes Augusto Monterrosa in the shortest short story on record. Similarly, for us, pretending that the dinosaurs are a dream is to ensure that they will be there when we awaken. The fierce patrimonialism of the ultraconservative emissaries of the past must be explicitly neutralized: their time is over; they are an obstacle to national development. In contrast, the PRI reformers—heirs to Colosio and Ruiz Massieu—should be encouraged.

Even these good internal guidelines must be translated so as to become the Mexican Moncloa, an agenda with which we can all identify without forsaking our principles or autonomy. Broad negotiations along these lines are still pending among the various political forces. A postelectoral transition is under way: the election could not and should not have fulfilled the agenda.

There is no need to alter the structural design of Carlos Salinas's economic reform in order to create additionally a deliberate policy to reduce inequality, increase savings, bring down domestic interest rates, free the forces of social organization, broaden access to information, and create the infrastructure we need to accelerate growth and increase employment (public works, education, health, housing).

We must leave Jurassic Park forever. No Elysian Fields await us, but neither do we face a vale of shadows. What awaits us is neither more nor less than community, city, the polis that is our public meeting place and cultural acropolis: a Mexico that is more hospitable and better prepared to enter the new century and the new millennium.

Appendix:
Dialogue between a Guerrilla and a Novelist

Zapatista Army of National Liberation,
Mexico, 27 June 1994

From: Insurgent Subcommander Marcos,
in the mountains of the Mexican Southeast, Chiapas

To: Carlos Fuentes,
Mexico City

Several ingredients are immediately perceived. One is the continuity of the social struggle in Mexico: the Mexican Revolution

. . . actually began the day after the fall of the Aztecs to the conquistador Hernán Cortés. The second is the tension, within that continuity, between the dynamics of modernization and the values of tradition. This implies, at every stage of Mexican history, an adjustment between past and present whose most original feature is admitting the presence of the past. Nothing seems to be totally canceled by the future in the Mexican experience: styles of life and legal claims dating from the Aztec or colonial centuries are still relevant in our times.

. . . Nearly seventy years after the death of Zapata, Mexico again faces crisis and the need for change. Enormous development has taken place, along with great injustice. Again, as Mexico searches for solutions in economic modernization, it must also find them in political modernization. The society, as in 1910, has outstripped the institutions. But, once more, modernization cannot be achieved at the expense of the small agrarian communities, the forgotten world of Villa and Zapata. . . . If Mexico is to achieve lasting growth, it must, at last, permit the strong central state to meet the peaceful challenge of self-government from below. The cultural element again becomes paramount, since the continuity of Mexican history implies an effort to admit the presence of the past, uniting tradition with development.

> —CARLOS FUENTES, foreword to John Mason Hart,
> *El México revolucionario*
> (Mexico: Alianza Editorial Mexicana, 1990*)

I do not know when you wrote these lines, but they are certainly valid in the year that dogs us now.

I find myself writing you this letter for many reasons and through a series of coincidences. I find myself seeking the words, images, thoughts needed to touch in you that synthesis of past and future embraced by your cultural and political activities.

I find myself wishing to convince you that this new crisis and the need for change, which caress and inhibit the air of Mexico, need your eyes, your word. I see myself without a face, without a

---

* The Mexican edition of the book I discuss above, in chapter 4.

name, leaving aside weapons and all the military paraphernalia that so oppress us, trying to talk with you man to man, hope to hope.

I am well aware of the fears and mistrust aroused by our moves since the dawn of this year; I am well aware of the skepticism aroused by our clumsy anonymous discourse, by our weapons and our paltry attempt to make for ourselves, by force of arms, a place in what the school history books used to call the "Fatherland."

But I must do everything I can to convince you that, for weapons to fall silent, ideas must speak—and must speak loudly, more loudly than bullets. I must convince you not only that we cannot, alone, carry this banner that ripples anew, with its indigenous blood, above our soil. I must also convince you that we do not want to carry it alone, that we want others, better and wiser than us, to raise it with us. I must convince you that the long night of ignominy that oppressed us all these decades ("What is the night?" asks Macbeth, and Lady Macbeth replies, "Almost at odds with morning, which is which") is not necessarily followed by a dawn, that the night might well be followed by another night if we do not, by force of reason, end it now.

I know it sounds paradoxical that an armed, anonymous, and illegal force should call for a strong, peaceful, and legal civilian movement to achieve the definitive opening of a democratic space in our country, free and just. I know it might seem absurd, but you will agree with me that if anything distinguishes this country, its history, and its people, it is that absurd paradox of opposites which meet (they clash, yes, but meet nonetheless in past and future, tradition and modernity, violence and pacifism, military and civilian. Instead of trying to negate or justify this contradiction, we have simply accepted it and recognized it and now try to turn our steps as it dictates, not so capriciously after all.

In any case, I want to invite you to the National Democratic Convention. Yes, a convention of civilians, convened by military men (revolutionary but military nonetheless). Yes, a peaceful convention, convened by violent people. Yes, a convention that insists on legality, convened by the outlawed. Yes, a convention of men and women with names and faces, convened by unnameable persons with hidden faces. Yes, a paradoxical convention, consistent with our past and future history. Yes, a convention that will raise those banners already aloft in foreign lands but forbidden on our soil: the banners of democracy, liberty, and justice. That is what I want—to invite you to attend. We would be greatly honored to receive you and hear you speak.

We cannot say much about ourselves in response to reasonable doubts. We say only that we are Mexican (like you), that we want democracy (like you), that we want freedom (like you), that we want justice (like you). What could be wrong with a meeting among Mexicans like us? Absurd and paradoxical? I know—but is there anything in this country that is not?

So, Mr. Fuentes, we felt we couldn't take this step without at least trying to take it together with Mexicans like Carlos Fuentes. I don't know if I have succeeded in inviting you, much less if I have succeeded in convincing you. I also know that, even if you wish to attend, you might not have the time to stop off in this corner of Mexico. However that may be, greetings to the man of letters, the diplomat, the scientist—but, above all, greetings to the Mexican.

5 July 1994

To: Subcommander Marcos,
    in the mountains of Chiapas

Dear friend:
Your letter compels me to think about many things. The first is the debate about the old and the new, tradition and modernity, that you cite at the outset.

The first debt I owe you is for having made us ponder anew what we mean by modernity. An excluding modernity, which leaves by the wayside those unable to enter the race toward progress? What is progress if it does not mean progress for the majority of a country's citizens? And what is progress without a tradition to nourish it? Can there be a living future with a dead past? Or should we rethink an inclusive modernity, which does not leave out any possible contribution toward a genuine future—that is, a future laden with a past, with experience, with memory?

The Chiapas uprising has provoked fierce reactions in the Mexican media. I have heard people say, "The Indians are an obstacle to progress and modernity." The inevitable corollary is "They should be exterminated." I have heard one person say, with macabre humor, "In Mexico there are ninety million people. If we were only thirty million, we would already be a First World country."

You have come to remind us that our modernity includes you. Not as an imitation of us but as yourselves, as what you are. The indigenous cultures of Mexico might be destined to disappear in the larger process of *mestizaje*. But until that happens, if it does happen, and while it unfolds, we must respect cultures that are ours because they live with us, proffering values that are possibly superior and doubtless necessary, to enrich our diminished ideas of modernity and progress.

Fernando Benítez, whom you should also invite, has seen it better than anyone else. The native cultures of Mexico value the ritual and mythical world, death, nature, a sense of community and capacity for self-government, which our makeshift modernity might well need to become more complete.

You have completed our modernity: our living more fully in the present. You also complete our idea of progress. You have made me see that there are two realities in Chiapas and, by extension, in the nation. There is the historical community, humiliated for five hundred years and visited first by the Conquest, which came to stay, and then by the Revolution, which came and went like a gust of wind. The Chiapas of centuries of exploitation and poverty has spoken.

But another Chiapas has also spoken, with extraordinary intuition—a Chiapas of the future, immersed in one of the most acute problems of the so-called global village. You have realized (and I repeat, your intuition has opened my eyes) that very soon —in a process of worldwide integration that, left in the hands of God, callously sacrifices millions of workers for the sake of efficiency, productivity, and benefits for the few—you, the exploited of Chiapas, would be worse than exploited. You would be thrust aside, forgotten, abandoned to your fate.

No wonder the extraordinary journalist Alma Guillermoprieto sees in you pioneers, men and women of the frontier, the vanguard who sounded the alarm before anybody else in Mexico: Be careful. We are going from exploitation to marginalization. At least exploitation generates a salary. Marginalization generates nothing but abandonment and death.

Somebody had to speak up, present petitions, join ancient and modern demands. Land but also credit, technology, education, transportation, access to markets, and, above all, justice, law enforcement, an end to that disheartening sense that justice has no home in Mexico.

A few years ago all these demands would have been stamped with the red-hot branding iron of anti-Communism. You are the first post-Communist actors on the stage of the Third World. Your aspirations can no longer be concealed or perverted as part of a Soviet world conspiracy. Only the shipwrecked of the cold war, bereft of Manichean enemies, can still believe that. Today, we must confront our social problems without ideological excuses. In 1968 Díaz Ordaz exterminated students in the name of anti-Communism; Mexico's problems were fantasies invented by the "philosophers of destruction."* In 1994, Salinas de Gortari admits that the problems of Mexico are the responsibility of Mexicans and, instead of extermination, chooses dialogue. You should at least grant that much to Salinas and give up your absurd demand that he resign. A breakdown in the constitutional timetable benefits no one but the PRI dinosaurs.

Furthermore, you have declared to all of us Mexicans that the aspirations of your communities can be fulfilled only through the exercise of democracy. And democracy is always preeminently local. You have the right to choose your companions, your friends, those who deserve your trust. There is no reason for you to suffer the humiliation of having the authoritarian center impose on you its governors, whose mission it is to support those exploiting you in Chiapas.

We owe you all this and something more: you have reminded us of all we had forgotten. Including ourselves.

Did you have to take up arms in order to achieve all this? I insist that you didn't. I insist that legal channels must be pursued until they are exhausted; and when they are, new political options must be sought. If exercised imaginatively, politics and the law are in-

---

* In his delirious search for scapegoats, Díaz Ordaz had explicitly named Herbert Marcuse as one of these destructive thinkers.

exhaustible. You have proof of this, I believe, in the excellent performance of Manuel Camacho Solís as peace commissioner for Chiapas. To deny the success of his mission is to deny the success of political channels, thus dangerously reopening the way for official policy in Chiapas, which is repression.

Were there no other paths open to you but to take up arms? I insist that there were. But I am not an indigenous campesino from Chiapas. Perhaps I lack the mental clarity or experience needed to put myself in your place and feel what you feel. As Carlos Monsiváis has so splendidly said, "When the weak rebel, we call it violence. But when the powerful exercise violence, we call it impunity." I hope our country will find paths to prevent violence, so that actions like those you undertook on 1 January will no longer be necessary.

Whether you could have taken another path is now a moot point. It's like debating whether it should have rained last night or whether the sun rose this morning. The real issue, Subcommander, is to join forces now so that the path you chose does not have to be followed again. But, as we all know, this implies a mutual political responsibility: democracy in Chiapas so there can be democracy in Mexico, and democracy in Mexico so there can be democracy in Chiapas.

You do not need to convince me: we must join forces to achieve the goal of a credible and democratic election on 21 August, so there will be no violent aftermath on 22 August. You speak of a citizens' convention with democratic goals, uniting the efforts of civil society.

Today, Subcommander Marcos, you have an opportunity to go beyond the very cordial personal invitation you extended me in your letter. I am part of a pluralistic group of Mexican men and women, partisan and nonpartisan, who wish to state the dangers of violent confrontation and avoid them through strict adherence to the spirit and the letter of democracy.

I very cordially suggest that you extend this personal invitation to other members of the pluralistic group that the press has baptized the San Ángel Group, which, I am sure, will open with you and yours, Indians and campesinos of Chiapas, new paths for political growth, understanding and concord, viable democracy, progress for the majority, and an inclusive modernity.

CARLOS FUENTES

8 : HAPPY NEW YEAR

....

A Lament for 1995

Left with Ourselves

When I was honored with the Cervantes Award for Literature in 1988, Alfredo Baranda, Mexico's ambassador to Spain, invited me to a dinner. Baranda was well connected in Madrid; guests at the dinner included Felipe González, president of the government, and his minister of the economy, Carlos Solchaga. Solchaga had just returned from Mexico and had been impressed with the discipline and farsightedness of the Mexican administration. President Miguel de la Madrid had devalued the peso so as to spare his successor, Carlos Salinas de Gortari, from having to make such a difficult decision. Echeverría had done the same for López Portillo, and López Portillo for de la Madrid.

Now, in 1995, this golden rule of Mexican politics—whereby the predecessor makes unpopular decisions and smooths the way for his successor—has been broken, with fatal results. But even if the rule had been maintained—that is, if Carlos Salinas had devalued the currency in November, as Ernesto Zedillo proposed—two of our most obvious problems would still be pending.

The first is the narrowness of the governing group, ever smaller and self-involved. Many of its members are graduates of Ivy League and eastern universities (Harvard, Yale, MIT). For them, the economy unfolds on a blackboard, never in real life; it is something that happens to statistics, not to flesh-and-blood men and women. This group is increasingly distanced from public opinion and the raw material of the nation. It holds out the promise of Adam Smith's optimistic eighteenth-century definition of economics—the science of human happiness—and ends up confirming Thomas Carlyle's pessimistic definition in the nineteenth: the dismal science.

The second problem is the unlimited power of the Mexican executive. Two ideas that are standard in Anglo-Saxon public law—accountability and checks and balances—are difficult to translate and virtually unknown among us. We must go back to the vocabulary of colonial law to find something like the concept of impeachment in the *juicio de residencia*, by which the Spanish Crown judged and held in check its royal officials in the Indies.

Everybody knows the magnitude of the Mexican economic crisis that ended our year of living dangerously. Policies to liberalize trade, reducing duties and tariffs, led to a wave of often frivolous imports far higher than our export capacity. Many small and medium-size industries went broke: the Mexican public prefers tennis shoes imported from the United States (albeit made in Hong Kong) to domestic shoes of higher quality. This is a triumph of status, of images of prestige, over economic reality. It is the result of incessant propaganda about the virtues of the First World, a universe inhabited by Cindy Crawford and Richard Gere, in whom the *India* Bonita and the *Indio* Magdaleno, yearning and resentful alike, aspire to see themselves. It is a universal phenomenon. When the Albanian boat people reached the coast of Italy in 1992, their first question was "How do we get to Dallas?" Immigration authorities in Europe and the United States have no right to complain: the consumer-based economy of the West has made the Second, Third, and Fourth Worlds believe that beauty and prosperity are at hand for whoever arrives, with whatever baggage, at the golden gates of the First World.

This wave of imports slashed Mexico's hard-currency reserves from a peak of $30 billion to a total of barely $6 billion—and that without even touching bottom. The economy became hostage to foreign investment in order to maintain the peso's parity and pay the current-account deficit. But foreign investment was concentrated mainly in stocks, bonds, and other short-term instruments: in the volatile and transitory paper economy. Only 15 percent of foreign investment went into the real economy, into the creation of factories, increased employment, and increased production. The country was threatened with an acute case of schizophrenia. A minority centered their lives on the New York Stock Exchange, and a majority on the price of beans. One economy was all gilded wrapping paper, the other all huts and untilled land. The former was the minority's, the latter the majority's.

Several elements, aside from the exclusiveness of the governing group and the discretionary powers of the president, led many to misread the situation. One—secondary, in my view—was the personal agenda of President Salinas, which was related to the successive shocks of 1994. The Chiapas revolt was not what had caused the economic upheaval; above all, it was a timely reminder of all we had forgotten. (President Zedillo has not dwelt on the nonsensical idea that "it's the fault of Chiapas," though it has become the refrain of the threatening "ultras" of the Mexican right.) Our financial problems began with the assassination of Luis Donaldo Colosio and the sudden awareness that he had represented a unique effort toward reform, change, and broad political alliances. On 6 March Colosio gave the most reformist speech ever made by any PRI candidate for the presidency, and two weeks later he was dead. The response of the Mexican legal system reassured nobody. Our perplexity and apprehension deepened with the September assassination of José Francisco Ruiz Massieu and, even further, with the actions and words of Deputy Attorney General Mario Ruiz Massieu, the victim's brother. His accusations against PRI President Ignacio Pichardo, PRI Senator María de los Ángeles Moreno, and Attorney General Humberto Benítez fostered suspicion that the PRI was disintegrating in a Sicilian paroxysm. And the lack of convincing explanations at all levels added to our feelings of insecurity, mystery, vulnerability. This was the other, psychological and emotional factor that paved the way for the December crisis, when the flight of capital began.

President Salinas thought that a devaluation before the August elections would be fatal to the PRI, and after August, it would harm his campaign to head the World Trade Organization, the body that succeeded the General Agreement on Tariffs and Trade (GATT). Salinas made a mistake. A timely, well-ordered devaluation without panic would have benefited not only the national currency but also Salinas himself, and now he is berated for the difficult situation he left behind. No cheese and no grapes.

Another misreading by the Salinas presidency was to postpone Mexico's democratic reform and to invoke the ominous example of the dissolution of the USSR, to argue that glasnost is not simultaneously compatible with perestroika, as evidenced by the Gorbachev disaster, the fragmentation and collapse of the Soviet world. But the comparison is not valid. The context of the USSR is not that of Mexico. The heirs of ancient Muscovy operated, through the centuries, on the basis of a territorial imperative: to gain territory, expand, subjugate neighboring nations and cultures, and then secure the frontiers of empire at any cost. What neither Gorbachev nor his successors could do was to shift the axis of Russian policy from this territorial imperative to the imperative of production and democracy. One hopes that they will. But in the meantime, the problem of Mexico is not one of territorial expansion or the defense of an imperial perimeter but, precisely, that which the Kremlin has been unable to deliver: production and democracy. The reasons for our respective failures are different; Soviet resources were devoured by a war economy and paralyzed by administrative incompetence, whereas in Mexico a purely economic reform would fail without the checks and balances, legislative oversight, accurate information, and other democratic mechanisms sanctioned by our new association with the two democracies of North America, the United States and Canada. For how long can our intractable, frozen authoritarianism coexist with the democratic fluidity of the United States and Canada?

Mexican authoritarianism has taken us to the brink of the worst dependency in our history. Only democracy can restore to us our sovereignty and some measure of fairness—increasingly difficult to secure—in our relations with North America.

Perhaps the other obscure object of Mexico's despotic desire is the Chinese model: authoritarian capitalism, development without democracy. Our experience with the Porfirian age and its developmentalism should have inoculated us against these fantasies. Given its size, population, geography, and tradition, China cannot possibly be a model for Mexico.

So we are left, once again, with ourselves. We are left, as José Agustín Ortiz Pinchetti writes, "with a great multiracial nation, at the crossroads of east and west, which has not yet borne the fruits that humanity might expect of us."

Nor will it, unless we learn the profound lessons of the crisis, understanding that while it may have manifested itself in the economy, it has its roots—and a solution—in politics. The wrong or overdue decisions that we now regret could have been avoided in a democratic regime that obliged the executive branch to report in timely fashion on measures affecting the entire nation, with the measures subjected to the checks and balances of public debate, accurate disclosure, and legislative oversight.

I remember another night in 1991 when a group of us, at the home of Jorge Castañeda, first learned from the pages of the *Wall Street Journal* of negotiations for a free-trade agreement with the United States. Had it not been for the *Journal*, that bastion of capitalism, we Mexicans could just as well have been on the moon. Hadn't Salinas rejected the likelihood of any such agreement, which he described in his campaign speeches as harmful to Mexican sovereignty? Paradox of paradoxes: the first convincing defense of a free-trade agreement I ever heard was expressed by Horacio Flores de la Peña, the openly nationalistic former minister of national patrimony. When I spoke with him in Rome in 1991, Flores de la Peña saw the agreement as the indispensable beginning of Mexico's incorporation into the world economy, not so different from Spain's decision to join the European Economic Community. There were dangers, we should be aware of them, but we could handle them. The price of protectionist isolationism had become far too high.

Yet, despite the ensuing publicity abroad, NAFTA was never publicly debated in Mexico, as Flores de la Peña would have wished it to be. Everything was done with the secrecy so dear to authoritarianism. Those who criticized the negotations were demonized—especially if they dared to express their arguments abroad—though men like Adolfo Aguilar Zínser and Jorge Castañeda argued, in turn, that Mexico's mass media would never air any direct opposition to the discretionary decisions of the executive branch.

Political parties, civil society, nongovernmental organizations, universities, intellectuals—all pointed out the defects that are now being discovered, with great lamentation, by the chorus of leaders who only yesterday exalted each and every decision of President Salinas. The timely criticism of neoliberal doctrines expressed at a winter colloquium held at the University of Mexico in 1992 was particularly useful in this regard. It seemed heretical then to speak against the new gospel preached by local disciples of Reagan and Thatcher. Today we are simply forced to recognize that no economic theory is invincible or complete in itself, whether it is the developmentalism of yesteryear or the neoliberalism of the present day.

Mexico and Latin America, orphans long bereft of reason and progress, have avidly sought theologies that would give us faith, if not reason, and security, if not progress. From Saint Thomas Aquinas to Karl Marx, via Rousseau, Comte, and Bergson and on to Keynes, Prebisch, Hayek, and Milton Friedman, we are forsaken communicants seeking a church. We swallow all Hosts, even if they be millstones. And if things go badly, we soon discover the devil who deceived us, preventing us from reaching the Promised Land of positivism, Marxism, developmentalism, or neoliberalism, as the case may be.

It is worth recalling that the prefix *neo* is particularly well suited to this doctrine, which already had its chance in Latin America during the last century. Throughout the nineteenth century, Latin America followed the precepts of laissez-faire and the magic of the market, and its nations implemented policies geared toward exporting raw materials while importing capital and manufactured goods. Powerful economic elites emerged from Mexico to Argentina. The hope was that the wealth accumulated at the top would sooner or later find its way down to the bottom. This did not happen. It has never happened. Instead, the wealth generated at the working base found its way up to the top and stayed there.

Latin American nation-states were strengthened during the twentieth century (by Batlle y Ordóñez in Uruguay, Cárdenas in Mexico, Vargas in Brazil, Alessandri in Chile, López in Colombia, Perón in Argentina) in order to ensure that the public sector would bolster a higher level of development and thereby benefit both the private and the social sectors. Indeed, it did benefit them. Policies regarding infrastructure, education, and health could be executed only by the state but ended up furnishing the homes of the bourgeoisie, who got cheap energy, communications, subsidies, capital, and labor, as well as a previously nonexistent population of consumers. In exchange, the private sector did not return society's favor wth an adequate distribution of income; it remained adamantly opposed to modern taxation systems, and pursued its vocation as lackey to international capital. The state, for its part, grew excessively in response to the unsatisfied demands of different sectors: workers, campesinos, the middle class, the business class, cultural sectors, armies, and, above all, foreign creditors. Incapable of satisfying all these constituents, the Latin American state succumbed first to military dictatorship and then to neoliberal reform. The straitjacket of extreme protectionism, subsidized consumption and production, captive markets, and lack of competitiveness needed to be loosened—and was. But in its stead came a demonization of national states, a delusional faith in the free play of market forces, and the cruel complacency of social Darwinism in lands of extreme hunger and need.

We now know that the shrinking or absence of the state ensures neither well-being nor order. Will public administration in Latin America recover its strength enough to impose social obligations and tax reform on the new elites? The repercussions in South America of the Mexican crisis of 1994–95—the "tequila effect"—attest to the continent's difficulty in doing so. But they also point to a solution. It is a social solution that depends on the capacity of civil society and political forces to ensure that strategies for investment, export, and savings are combined with corrective social measures, tax reform, and renewed social services.

With what eyes shall the blind lead the blind?

The Mexican crisis and its Latin American repercussions should oblige us to open our eyes and realize that we are blinded only by seduction, convenience, or hypnotism. Peter Drucker, the apostle of the new economy of information, urges us to forget the neoliberal illusion that the state must disappear. Modern capitalist societies (or postmodern, in the fashionable phrase) need neither more nor less government but *better government.*

Neoliberal governments, in their purest Reaganite and Thatcherite manifestations, generated more expenditure and regulations than ever before in the United States and Great Britain and brought about the largest deficits in those countries' history. Mrs. Thatcher's deficits did nothing but grow, even as the rusting Iron Lady tried to limit government. Both champions—Ronnie and Maggie—attempted to eliminate government by increasing debt and ended up saddling government with heavier obligations than ever before.

What does Drucker mean, then, by better government? Concentrating on what works. Not what helps the patient feel better but what cures and ministrations that keep him in good health: adequate fiscal policy, investment in knowledge and human resources, infrastructure, and facilitated savings and production. In a society in which economy and information are virtually synonymous, education is the very basis of progress because, for now and the foreseeable future, the wealth of a nation will be measured not by the quantity of its capital but by that capital's productivity. Traditionally, for instance, a bank profited by the differential between what it paid for money and what it charged for money. Today that margin is shrinking. Banks profit only by charging for the information they provide.

The initial advantages of early exploitation and application of information, as Drucker explains, become permanent and irreversible. They establish a learning curve that affects all of society. We are entering an era of constant, lifelong continuing education; its purpose will be to train people for not only their first jobs but their last jobs as well.

In other words, there will be no productivity without information or information without education. This is one of the ports of entry into the twenty-first century. But it is not enough for a country like Mexico. I once asked the futurologist Alvin Toffler what such a country needs to progress from the "second wave"—smokestack industries, an economy based on quantity—to the "third wave"—an economy of services, technologies, quality rather than quantity. Toffler replied, "Food and education." A country that cannot feed or educate itself will always remain backward.

In my view, these goals exclude totalitarian economic doctrines, from the left or the right, which exclusively benefit either the state or private enterprise. Rather, they require a balance of the economy's sectors, demonizing none of them. Latin America has put a lot of effort into establishing viable nation-states. Without the nation-state created by Juárez and the reform of 1857, Mexico, harmed by U.S. expansion and by internal wars, might not exist today as a country. Without the nation-state conceived by Carranza and the Constituent Assembly of 1917, Mexico would not have made the imperfect but tangible advances that today make it, despite all its problems, one of the strongest and most promising communities of the coming century.

At the same time, we need private enterprise that is not, in José Iturriaga's words, deprived of enterprise. The Mexican state has been magnanimous with its private sector, endowing it with all sorts of incentives, but in an excessively protectionist framework. It is not true that all the ills of Mexico began forty years ago, when "the state took over the economy," as a misguided member of the Zedillo government said recently. The president then was Ávila Camacho, who was succeeded by Miguel Alemán Valdés—a president who coddled the private sector as few have done.

Rather, we should respect and consolidate the advantages and obligations of each sector. The public sector is entrusted with defense, justice, foreign relations, and monetary policy. The nation-state has an obligation to feed and educate the population, create infrastructure, and collect taxes. The private sector must look after investment, production, and business. But today all societies, especially the most advanced, recognize the need to protect their social sector, the satisfier of social needs and promoter of citizen identity.

The Ten Commandments

In Mexico and Latin America, we want to go from the concept of population to that of citizenry, from number to quality, from a resigned sense of fatality toward a commitment to community. This takes us back to politics, for all politics are local, as Günter Grass said in Germany and Tip O'Neill in the United States.

The problems now besetting us are a disheartening repetition of situations we experienced in 1978, 1982, and 1988. If there can no longer be a presidential succession without trauma in Mexico, it is because the system that worked, more or less, from Cárdenas to López Mateos collapsed at Tlatelolco in 1988. All the king's men cannot put Humpty Dumpty back together again.

We must take a definitive step toward full democracy in Mexico. I have been advocating a Mexican Moncloa, an agreement parallel to the one enacted in 1977 to promote democracy in Spain, that would unite government and political parties and define specific actions and political contracts binding on everyone. Will Ernesto Zedillo be the Adolfo Suárez of Mexico? If he can achieve a Mexican Moncloa, Zedillo will save his government, himself, and his country.

What would a Mexican Moncloa consist of?

A decalogue for democracy, liberty, and justice should include, first of all, an agreement to finish carrying out electoral reform to translate into law the loose ends of the recent civic contest, agreeing on the principle of alternations of power, creating an autonomous electoral agency with its own status and resources, and establishing strict criteria for party finances and access to the media. These things are essential for electoral credibility and for ending the postelectoral conflicts that mar, discourage, and at times bloody political life in Mexico.

Federalism, a separation of powers, an electoral statute for Mexico City, and insistence on the rule of law and law enforcement are four more items in the desired decalogue.

The sixth commandment concerns the media. We won't avoid the mistakes we so regret today if the press—and especially television—neither informs nor criticizes nor stands apart from the presidential perspective; if newspapers cannot obtain timely information; if editors are threatened, beaten, and even murdered.

Human rights are the seventh commandment. Carlos Salinas accorded an important place and gave impetus to the culture of human rights by establishing the National Human Rights Commission and its statutes. But that culture must suffuse the authorities' actions and offer guarantees to citizens.

This leads to the eighth item of the decalogue: reforming the security agencies and understanding them as institutions for citizen security and public security but also of national security—that is, as institutions concerned with foreign relations, drug trafficking, and the defense of strategic industries like PEMEX. To challenge the national status of the petroleum industry, for example, is to issue a suicidal call for division within the country and civil strife among Mexicans and to renounce a symbol equivalent to the national seal or flag.

The ninth commandment in this decalogue involves respect and encouragement for the organizations of civil society. Only they can give full meaning to the community's social sector.

And the tenth article is, at long last, a model for development with justice, a market economy with social commitments, a balance between the public and private sectors by means of a stronger social sector. We might then arrive at a representative pact, not one imposed from above. To complete the virtuous circle, this pact would also require independent and aggressive labor unions serving as interlocutors and capable of providing the necessary balance among healthy finances, increased production, and worker protection.

The accord signed by the government and the political parties on 17 January 1995 gave a name to this commitment: the Los Pinos Pact. It is only a beginning, and it encompasses only the first commandment of the decalogue. But a comparison with the Spanish Moncloa is still valid: as it was in Spain in 1977, the issue in Mexico in 1995 is to join the raw economic, social, and cultural substance of the country with new political forms. In Spain, as in Mexico, society no longer fits into the obsolete political framework.

Federico Reyes Heroles is right: we must draw up an unbiased ledger of the last few years and make a distinction between light and shadow. Revenge is not a good political adviser. In Dickens's *Tale of Two Cities*, the righteous Madame Defarge sits at the foot of the guillotine knitting her register of those who will die and counting the heads as they fall. Rather than guillotine the recent past and its figures, we Mexicans would perhaps do better to find laws, rules for coexistence, liberties, and agreements, to prevent the repetition of political vices derived from a system without accountability or checks and balances. The possible benefits of our crisis—increased Mexican exports, better foreign investment, more job sources for Mexicans, increased productivity and salaries, better utilization of the advantages of NAFTA—will not accrue without political reform. And that will not come about without opposition parties. The PAN and PRD, living through their own restructuring crises, must distinguish between what benefits the opposition and what benefits the nation: the two do not always coincide.

In Chiapas, the spokespeople of the Zapatista army have argued that not only the region's problems but those of the country as a whole must be attended to. An agreement for democracy—a Mexican Moncloa—would prove them right and would also neutralize one of the arguments put forth by Subcommander Marcos.

What Went Wrong?

If in 1994 we lived dangerously, in 1995 we might have stopped living altogether; we must shift three axes in our national life with energy and true reformist determination:

First, we must move the exercise of authority from an authoritarian to a democratic axis.

Second, we must move our economy from a speculative to a productive axis.

Third, we must move our diplomacy from a supplicant to a resistant axis.

To the dangers I have already discussed are now added threats that were until recently hardly conceivable. One of them is the power vacuum. If Zedillo does not assert presidential power—not presidentialistic and authoritarian, but political and juridical, or *democratic*—Mexico may drift toward a vacuum, and a vacuum never stays empty for long. The financial and political crises of Italy and Germany after the First World War led not to democracy but to fascism.

Salinas denied Zedillo hope and, with it, power. Perhaps now it it time for Zedillo to give the country, if not hope, then a minimal degree of confidence and proof of his commitment to democracy, so that Mexicans will acquire the personal power that our accidental president still lacks. The cabinet must be renewed; those who function well should be confirmed, and those who do not should be sent away to study or tell jokes. Above all, the composition of the cabinet must reflect breadth and representativeness— in terms of age and diversity—which in turn will devolve power back to the president. The generation of change should be both older and younger than the group currently in place, which is destined to rule, according to Foreign Minister Ángel Gurría, for another twenty-five years. There are Mexicans who contemplate suicide at the very thought.

Another source of confidence and credibility would be the prompt solving of the assassinations of Colosio and Ruiz Massieu. Accomplishing this could do for Zedillo what jailing the corrupt union leader La Quina did for Salinas.

Zedillo needs a national cabinet with a national policy. We are on the verge of allowing power vacuums to develop that only extremists can fill. From the Sinaloa right to the Chiapas right, Mexican fascists are beginning to manifest themselves, demanding blood, order, intolerance. They seek a Berlusconi. They might find a Pinochet.

Only a rapid transition toward democracy, law enforcement,

perseverance in negotiation, an emphasis on *making* politics rather than on *suffering* them, and the active presence of all political, social, and cultural groups—the promise and backbone of our country—can restore us to the path leading to our desired goal, a Mexico of economic development with political democracy and social justice.

A shift in economic thinking from a speculative to a productive axis will be required. Salinas's macroeconomic strategy achieved some notable victories: curbing inflation, balancing the budget, restoring public finances to health, opening the country to the global economy, and maintaining hard-currency reserves at a very high level for a long time.

What went wrong, then?

First and foremost, the neglect—Solidarity notwithstanding—of the economy's real object, citizens—human beings and their families. True, the sacrifices imposed on salaried employees were made for the sake of future abundance and felicity. And Mexican unemployment had its escape valve, even financial justification: labor migration to the United States and dollars sent back to Mexico by our workers. But the structural changes that should have accompanied the macroeconomic revolution did not materialize.

In the second place, our financial borders were opened, in the belief that speculative investment would always cover the deficit in the current account. But foreign capital flowing into emerging markets is, by nature, volatile and speculative flight capital. It cannot be otherwise. Financial capital has no national allegiance. It pursues its own interests, not those of the nations it visits. It can be no more than a highly suspect auxiliary to a nation's productive base.

And this base was neglected. People believed in impossible miracles. They forgot the evidence offered by those much-envied models of development the Asian tigers, which finance 75 percent of their development and foreign trade with domestic savings. This, not the vagaries of speculative investment, is the basis of their success. In contrast, domestic savings are virtually nonexistent in Mexico. To promote and restore savings is the only way for Mexico to achieve growth with justice and well-being without falling prey, time and time again, to the whims of foreign investors. It is worth recalling that during the Salinas administration foreign investors channeled only 15 percent of their investment into production, and the rest into speculation.

Are we still in time to change our economic course and give Mexican growth a solid basis in domestic savings? One might well be skeptical. But Chile, which also experienced a catastrophic devaluation in the early 1980s, maintained its currency at competitive levels, curbed inflation, and increased exports through a determined policy aimed at promoting domestic savings—albeit under the iron fist of a military dictatorship—Chile has taken full advantage of its public and private pension funds; Mexico has barely begun to do so, but without it, it is difficult to capture savings.

If Mexico does not develop internal savings as a basis for production and foreign trade, if it does not include in its economic book a social chapter (comparable to that in the European Union), Mexico will suffer the consequences of NAFTA instead of enjoying its benefits. This aspect is further and enormously complicated by the timing: Mexico's current crisis is happening at the worst possible moment vis-à-vis the United States.

Intimate partners as we are with the United States, we have depleted our financial and political resources in exchange for fairer treatment, and in return, we are caught in the most negative North American environment in recent years. Disoriented by the end of the cold war, the United States, a country that needs a reliable external enemy, does not dare see one at home. President Clinton has tried weakly and vainly to put forth an agenda for the post–cold war era. Public health, tax reform, urban violence, deteriorating services, education, infrastructure, correcting the budget and current-account deficits left behind by Reagan and Bush—the people of the United States do not want to hear any of it, much less pay for it. They would rather revive archaic certainties and restore lost mirages. The 1994 congressional elections reiterated the conservative illusion that it is possible to eliminate the state, cut taxes, and still increase defense spending.

Malaise in the United States is accompanied by the need for a foreign enemy, whose presence then becomes a reassurance. Great Britain, Mexico, Spain, Germany, Japan, the USSR, Korea, Libya, Iran, Iraq, Cuba, Grenada, Nicaragua, Panama have all played, some repeatedly, the role of an international Erich von Stroheim: the nation you love to hate. Efforts to assign this villainous role to

Japan have failed. It is not possible for U.S. citizens to hate a country that sends them good cars.

Yet the perfect enemy lies waiting at the very doorstep. With a common border stretching over two thousand kilometers, Mexico is seen by many Americans as a country that is suspect, unreliable, eternally underage, unable to govern itself, financially inept, and socially unjust. Mexico exports workers because it is incapable of employing them. Mexico begs for loans because it is incapable of handling its economy and, as a result, incapable of paying them back—unless the United States obliges it to honor its commitments.

It matters little that California crops would rot in the fields without Mexican workers, that produce prices would skyrocket, the service industry go into crisis, and the labor market collapse. Mexican villains are indispensable as scapegoats. They bear the guilt for the U.S. deficit, for the end of the war economy and subsequent unemployment, for the decline in education and health, for the lack of programs for industrial reconversion and labor retraining. Proposition 187 in California, xenophobia, barely disguised racism— these are all directed against the identified enemy, Mexico. Can Mexican immigration be curbed by denying education to children and health care to the sick? Do Mexican workers emigrate in search of schools and hospitals or in search of jobs? Never mind that they are perhaps lured by demand among U.S. employers and that they contribute more in taxes than they draw out in social benefits. None of that counts when xenophobia and discrimination rule the day. There is evidently something politically orgasmic in erecting fences and digging ditches to "secure the borders." Erotic perversion reaches its extreme when Mexicans are murdered just because they are Mexican. Natural-born killers and natural brown victims.

Mexico's financial crisis coincided with the resurgence of the political right in the United States. The $40 billion Mexico requested from the United States came not only out of Clinton's goodwill but as the result of a government policy that posits Mexican stability as important for U.S. stability. Mexico is the world's second-largest buyer of U.S. goods. A crisis in Mexico could shut down the Mexican market, which is annually more or less equivalent to the sum requested.

The $40 billion asked for Mexico under the 1990 Credit Reform Act required approval and oversight by a Congress now dominated by religious and nationalistic extremists. It was not to be given for free: there were public discussions in Washington about the concessions to be wrested from Mexico in exchange for it. Senator Barbara Boxer asked that Mexico close its border, preventing Mexican workers from entering the United States. Other lawmakers asked that PEMEX be handed over as a loan guarantee. Senator Jesse Helms, the reactionary chairman of the Senate Foreign Relations Committee, asked that Mexico "separate" itself from Cuba, and others that the Drug Enforcement Agency be allowed the run of Mexico. Most agreed that Mexico should pay as much as 10 percent of the loan, just to secure it. Still others—liberals and Perot followers—that NAFTA be abrogated or that the United States be allowed, at least, to intervene in Mexico's labor and environmental policies. Ominously, this could all be summed up in a new title for our country: Mexico, Protectorate of the United States of America.

How about the Calvo Doctrine, which denies foreign investors any guarantees beyond those allowed national investors? Or the Drago Doctrine, denying the right of creditor nations to force payment from debtor nations? Calvo? Drago? Those dishes are out of fashion; nobody eats them anymore, not even with *chimichurri*. Instead, we now have the Shylock Doctrine: loans are to be repaid with a pound of flesh.

The Free and Associated State of Mexico? The rapid erosion of our sovereignty is both overt and covert, explicit and implicit, and to reverse it will require of Mexicans the effort, lucidity, agility, and integrity of a Juárez or a Cárdenas. Mexico has had no shortage of diplomats able and willing to respond to the needs of the nation. Suffice it to recall the recent examples of Tello (and later of Tello, Jr.), Padilla Nervo, García Robles, Rabasa, Castañeda, and Sepúlveda. But today, rather than rely on the providential appearance of such men, the entire country must shift authority from authoritarianism to democracy, the economy from speculation to production, and its diplomacy from supplication to resistance.

To his credit, and that of all citizens, President Zedillo stated on 25 January, "We will not accept any commitment that infringes on our national sovereignty or undermines the legitimate interests of Mexicans." This declaration is binding on us all, but it by no means excuses us from exercising critical oversight and drawing our conclusions from a crisis whose end is not yet in sight.

In effect, President Clinton withdrew the original $40 billion loan requiring Congressional approval and gave Mexico $20 billion out of a discretionary fund. Strings were attached: Mexico's oil revenue would serve as collateral and be paid directly into the Federal Reserve Bank in New York. President Zedillo didn't even blink at this onerous condition and both Zedillo and Clinton knew that the U.S. lent Mexico money to repay U.S. banks, and investors, who had already harvested enormous earnings in their Mexican ventures. Production, employment, salaries, education, and social services—the real saviors of the Mexican economy—were once more postponed. Sovereignty was severely affected: the agreement gave the U.S. the right to monitor Mexico's economic policies.

Tequila on the Rocks

The lessons of the Mexican crisis are clear. The first one concerns *information* as opposed to *secrecy*. The Mexican government is to blame for not reporting the real state of our economy, the lack of hard-currency reserves and the true value of the peso. But the crisis is also the fault of the U.S. government, which was aware of the real situation and failed to react or sound the alarm, even to protect its own investors. They, too, are to blame; knowing that the Mexican economy was increasingly precarious, they chose either to take their capital out—thus precipitating the crisis—or to keep it in, assuming greater risks for the sake of greater (though short-term) gain. Henry Kaufman of the *Wall Street Journal* notes that the analysts who guide banks, insurance companies, and mutual funds no longer consider the long term. Their professional bias leads them to look myopically only at the short term—at immediate, high-risk profits, which is why this capital is not productive.

In any case, the Mexican crisis revealed the nature of present-day international capital. In 1982, Mexico was able to negotiate its debt crisis with a handful of banks. The parties involved, even counting Jesús Silva Herzog, all fit into one room in New York's Plaza Hotel. Today, to meet with its aggrieved parties, Mexico would have to rent Yankee Stadium. Millions of large and small investors have been affected by the handling of Mexican finances. We are dealing with management funds that are uncontrollable, volatile, and enamored of the short term—enemies of productive investment, they are so diversified that whatever happens in Mexico affects the economies of Brazil and Hong Kong. Large corporations are involved, but so, too, are millions of individual investors, banking portfolios, and insurance, mutual, and pension funds. This type of capital easily eludes oversight either by governments or by institutions like the International Monetary Fund and the World Bank.

The first great crisis for this new capital erupted in Mexico, giving our country the dubious distinction of having the world by the balls and proving that, if there is one thing we are good at, it is making misfortune universal. We did not know with whom or with what we were dealing, or we played dumb for internal political purposes. But in contrast, financial investors did not deceive themselves. As long as the recession—and low U.S. interest rates—lasted, they looked to Mexico. The moment the recession ended and interest rates rose, they took flight for warmer nests; only the blind and the suicidal stayed behind.

Even after taking into account the executive branch's lack of controls, its internal agenda, the tradition of secrecy, and the deluded complicity of Washington, a bitter doubt remains in Mexico. If the devaluation of the peso was not done in time, why was it also done so badly? What happened to the technicians, the economists, the boys at the blackboard? Why did they not negotiate with the U.S. government before the devaluation, so that credit could be obtained at less risk to our national sovereignty? Why was it all done so late, so ineptly? In the last days of January 1995, when the illusion of a rescue loan was fading, our supplicant diplomats returned home with empty hands, equipped only with nails to scratch ourselves with.

Once again, international institutions show how much they lag behind the new world realities. Just as Mexican society no longer fits into the corset of its PRI authoritarian government, the world economy no longer fits into the obsolete institutionality of the IMF and the World Bank. In the fiftieth-anniversary year of the United Nations, that world organization must urgently be updated.

In the meantime, Mexico remains subject to Mexico: we must

find solutions within ourselves, our tradition, our culture . . . and our evils. Every light in our tunnel has a shadow. The hope for greater exports thanks to a devalued peso will generate negative reactions among U.S. exporters, impoverished by our poverty. The hope for productive investment will not curtail emigration to the United States. And while Mexico reorganizes itself to initiate a new phase of its development, unemployment, falling salaries, inflation, crime, personal insecurity, and threats to intellectual and informational freedom (like those suffered in January by the poet José Emilio Pacheco and his wife, Cristina, a journalist) will further blight this unhappy new year.

We should retain the good ideas of the recent past: our unavoidable opening to the world, our efforts toward greater productivity. We should not waste time on vendettas because of internal political mistakes shared by the U.S. government, with foreign investors, and with international financial institutions. Twice we have been unwitting and obtuse victims—of the debt crisis in 1982 and of flight capital in 1994. We must not repeat these mistakes. We believe in clear norms for public accountability and limitations on the government's discretionary powers.

Production and savings, better jobs and better salaries take time and determination, but they also require democracy. The municipalities of Mexico can be the basis of labor, creativity, and wealth—but only if they are not abjectly exploited, if their politics and economy are managed by their own citizens. Industrial workers will become more productive when they feel better protected by the law and better represented by their unions. Business leaders will be more socially responsible when their property guarantees go hand in hand with a better standard of living and a higher consumption potential in the marketplace.

That is why true democracy is equivalent to a true economy.

A beautiful country with a magnificent people and an ancient culture could slip through our fingers. We must recover Mexico. Our time of illusions, grandiloquence, and arrogance has passed. The time has come for work, modesty, and a collective Alka-Seltzer.

Salinas versus Zedillo: The Skirt of the Goddess Coatlicue

"It's straight out of Valle-Inclán."* Thus did Jorge Semprún describe the farce staged by Lieutenant Colonel Antonio Tejero Molina in front of television cameras in the Cortes of Madrid on 23 February 1981, when, flashing a pistol, he tried to cow the Congress and take over the government in a *coup d'état*.

We have been sorely, at times irresistibly, tempted to make Valle-Inclán jokes about the recent posturings of Carlos Salinas de Gortari, our former president. Ever since his decision to go on a fast, cartoonists have depicted him as a Creole Gandhi, an exhibitionistic fakir, or a Christ who nails himself to the cross, muttering, "Forgive me, Lord, for I know not what I do."

But Carlos Salinas knows exactly what he is doing. We would be wrong to underestimate him. He is a highly complex and intelligent man, worthy of an in-depth study like Gregorio Marañón's of Tiberius Caesar or, more recently, the studies of power by Gabriel García Márquez (Simon Bolivar) and Richard Kapuscinski (the Negus and the Shah). If his enemies underestimate him, Salinas will gain a great advantage over them. His script was written not by the author of *Carnival Tuesday*, Valle-Inclán, but by that of the Long March, Mao Zedong.

Salinas, the young Maoist, rookie traveler to the People's Republic, experienced technocrat, universally acclaimed president, felt threatened by the new Mexican government's actions. He tried to stop the course of events by force, sending an armed escort to rescue his brother Raúl, accused of masterminding the murder of Francisco Ruiz Massieu. He ran into the army and decided he'd better retreat to his populist base, the San Bernabé quarter of Monterrey, a working-class neighborhood that reaped the benefit of Solidarity, the social program of his presidency. The Hunan caves of Carlos Salinas de Gortari.

Once there, he reasserted his threefold position on the events besetting Mexico. He believes in the innocence of his brother. He demands that he himself be cleared of any suspicion of a cover-up

---

* Ramón del Valle-Inclán (1866–1936) revolutionized Spanish prose and theater with his *esperpentos*, or grotesque farces, based on his theory that Hispanic life can be reflected only in the mirrors of deformity.

in the assassination of Luis Donaldo Colosio. And finally he asks that the Zedillo government take full responsibility for the crisis caused by the devaluation of the Mexican peso in December 1994.

In defending his brother Raúl Salinas, the former president reminds us that the opening ball in this violent jai alai game of Mexican politics was thrown by Zedillo, that the current president was the one to seek a break with his predecessor. Why did he do so? To assert his own power, weakened by the crises of his turbulent first hundred days—devaluation, financial turmoil, Chiapas, humiliating negotiations with the United States? Because he knew of political maneuvers by the former president that might have been dangerous to him? To fulfill the parricidal ritual of Mexican politics, which must take place every six years? Or, simply and truthfully, because he had new and precise information incriminating Raúl Salinas and decided to enforce the law over and beyond any other consideration, whether personal or political?

Even if the latter were not the case, for the good of Mexico we would have to give Zedillo the benefit of the doubt, believe that it was his almost puritanical quest to reform the judicial system, his insistence on the rule of law, that led him to initiate this sequence of events. Yet he could not help seeing that he was, in effect, carrying out the Aztec six-year ritual, that his action would bring him immediate popularity and project the image of a strong president. It also exposed him—did he foresee this?—to a vigorous response from Salinas. And Salinas broke the golden rule of Mexico's patrilinear transmission of power, which requires a former president to bear everything—calumny, mockery, contempt—so that a new one may consolidate absolute power.

But in this bartering, the former president must never open his mouth again; in exchange, the new president must never touch his predecessor's money or family. In this sense, Zedillo's break with Salinas was more brutal than the one often recalled these days, that in 1935 between the new president, Lázaro Cárdenas, and the former president and maximum leader of the Revolution, Plutarco Elías Calles. But Calles reluctantly accepted exile, and Cárdenas, once he had claimed the power and dignity of his office, went on to implement his own policies.

The issue now is to determine whether this system can be perpetuated or whether it should be renewed or replaced by another.

Thus the confrontation between Zedillo and Salinas goes far beyond their personalities and places us at the very heart of Mexican political history. We have reached a limit. The old system can go no further. It is no longer sustainable in social, economic, or political terms. While it ensured stability and development in exchange for democratic freedom, it was tolerated and even admired. When its only fruit is economic crisis, instability, corruption, and impunity for all its players, what is the point of it? And what can replace it?

The answer is not long in coming. Democracy. But all the political parties of Mexico are in crisis, in a process of recomposition. The PRD (Party of Democratic Revolution) has a social-democratic wing and another on the extreme left. The PAN (National Action Party) has a collaborationist wing and an independent one, a democratic tradition and a Falangist one; almost always, however, it has a conservative social agenda that is puritanical, homophobic, and antiabortion. And the PRI has one progressive wing and one dominated by dinosaurs.

At the start, Zedillo emphasized above all else the need for a separation between party and government—without, however, renouncing his own party affiliation. But on 4 March, while celebrating the sixty-fifth anniversary of the PRI's founding, he reasserted with unusual energy the government's firm alliance with the party. A few hours earlier, the attorney general had made Salinas a present, as they say, giving in to his demand to be cleared of suspicion of a cover-up in the Colosio case. Zedillo had to go back to the PRI to reclaim his power base while, to reassert his, Salinas went back to San Bernabé and the Solidarity movement (perhaps the future Solidarity party?).

We must note the third matter raised by this very active and intelligent former president, who, not surprisingly, has committed Machiavelli's *The Prince* to memory and knows that the best defense is a good offense; without denying his own failings, Salinas blames the Zedillo government for having made a "problem" into a "crisis" with the December 1994 devaluation of the peso. In my view, Salinas is wrong. But it is only natural that he has difficulty acknowledging the collapse of the neoliberal economic model, the voodoo economics once denounced by his friend George Bush, the deluded belief that wealth accumulated at the top will trickle down to those waiting below, which he and his men made into a religion.

The neoliberal model takes place in the celestial spheres of the macroeconomy. But most people live in the microeconomy. And though the macroeconomy might solve cash-flow problems—as the always alert Gabriel Zaíd has said—there is a high price to be paid in the punishment imposed on individuals and companies, on savings and productive investment. The government of Carlos Salinas was governed by neoliberal dogma, sweetened by the Christian balm of Solidarity: balanced budgets, single-digit inflation, substantial hard-currency reserves, an opening to the world, and a warm welcome to foreign capital. But as we have seen, this capital was scarcely invested in the productive sector at all and was mainly sunk into speculation, subjecting itself (and Mexico) to financial fluctuations over which no government has control. It quickly took wing as flight capital.

The black swallows of flight capital having flown, we were left with the empty nest of an untenable foreign debt disguised as domestic debt, with growth sacrificed to the fetish of low inflation; with frantic trade liberalization (which will cancel out the obvious and proven benefits of NAFTA), with excessive imports financed with flight capital, with a growing deficit in the current account, and, despite everything, a dogmatic belief that the best and only possible path had been taken.

Zedillo handled the crisis badly, but he was not solely responsible for the "mistakes of December," as Salinas claims. Still, the crisis occurred at the worst possible moment for Zedillo, and Salinas knows it. As the Mexican congress debates the financial-aid package organized mainly by the U.S. government, Mexico is pledging to follow an economic policy that is precisely the one that led to the current situation: zero growth in the money supply, cuts in government spending, and more privatization. This is a renewed formula for disaster in a country that needs to stimulate growth even at the risk of inflation, as Brazil has done (though one need not go to the same extremes). Mexico has yet to learn the lesson that economists everywhere else have deduced from the crises perpetrated by the supply-side economics practiced during twelve years of Reagan, Bush, and Thatcher: that to restrict money supply and spending during a recession leads to depression, not recovery. Mexico's private sector, starved for credit and bloated by debt, needs more public spending to have more consumers. The deputies who wish to restore confidence in Mexico should vote against a package that is morally, politically, and economically deleterious. It resolves nothing and postpones everything.

That this unworthy agreement got as far as our congress speaks ill indeed of our diplomats' capacity to make the U.S. public understand that this is a crisis shared by Mexico and the United States, both bilaterally and as members of a global economy. (The U.S. government, of course, does understand but pretends not to for its own political reasons.) Our communications have broken down. We should recall Franklin D. Roosevelt's way of persuading Congress to pass the at first extremely unpopular Lend-Lease Act, designed to help Great Britain in 1941. "Suppose my neighbor's house is on fire," said FDR, "if he can take my garden hose . . . to put out his fire . . . I don't say to him . . . 'You have got to pay me $15 for it.' " Some fire. Some hose.

The danger of the Mexican bomb is that it could explode along any one of three fuses: the banking crisis, the business and employment crisis, or the discontent that stirs popular uprisings like those in Venezuela during the second term of Pérez's presidency. Rather than postpone these dangers, Mexico should accelerate the moment of truth. That needn't mean a drastic call for a debt moratorium or a suspension of payments; instead we should do as we have done since the time of our first president, Guadalupe Victoria, and call our action "debt renegotiation." We have always been good at it and should now be even better, as experienced negotiators like Jesús Silva Herzog, Bernardo Sepúlveda, and—God help us—Ángel Gurría, the current foreign minister, well know.

We should renegotiate the debt with imagination, daring, and patriotism and, at the same time, design a new development policy. We should get a moderate inflation rate compatible with growth. Exercise greater selectiveness in investments, preferably those for productive purposes. (Both the Copenhagen summit and the *Wall Street Journal* have called for taxes on speculative foreign investment.) Increase savings in pension and mutual funds. Give more protection to export companies able to reverse the balance-of-payment situation.

The political challenge gives Zedillo an opportunity, which no other president has really had since Cárdenas, to redefine a determined policy for national salvation. Building on the achievements of the Salinas administration, that policy should, in the new international context, renew the energy and capacity for work, savings, and productivity of the thirteenth-largest economy in the world. No longer a prisoner of petroleum, Mexico now prides itself on 80 percent nonoil exports.

Zedillo cannot afford to be passive, either for the country or for himself. Let him find support in the PRI or whatever is left of the PRI—but especially in the society, business and labor, the opposition, and, of course (for we must be realistic), the army. A constitutional president of Mexico, lawfully chosen by 51 percent of the electorate, has all the tools he needs to turn the country around.

The point is not to imitate Lázaro Cárdenas. It is not 1935. Then as now, however, the specters of Depression, bankruptcy, and unemployment, the fear of something worse, encouraged by the army, by the dinosaurs, or by the agents of high finance, might engender a populist response. In the capitalist world, Hitler and Mussolini built their strength in just this way. In the precapitalist world, Mao built his in an inflation-ridden, violent, and divided China, which could not see that a historical era had come to an end.

Perhaps Carlos Salinas understands this better than Ernesto Zedillo does. As the Argentine novelist Julio Cortázar would say, however, who will win the last round? We can only hope it will not be our cruel and mysterious mother, the unfathomable goddess of the shadows, Coatlicue, wrapped in serpents. Let us hope that Zedillo will at least give her a fashionable miniskirt.

Neither Hitler, nor Mussolini, nor Mao, the president of Mexico now has a chance to translate his legal puritanism into political realism: democracy with progress and justice. Now or never. For in politics, "too late" often means "never."

In Memoriam: Luis Donaldo Colosio

I met Luis Donaldo Colosio four years ago at the home of José Luis Cuevas, in the company of Daisy Ascher, Enrique González Pedrero, and Fernando Benítez. He later invited me to speak at a seminar on "Freedom and Justice in Modern Societies" and explained his concern about the inevitable tension between not only nationalism and globalization but also freedom and justice, the individual and the community. When I gave my lecture in June 1993, he accompanied me in a friendly way, found a seat in the auditorium, and took notes. Then my wife, Silvia, and I had the pleasure of receiving him and his wife, Diana Laura, at our home, at a celebration for the English historian Hugh Thomas, whose book on the Conquest of Mexico had just been published. After Colosio became a candidate for the presidency, our meetings grew more intensive, as did his concerns about the future of Mexico. Jorge Castañeda, Héctor Aguilar Camín, Miguel Alemán Velasco, Mario Moya Palencia, Gabriel García Márquez, Víctor Flores Olea, and Enrique González Pedrero joined this discussion with Luis Donaldo. What most impressed me in our conversations was Colosio's effort to find a balance between the poles of ideological and geopolitical division, between outdated development models and new forms for social participation, between Mexico and the world. What most grieves me about his death is the impossibility of pursuing that dialogue, and now I stay awake wondering what this open, warmhearted, concerned, and sensitive man might have thought and said about us Mexicans now. Perhaps in describing him I am describing the best in our country; perhaps my dialogue with Luis Donaldo Colosio will continue in a dialogue with Mexico. If our future proves good, we will find Colosio in it. If it doesn't, we will mourn his loss all the more. But in either case his sacrifice will not have been in vain. There are many ways to honor him, and all converge in one word, *democracy.*

On 6 January 1994, he wrote me a letter asking me to continue pursuing initiatives that might lead to "the democratic transformation of Mexico." He was referring to, among other things, a failed meeting I had tried to organize between him and the left-wing presidential candidate, Cuauhtémoc Cárdenas of the PRD. After accepting, Cárdenas backed out, rescheduled, and finally called off the meeting. I felt that his initial response had been spontaneous and creative, but perhaps some of his more intransigent counselors convinced him not to have contact with the standard-bearer of the detested official party. Will we ever know if Cárdenas, who many (including himself) thought had been fraudulently deprived of victory in the 1988 elections, was right in denouncing Salinas as an illegitimate president and refusing all contact with him? Would Cárdenas, his party, and the country, have gained if, negotiating from strength, the left had secured positions and won electoral rights for the people? As it was, Cárdenas maintained his rigid, aloof, and unbending denial of Salinas, Salinas nurtured his own hatred for Cárdenas, and PRD members were politically and physically attacked throughout the Salinas administration. Then Cárdenas sacrificed the possibility of overcoming this impasse and initiating a new dialogue with a new man in a new situation.

As Colosio drifted further and further from both Salinas and Salinas's men (notably the Fouché-like chief of staff, José Córdoba), he became increasingly lonely, misunderstood by Cárdenas and perhaps also by his potential rival within the official ranks, Manuel Camacho. His loneliness was apparent by 6 March, when he made his reformist speech at the Monument of the Revolution. What indeed was he proposing? Separation of party and state, a quickened pace of democratic reform, recasting of progressive alliances in Mexico. According to recent reports in *Proceso* (November 1995), Colosio received a fourteen-page draft of this speech from Córdoba, tore up twelve pages, retained just two, and then wrote his own draft, consulting no one. That the distance between Salinas and Colosio had grown is certified by none other than Zedillo, Colosio's campaign manager at the time. In a letter written on 20 March, two days before the assassination, he begged Colosio to mend his relation with Salinas and reach "a political alliance with the president," for such an alliance had become nonexistent.

My friends and I had agreed to have a second luncheon with Colosio on 18 March, which happened to be the anniversary of Lázaro Cárdenas's expropriation of Mexico's oil in 1938, as well as the birthday of Miguel Alemán Valasco, who was to be our host. That day Senator Alemán was informed that candidate Colosio would be unable to join us. The reason: he had changed his campaign schedule and had advanced his trip to Tijuana, Baja California, by several days. In Tijuana on 22 March, Colosio was assassinated. He had gone to his appointment in Samarra.

The sloppiness, the zigzags, the sheer snail's pace of the murder investigation have created immense anguish, doubt, and suspicion in Mexico. Who would want this decent, conciliatory, creative man out of the way? It is hard to believe that President Salinas would have wrecked his own political strategy and jeopardized his place in history by having his anointed heir murdered and plunging the country into disaster.

Yet when I consider the fate of Colosio, I always recall that of the Italian Socialist deputy Giacomo Matteotti, the last independent representative in the Fascist-dominated lower chamber, who in 1924 waged a war of words against Mussolini and was assassinated by Fascist gangs. No one could blame Mussolini himself, one could only point to the officious members of his entrourage who believed that by killing Matteotti they would please Il Duce. The Matteotti case discredited Mussolini before he openly imposed his dictatorship in 1925—and it also permitted him to impose that dictatorship.

The Pandora's box of corruption in Mexico, whose lid was only barely lifted with the arrest and imprisonment of the former president's brother Raúl in early 1995, popped wide open late in the year with the arrest of Raúl's wife, Paulina, as she was about to withdraw $84 million from a Swiss bank account of her husband's obtained with fake documents and a fake passport. As the sinister plot unfolded, it linked Raúl and his wife to drug trafficking, money laundering, and assorted other crimes. Corruption, fraud, drugs, money laundering—were these the horrors that had, together, murdered the democratic, seemingly incorruptible Luis Donaldo Colosio? Since the Mexican melodrama has not come to its final chapter, I cannot say. But if the Colosio case is left unsolved, the goals he outlined in his 6 March speech will not be achieved: a democracy with no trace of authoritarianism; an executive branch subject to constitutional limitations; a Mexico of Indian communities willing to participate in the national society and unwilling to postpone their demands for justice; a Mexico of campesinos able to respond to good incentives for production and justice; a Mexico of workers who receive the training and employment they deserve; a Mexico of youths who are offered the support and education they need.

Colosio spoke of the great inequality and poverty in Mexico, of the social reforms necessary for overcoming them, and of the political reforms on which to base all the other measures for change.

The question remains: Who took these promises so seriously that they decided to eliminate Colosio? Who opposed these reforms so violently that they believed in Colosio's will to implement them? Will we ever know the truth? If we don't, Mexico, its institutions, its democratic promise will be tragically postponed. We do not know what will take their place. We will have to fear the worst.

One Hundred Years of Cárdenas

> *On the centenary of his birth, I reiterate to Lázaro Cárdenas, his memory and legacy, the trust, affection, and respect of a citizen.*

I have known all the presidents of Mexico from 1934 to the present. Some have been more intelligent than others, some more politically astute, some more cultivated; but only one has attained true greatness: Lázaro Cárdenas. By greatness I mean, over and beyond tactical skill, energy, and determination, the concept of nationhood, the lofty vision that Cárdenas had of Mexico, its people, its history and culture, its destiny. He never thought small; he never belittled Mexico or its people.

Now that so much emphasis is placed on comparing the break between Salinas and Zedillo and that which took place, sixty years ago, between Calles and Cárdenas, it is worth recalling that Cárdenas broke free of Calles to launch his own policies. To that end, he sought to bolster his power by consolidating political alliances among the various sectors of production: businesspeople, workers, campesinos, intellectuals. First of all, he built on the strength of the citizenry. Then he was able to implement policies that revolutionized Mexico from top to bottom, revitalizing the spirit of the Mexican Revolution, which had become fossilized.

Agrarian reform, education, labor policy, nationalization of the oil industry—in all these areas, Cárdenas faced fierce opposition from the sectors adversely affected. He overcame these obstacles thanks to the people's support for their courageous, clearheaded, determined chief of state. More than on elevated macroeconomic designs, Cárdenas counted on the human capital of Mexico, on the permanent, essential wealth constituted by the human resources of the nation. Parting from them, he returned to them, giving Mexicans the fruits of an effort shared by people and government alike.

A fundamental aspect of Cardenista policy was the independence of his foreign policy. Mexico's nationalization of the oil industry caused the industrialized democracies to rise up against us; the subsequent boycott obliged Cárdenas to sell oil to his ideological enemies, the Nazi and Fascist powers. But he committed himself to a policy of negotiation, negotiation, and more negotiation. He decided—granted, within an economic context that was far less globally interdependent than now—to suspend international payments, arguing that he would not sacrifice his domestic-development and social program to them. England and Holland severed diplomatic relations with Mexico, but the United States responded more positively.

The renegotiation of the petroleum debt, headed by two eminent Mexican statesmen—Treasury Secretary Eduardo Suárez and Mexico's ambassador in Washington, Francisco Castillo Nájera—was a decisive moment for the good-neighbor policy of Franklin D. Roosevelt. Beleaguered by the interest groups that since 1821 had been demanding war against Mexico, invasion of Mexico, dismemberment of Mexico, suffocation of Mexico, Roosevelt courageously played the card of negotiation. Both Mexico and the United States came out winners. The United States gained an ally in the approaching world war, and Mexico was able to pursue its policies for development.

Under Lázaro Cárdenas, Mexico did not cease to be the country of inequality that Alexander von Humboldt described in 1806. But never in our history have we had more equitable development, in which all classes and sectors grew together, laying the foundation for the 6 percent annual growth rate that collapsed only with the foreign-debt crisis of 1982. Lázaro Cárdenas, reviled by the Mexican bourgeoisie, furnished the empty home of Mexican business —much as President Franklin Roosevelt, reviled by the American right, saved U.S. capitalism from itself. He freed the campesino from the slavery of the hacienda, promoted internal migration, urban development, universal education, and an industrialization based on cheap labor, often derived from the rural proletariat. In a word, he gave the bourgeoisie cheap energy, and wealthier and better-educated consumer credit institutions and fiscal incentives for private enterprise, even as he bolstered the lower classes and the incipient middle class.

The shortcomings of the Cárdenas administration are well

known but were not always attributable to it alone. The symbiosis between the state and the PRI, the PRI's corporative structure, the Scholastic politics of traditional Mexico—which have always placed the common good above the risks of democratic pluralism —and the demagogy that often accompanied agrarian reform are only a few. In contrast, later policies dismantled or rendered ineffective many of Cárdenas's revolutionary advances. Continued agrarian reform would have required credit, machinery, seed, cooperatives managed honestly and democratically. Popular organizations needed to do more for their constitutents and less for the state and private enterprise. "I delivered strong organizations to the workers and campesinos," Cárdenas once said to me, implying that what happened to them after 1941 was not what he would have wished.

"You should have stayed in the presidency until you completed your task," Fernando Benítez told the general. Cárdenas replied in his deliberate and thoughtful way, "I would have become a Trujillo." In order to ensure the power and independence of the executive, Cárdenas set the rules required to prevent absolutism, coups d'état, and military tyrannies in Mexico: no reelection; all power to Caesar, but only for six years, and only once.

Mexico today is not the Mexico of Cárdenas, but it is what it is, for good and for evil, thanks to Cárdenas. His goals of a just and shared progress, his trust in the country, his conviction that economic life does not occur on blackboards but in kitchens, streets, fields, factories, and the privacy of the home are still valid today. Like no one else, Lázaro Cárdenas was willing to bet that our human resources are Mexico's first and best capital.

My personal memory of Lázaro Cárdenas is warm. He offered me friendship and good counsel at the beginning of my literary career. I traveled with him through many regions of our splendid, energetic country, so often impeded, humiliated, and maligned yet patient, willing to give the best of itself if only it is treated with a little trust and respect. From La Piedad to Querétaro, from La Barca to Uruápan, from Guanajuato to Guadalajara, I have never seen a Mexican more loved, respected, and followed than Lázaro Cárdenas. To understand why one had merely to hear him talking with people: Cárdenas loved, respected, and followed the people of Mexico.

9 : SO FAR FROM GOD

. . . .

Mexico and the United States

I

The most famous saying about Mexico and the United States has been attributed to Porfirio Díaz, the old dictator who ruled my country with an iron hand from 1877 to the outbreak of the Revolution in 1910: "Poor Mexico! So far from God and so close to the United States!" In the present circumstances, we would be well advised to change this celebrated saying and exclaim instead, "Poor Mexico and poor United States! So far from God and so close to each other!"

Our two countries have become extremely interdependent yet also have an extremely lopsided power relationship—the United States is strong, Mexico is weak—and both elements are dramatically heightened by the fact that we share a common border, one of the longest, most conflictive, and most challenging borders in the world: three thousand kilometers long, from the Pacific Ocean to the Gulf of Mexico, from San Diego–Tijuana to Brownsville–Matamoros. A cultural frontier where two different civilizations face, challenge, and enrich each other—cultures as different as those of the United States and any Asian nation. A labor frontier, with five thousand Mexican workers, both legal and illegal, crossing each day, acting on the demand of the United States economy. And, of course, an economic frontier, with Mexico the third-largest client of the United States (after Canada and Japan) and the United States the largest market for Mexican goods.

The porousness of the border is more than a matter of products: 300 million people cross the border in both directions every year, and with them, ideas, habits, information, and cultural trends come and go. The vast asymmetry of power between the United States and Mexico is less and less significant with each passing day.

If in the past, Mexico got pneumonia when the United States caught a cold, today we get the flu together and have not developed an efficient vaccine against our increasingly common ills.

It is not an easy border. True, it is unmilitarized. For how long? Ultraconservatives in the United States demand that, the Berlin Wall having fallen, a new wall now be constructed between the United States and Mexico.

It is not an easy border, because its significance is unique. It is the only visible border between a developed postindustrial state and an emerging, developing nation, between the First and the Third Worlds. All the frictions, all the lessons, all the opportunities of the north-south relationship in the twenty-first century are bound to manifest themselves along that line from the Pacific to the gulf.

But this is not only a border between Mexico and the United States or even between a developing and a developed nation. It is also a border between the United States and *all* of Latin America, which begins south of the river that you call the Rio Grande and we call the Río Bravo. What happens on the line between Nogales, Arizona, and Nogales, Sonora, is bound to affect the relationship between the United States and the rest of the Western Hemisphere.

Not an easy border, no. Is it more than a border, asks a character in my novel *The Old Gringo*. Is it a scar? Will it heal? Will it bleed again?

This will depend, of course, on our policies with regard to the main issues on the U.S.–Mexico agenda, starting with trade and migration but including many other areas of the increasing interdependency of the two countries.

The North American Free Trade Agreement (NAFTA) among Mexico, the United States, and Canada was designed as the first stage in a new, more constructive and integrated relationship. It became part of a central thrust in the post–cold war world: sharing the possible benefits of free trade out of a conviction that a growing exchange of goods, services, capital, and labor in an interdependent world is not a zero-sum game, since output and investment are not fixed, and that economies in free trade should grow prosperous together, not at one another's expense. Free trade is a positive-sum game: this is the philosophy that stimulated the NAFTA.

While the treaty was being discussed, I made a bet with my

friend the Mexican writer Jorge Castañeda: if NAFTA was approved by 1 January 1994, he would invite me to dinner; if it wasn't, I would invite him to dinner.

It was a win-win situation, for we enjoy each other's company. Castañeda was a staunch opponent of NAFTA as it stands. While sharing many of his criticisms, I always thought the treaty would be approved for the very simple reason that it serves, above all, the national interests of the United States. But you would not think so to hear the Texagogue Ross Perot thunder on about the "sucking sound" of jobs heading from the United States to Mexico.

This argument should be disposed of quickly. First, labor-intensive jobs in the low-tech industries of the past are going to go to low-wage workers, NAFTA or no NAFTA. With NAFTA, they will go to Mexico and therefore strengthen the U.S. strategic position vis-à-vis the other two great trading blocs, Asia and Europe; without NAFTA, they will certainly go to Indonesia, China, or Malaysia and improve Japan's position. But if low wages were the principal factor in attracting jobs, Bangladesh would be an employment paradise. It is not.

Mexico is also the United States' fastest-growing export market and second-largest trading partner. About three-quarters of every Mexican dollar spent on imports is spent on U.S. goods, and for every dollar's worth of growth, Mexico spends 20 cents in the United States.

Does the growth of U.S. exports to Mexico mean U.S. employment grows along with them?

This is what the partisans of NAFTA affirmed and its foes vehemently denied. The partisans argue: If each $1 billion of net improvement in the U.S. trade balance signified 20,000 new American jobs, it was conservatively foreseeable that within two years the $42 billion in U.S. exports to Mexico (the figure for 1992) would jump to $52 billion with NAFTA, and the $30 billion in U.S. imports from Mexico would rise by $5 billion; the new U.S. trade surplus would create nearly 200,000 new export-related jobs.

The United States also stood to lose some 100,000 old jobs, but not just because NAFTA would negatively affect a number of labor-intensive industries. Those jobs would migrate or be lost, in any case, if the United States did not stand up to its real competition, the high-tech, high-productivity, high-salary club in the Pacific Basin and the European Economic Community. To think otherwise is to give Mexico a truly bum rap.

NAFTA, by integrating a population of 360 million people with a $6.5 trillion trading bloc—the largest in the world—would in any case enormously strengthen the U.S. position in the highly integrated, capital-scarce, technologically advanced economy of the twenty-first century. This is what was really at stake for the United States: Where would it focus its energy in the new global economy? How would it stand up to German or Japanese competition?

U.S. indecisiveness in these issues makes one wonder whether the federal republic founded in 1776—the sole great power in history to be blessed with only two neighbors, both of them weak—can enter the twenty-first century with a sure step and a sense of its true duties. Or will the United States be content as a backwater from the second industrial revolution, a Luddite widow set to repudiate advanced technology in the name of full employment and the narrow interests of pressure groups?

Like all other industrialized nations today, the United States faces the cruel paradox of "jobless productivity," in which the more you produce, the less employment there is. It is not the Third World that is taking jobs away from the industrialized world. Technology is. Blame yourselves. Don't blame Mexico. And the humane political and social resolution to the paradox lies within U.S. borders: it is the retraining, education, and development of workers for new jobs.

Granted, this is not an easy situation. Konrad Seitz, the outspoken director of strategic planning at the German Ministry of Foreign Affairs, bluntly states that a high standard of living in the future will be available only to nations or groups of nations that possess the most advanced production technologies. A country that manufactures products of the first or second industrial revolutions—automobiles, steel, and so on—will have to content itself with "the salaries of Mexico or Korea," he says. High salaries will be reserved for those who make products of the third industrial revolution—what Alvin Toffler calls the "third wave": space technology, cyber-information, biotechnology, services, and so on.

Will the three big blocs resolve the struggle over these resources peacefully or with strife? And who will accompany them into the twenty-first century?

After 1989, the government of President Carlos Salinas de Gortari decided that Mexico's best opportunity lay in having at least a foot instead one of these blocs. It seemed natural to profit from the border situation and the de facto integration taking place between the U.S. and Mexican economies. It also seemed advantageous to eliminate a noxious protectionism from our relations.

Lest we forget, NAFTA signifies the only dynamic U.S. initiative toward Latin America in a long, long time. Our relations were strained by President Reagan's obsession with Nicaragua and President Bush's efforts to prove he was not a wimp by invading Panama and kidnapping General Manuel Noriega. In the meantime, economic realities made Latin America the only area in the world where the United States had a trade surplus. From the Rio Grande to Cape Horn, this was the fastest-growing market for U.S. goods. (In 1993, while U.S. exports to Latin America increased by almost 33 percent, to the rest of the world they increased by only 4.4 percent.)

The regional subgroups that have been gaining strength in Latin America—Mercosur, the Andean Group, the Central American Common Market, the Mexico-Chile Free Trade Agreement, the G3 Agreement among Colombia, Mexico, and Venezuela—all eagerly anticipated the first step called NAFTA. I hope a North American trade pact will raise the levels of investment and employment in Mexico. I hope this will lessen labor migration to the United States and boost salaries in Mexico through higher productivity as well as greater independence and aggressiveness of the labor movement.

But Castañeda is right in many of his criticisms.

NAFTA is not a panacea. It will never take the place of hard work, internal investment, greater political democracy, and social justice in Mexico. So the only certain beneficiaries of all this were Castañeda and myself. We had a great dinner together on New Year's Day, 1994.

II

During NAFTA's first year, many of the optimistic predictions came true. Mexican imports from the United States rose spectacularly, and Latin America continued to be the world's fastest-growing market for U.S. goods.

Mexico, which in 1986, in the midst of the international debt crisis, imported goods worth a mere $13 billion from the United States, imported $50 billion (only slightly less than Japan) in 1994. The trade balance favored the United States, which imported $40 billion from Mexico, to the amount of $10 billion.

The Mexican imports signified enormous benefits for many states and regions of the United States. Our imports from Texas in 1994 were as high as $13 billion—one-third of the state's total exports. From Michigan, Mexico imported $6 billion, equivalent to one-fifth of that state's total exports. Similarly, one-fifth of Arizona's exports went to Mexico, as did one-fifth of New Mexico's. And from California, our yearly imports were in the range of $5 billion. Whole regions, such as the traditional Rust Belt, have in the last few years registered a trade surplus for the first time in many years, due entirely to exports of machinery and capital goods to Mexico.

The interdependency is so extended that even a recondite state like Delaware became a major exporter of chemicals to Mexico, and a relatively invisible state like Kansas established a lively trade of crops and processed foods with Mexico.

What NAFTA did was to institutionalize the growing relationship among the three North American economies. That relationship would have increased with or without NAFTA, but NAFTA spelled out opportunities, rights, and duties that would otherwise have gone unheeded or been insufficiently stimulated.

The philosophy governing NAFTA was—and is—quite correctly that free trade is not a zero-sum game. Output and investment are not fixed. More output and investment in Mexico does not occur at the expense of more output and investment in the United States. Economies in free trade grow rich together, not at one another's expense: as each country prospers, it becomes a bigger market for the other's exports. New investment opportunities at home and abroad call forth an increased supply of capital to invest, and investment raises incomes and savings and stimulates further investment.

NAFTA enshrined these hopes and principles, and what we now may call NAFTA I—1994, the initial year of the Treaty—bore out their validity. The export–import relationship between Mexico and the United States grew astonishingly, producing the largest increase in our history, and 700,000 United States jobs became dependent on Mexican imports—giving the lie to that great sucking-sound theory that U.S. jobs would go south. Ross Perot's theory in effect undersold one of the greatest strengths of the U.S. economy: its unequaled capacity to move capital and labor across space, social class, and economic activity.

Yet it is also true that these strengths were undermined by the post–cold war recession in the United States, which sent interest rates down and created pockets of unemployment in areas hit by the closure of defense industries and by a lack of worker-retraining programs, circumstances that have at times been unjustly ascribed to Mexican labor migration, which plays the role of scapegoat for deficiencies in the U.S. economy.

And Mexico, battered by the debt crisis of the 1980s—the lost decade of development, which affected all of Latin America— sought strong and revolutionary macroeconomic solutions, first under the de la Madrid administration, and then more fully under the Salinas administration. These measures included bringing inflation down to single digits, balancing the budget, increasing foreign reserves, welcoming foreign investment, keeping interest rates competitively high, and privatizing as much as possible. And enshrining supply-side economics, known in Latin America as neoliberalism, the equivalent to the trickle-down theory (or voodoo economics, as candidate George Bush called it back in 1980).

President Salinas tried to blunt the harsh social effects of this policy through Solidarity, his social giveaway program, but it was not enough. Mexico needed—and did not get—policies encouraging investment in activities that would further employment, wages, growth, and savings. Instead, the Salinas reforms provoked a flood of speculative, unregulated capital that did not go into productive areas. Like flight capital in any other emerging market, it stayed in Mexico as long as it was profitable to stay and fled as soon as dark clouds started accumulating in the sky. Recession and low interest rates in the United States sent this flight capital to Mexico; recovery and rising rates sent it back to the United States.

Never has Mexico received as much foreign investment as it did during the Salinas years: almost $59 billion between January 1989 and September 1994, but of that enormous sum, almost 85 percent was speculative flight capital.

Spurred by the Salinas reforms and then by NAFTA, however, the 15 percent that represented productive capital achieved excellent results. It created more than five thousand new businesses in Mexico, along with almost 1.5 million new jobs. Most of these jobs and enterprises were closely related to NAFTA: firms were positioning themselves for NAFTA or were created as a result of the passing of the NAFTA laws.

This was not sufficient to offset the negative effect of a number of factors. First, the excessively quick opening of the traditionally overprotected Mexican market led to a veritable shopping spree by Mexican businesses and middle-class individuals, who sometimes imported prestige items like mineral water and tennis shoes that could be had for less in Mexico at comparable quality. Larger imports of U.S. machinery, vehicles, telecommunications, and other manufactured goods forced the government to pay with its decreasing foreign-currency reserves. These fell from a height of $33 billion in February 1994, after the Chiapas uprising, to $17 billion in March, after the assassination of Luis Donaldo Colosio; to $4 billion in November, as the political mystery deepened with the assassination of Francisco Ruiz Massieu; and then to less than $1 billion as the Zedillo administration took over on 1 December.

No longer able to meet its financial obligations, the Zedillo administration drastically devalued the peso on 19 December, without first arranging for safety nets and rescue operations, and only four days after having assured leading financial institutions in the United States that no devaluation was foreseen for the overvalued peso. *From $33 billion to nil in one year.*

Why were no alarms sounded? Who is to blame?

Again, given the interdependency of our two economies, fault should be spread with some kind of rough justice. The principal culprit is the Mexican government.

The Chiapas rebellion in January 1994 revealed that, if Mexico had one foot in the First World, it still had the other foot in the Third World: it is a country with 40 million people living in poverty, 17 million in *extreme* poverty, out of a growing population of 90 million (which will reach 100 million before the century is over). How do we feed, educate, provide jobs for, and simply raise these millions out of misery or at least offer them a measure of hope?

The neoliberal model espoused by the Salinas administration responded by fighting inflation, balancing the budget, inspiring confidence in Mexico, attracting investment, concentrating wealth in a few competitive firms and individuals, and hoping that trickle-down would take effect. But the hope was undermined by evidence that the economy was not growing, that fighting inflation had become a fetish, that excessive foreign spending was not compensated for by increasing local production, that real growth was hindered by one of the lowest savings rates in the world, and, finally, that flight capital had become unmanageable.

Yet the deeper reason for the crisis has simply to do with democracy in Mexico. The secrecy surrounding our economic realities is related to the absence of something well known in Anglo-Saxon law for which there is not even a proper term in Spanish: accountability, checks and balances. These are part of a democratic system of government with a real separation of powers, in which the legislative and judicial branches balance and offset the executive. In Mexico, from the Aztec emperor Moctezuma right down to Carlos Salinas, the executive has been all-powerful, untrammeled, subjected neither to accountability nor to checks and balances.

To a great degree, the present crisis is due to the capricious nature of the Mexican presidency, to the fiat that one person, or a small group, can dictate unchallenged.

With its growing middle class, its increasingly diversified economy, its natural trend toward decentralization, as Guadalajara, Monterrey, Juárez, Tijuana—cities other than the gigantic federal district of Mexico City—grow in strength and population, Mexico has made enormous strides in advancing freedom of the press (including radio, though not yet television, coverage) and of independent social organizations such as agrarian co-ops, trade unions, women's groups, volunteer services, religious groups, business and neighborhood associations, if not the official corporative unions affiliated with the PRI. Mexicans understand that you can achieve development by dictatorial means—look at Chile, look at China. But authoritarian capitalism clashes with NAFTA, and besides, Mexicans want development with democracy and social justice.

Mexican society, I mean, has gained enormously since the massacre in Tlatelolco Square in 1968 signified the end of the "Mexican miracle," which had been built on a specific trade-off. When the Revolution was institutionalized in 1929, the government had said, We shall assure economic growth and social stability in exchange for your forfeiting democratic freedoms; the PRI will take care of politics. This trade-off worked for four decades. But it has now failed. Only a fully democratic system can solve the political problems in Mexico, but a transition to democracy has been immensely complicated by our economic crisis.

The United States will certainly be puzzled by the prospect of forthcoming political dramas in Mexico. Since World War II, Washington has depended on a basically stable nation on its southern border. The authoritarian sins of the PRI were forgiven because it gave the U.S. a secure southern flank. Mexico's independent foreign-policy forays were irritating but finally condoned: Mexico's maintenance of diplomatic relations with the Castro regime in Cuba is a good example, and in any case it provided a much-needed lifeline between Washington, Mexico City, and Havana. But now, as the left-wing PRD self-destructs in internal polemics and petty divisiveness, as the PRI disintegrates in incompetence, economic crisis, bloodbaths, and the loss of the Mafia-like *omertà* among its members, perhaps the U.S. will be tempted to foster the fortunes of the center-right PAN, to support it as the alternative to the PRI, and to bank on the electoral victories that could, with minimal strife, take it to victory in the 1997 legislative elections and in the general elections in 2000. Besides, in 1997, the mayor of Mexico City will be chosen, for the first time, at the ballot box, transforming him—or her—into the second most powerful elected official in the country. Imagine how the president and mayor are going to get along!

The PAN has been garnering impressive victories. In 1996, it controls four state governorships and eleven mayoralties of state capitals. Unfortunately, Mexican politics are not subject to predictable calendars. President Zedillo's lack of political expertise permits many negative factors to surface and many democratic slogans to be perverted. For example, given the weakness of presidential leadership, the banner of federalism is quickly becoming a fig leaf covering a return to old-fashioned *caciquismo*, or domination of the federal states by local authoritarian political bosses.

In Guerrero, Governor Rubén Figueroa has not been called to account for the massacre of protesting campesinos in the town of Aguas Blancas. In Tabasco, Governor Roberto Madrazo defies the federal executive in the name of federalism so as to avoid charges of violating electoral laws on campaign spending.

The United States is imbued with faith in the two-party system, a system that is not responsive to Mexico's more pluralistic political makeup. Perhaps we shall end up with two parties arising out of a divided PRD and another two parties out of a divided PRI. The PAN hides its internal differences and values its unity. Yet the real answer to Mexico's political needs is a left-of-center social democratic party along the lines of the German, French, or Spanish model. Developing such a party takes time, and three factors in the equation—the U.S. government, the PRI dinosaurs, and the exasperated Mexicans themselves—can tax the rationality and patience required to rebuild Mexico's political system.

President Zedillo has repeatedly spoken in favor of democratic presidential authority. It is up to him to stimulate and expedite a political pact based on deep reforms of the system and a overhauling of the electoral rules so as to make them truly democratic, modern, and fair. But whatever the tempo of executive-inspired reforms, the other branches of government, the legislative and the judiciary, as well as Mexico's civil society and its organizations, should propose dynamic ideas, shed old habits, adopt new democratic forms.

In the meantime, here we are, caught between the promises and the dangers of Mexico and the United States' shared crisis but perhaps not fully aware of the obligations the new situation imposes on us.

Mexico's obligation is primarily to put its house in order. The draconian self-discipline imposed by the Zedillo administration, though temporary, is, by the president's own admission, cruel: steep increases in the prices of gasoline and transportation, a 50 percent increase in value-added taxes, cuts in government spending, and almost total credit restriction. These are coupled with a 2 percent fall in the GNP, 750,000 people out of work, 42 percent inflation, and only 10 percent in wage increases.

Three short fuses may set off the Mexican bomb: bank failures, company closedowns, or street demonstrations and acts of vandalism, as in the Venezuela of President Pérez's second term—a Mexican reprise of that *caracazo*.

I certainly hope that none of this occurs. The Mexican people are extraordinarily patient, though most have never known anything but misfortune. But in 1982 the debt crisis struck a middle class with money in its pockets thanks to the oil boom. Today, Mexican middle-class families will be unable to pay the mortgages on their two-bedroom apartments, the monthly payments on their Volkswagens, and maybe even the rent. Their dramatic pauperization is evident in every corner of our larger cities.

Do we have time to set the stage for economic renewal?

Again, the answer to this question is intimately linked to the interdependent Mexican and U.S. economies.

To renew growth in Mexico, a policy based on internal savings has to take hold. This is the way that Chile came out of a comparable financial crisis in 1982—though, admittedly, under a brutally iron-fisted military regime.

More than this, Mexico can dramatically increase its inherent strengths, notably in export-led growth. The relationship with the United States comes into play here at two important levels. One of the original considerations of NAFTA was that all three partners —Mexico, Canada, and the United States—shared large current-account deficits, large foreign debts, and a need for export-led growth. All three came together because all three needed to enhance the international competitiveness of companies in North America. The pact has worked very well for U.S. and Canadian firms in Mexico, as trade figures show.

But now the present crisis is already hurting the United States economy. U.S. goods will become far more expensive in Mexico. Mexican goods will become far cheaper in the United States. The balance is bound to change in Mexico's favor: already, right on the border, trucks are backed up on the Mexican side to enter the United States, but U.S. trucks are not heading south in comparable numbers.

The U.S. will lose export-related jobs: it lost 30,000 after the peso's devaluation, and 700,000 more are at risk. The ugly tactics that may be used will tarnish NAFTA. Already, some firms in the United States, threatening to move south, have imposed two-year wage freezes on U.S. unions. Already, a wildcat strike among bonded factory workers in Juárez has thrown 1,300 workers out of their jobs at plants in Indiana. But at the same time, General Electric, whose exports to Mexico went up by 70 percent in 1994, is planning to export *from* Mexico to the United States, furthering a trend: in 1994, the company sold $300 million to Mexico but sold $1 billion *from* its Mexican plants worldwide.

General Electric seems to have found a way to protect itself from currency hurricanes, by balancing its peso and dollar revenues, its export and import markets, its real-estate projects with leases payable in dollars, and its exports from the United States to Mexico with exports from Mexico to the world.

In this wider picture of opportunity, a company comes out ahead even if Mexican salaries go up, as we hope, and investment and production costs in pesos come down. Revenues in dollars will still rise.

No wonder that Nike is planning to produce all its shoes in Mexico—for Mexicans, other Latin Americans, and then U.S. consumers. Mexico has become extremely cheap: immense opportunities are to be had, and they will build up the strengths of a country that, despite all its troubles, is destined to grow economically.

I have spoken out against the U.S. government's $20 billion rescue package, which, even with a further $31 billion collected from other sources, does nothing to set Mexico on its feet and back on the road to greater production. It merely permits us to attend to debt repayment with financial obligations called *tesobonos*, designated by peso value but payable in dollars: this is a grievous mistake, disguising foreign debt as internal debt, which, owing to the executive branch's lack of accountability, was not scrutinized in the Mexican congress. Notes of $71 billion were due in 1995. Repaying them meant freezing investments favoring production, employment, and social services, the real spurs to economic recovery.

The hour of truth has been postponed. But sooner or later Mexico will have to renegotiate its foreign debt without using the traumatic phrases *suspension of payment* or *moratorium*. Meanwhile, by accepting the U.S. package, the country has paid a very high price in sovereignty without gaining renewed investor confidence, as the package intended it to. For who can trust a country regarded as a perpetual minor, its economic policies dictated by Washington, its oil collateral held at the Federal Reserve Bank in New York in case of default—or disobedience? We must not postpone the moment of truth: we have a liquidity problem and must renegotiate, as so many other nations have done over the centuries.

We must build on our strength.

Let us have a renewal of growth at the risk of some inflation.

Let us stimulate direct foreign investment by showing that we do not care as much for speculative flight capital as we do for productive, permanent investment. Rather than worry about paying U.S. bondholders, let us worry about U.S. exporters who risk losing jobs and profits, U.S. exporters interested in creating platforms in Mexico.

Let us, as even the *Wall Street Journal* now suggests, tax speculative capital and require that it stay in the country a minimum period before flying back home.

Let us fortify the very basis of a rebounding Mexican economy: direct foreign investment, rules for flight capital, export-led growth, productivity, employment, savings.

Let us strengthen NAFTA by adding, as the European Economic Community has, a social component to its free-trade dynamics, admitting that the private sector needs more investment but also better wages, more jobs but also better productivity, better technology but also more training, better infrastructure but also more education.

Let us not put the cart before the horse. Investor confidence will return when Mexico starts producing again, and producing more and better means paying attention to the economy's social factors. We cannot enter the First World with 42 out of 90 million Mexicans living in abject poverty. We should pay attention to the priorities of human development, without sacrificing fiscal discipline, currency stability, and access to financial markets.

At the United Nations development summit held in 1995 in Copenhagen and headed by former Chilean president Patricio Aylwin, my fellow members of the Latin American commission and I proposed a policy to increase productivity among the poor through stimulation and assistance: worker retraining, access to credit, technical aid, and systems to commercialize and distribute the goods of small- and medium-size producers. This is vitally important in Mexico, as it is throughout the world: Latin America has the highest income per capita of any of the world's low-income regions, but it is also the region with the worst inequality in the distribution of wealth. Income is more and more concentrated, the gap between rich and poor is ever greater, and growth by itself does not eliminate poverty. (Between 1950 and 1980, Latin America's GNP grew by 80 percent, but poverty grew by 10 percent in the same period.)

The U.S. should attend to this situation as well as to a fundamental solution, fiscal reform. It was achieved in Chile after 1990, when taxes were raised by agreement of the government and the political parties, who affirmed that there is no market economy without a sound tax basis. In its absence you get the deformity that permits twenty-five individuals in Mexico to earn more than twenty-five million people do. Without tax reform in Latin America, we will never have good education, health, food, and housing. How long will the millions of Latin Americans living in poverty tolerate an economic model obsessed with achieving First World single-digit inflation while sacrificing growth, employment, and social policies? How long before political instability or social explosions defy trickle-down economics? The true Latin American and Mexican miracle is that so many people manage to survive under conditions of such penury.

Governments are offering only imaginary change in Latin America. The people are waiting for the imagination of change.

The United States should also be aware that solving basic local problems is the best way to exercise responsible global power. As the Mexican writer Julieta Campos asserts in her trenchant volume *What About the Poor?*, "Global problems are found in the growth of local spaces, and they should be understood and attended to locally if they are to contribute to authentic world change."

This, in the end, is the soundest way of dealing with the other paramount problem in U.S.–Mexican relations, immigration.

III

On 12 June 1992, Michael Elmer, a U.S. border patrol agent, shot and killed Dario Miranda, an undocumented Mexican worker, in a place called Mariposa Canyon, in Arizona. Using an unauthorized weapon, Elmer lodged two bullets in Miranda's back. Then he tried to hide the body.

Accused of murder, assault, and obstruction of justice, Elmer was pardoned by a state-court jury. The flagrant injustice of this decision led to a new trial in federal court, where once again Elmer was exonerated, this time by a jury of one black and eleven white Americans.

These bare facts shed a terrible light on the wave of antimigrant hysteria and xenophobia that grows day by day along the tense border between Mexico and the United States.

Through the bodies of workers such as Miranda's, the border is bleeding again.

What is the basis of the anti-Mexican phobia, particularly in California? During a recent visit to Los Angeles, I heard the same arguments over and over. Mexican workers, it seems, are the principal cause of the state deficit. Supposedly they receive excessive social benefits, do not contribute to the state economy, and overburden it with educational and health expenses. They are also the reason for unemployment in California, and, last but not least, they introduce drugs.

These are just plain lies.

Drugs do not enter the United States through Tijuana and San Diego tied up in migrant workers' kerchiefs. They arrive in planes belonging to U.S. dealers whose names no one knows and who are never the objects of the sort of publicity and persecution given their Latin American counterparts.

The United States has washed its hands of its drug barons—and laundered their money. All guilt is in the offer, none in the demand. It is easier—and more pharisaical—to militarize Bolivia than to militarize the Bronx.

Nor is unemployment caused by the use of Mexican labor. It is part of a long-lasting recession, complicated in California's case by a cutback in defense industries, and nationally, by the paradox of a third industrial revolution, which brings about unemployment even as productivity grows. The United States has not adopted a wise policy of industrial conversion and worker retraining; and it has not faced up to the labor complications derived from the post–cold war expansion of technology.

Blame all these realities, but not Mexican workers, who respond to the demands of the U.S. market and do work that no one in the United States is willing to perform.

Finally, the U.S. deficits in California and elsewhere are the product of twelve years of voodoo economics under Ronald Reagan and George Bush. You cannot cut taxes, raise defense budgets, and expect surpluses. Undocumented workers do not apply for welfare benefits. But as consumers they pay taxes far in excess of any benefits in health care and education they may in fact receive. The Mexican worker is a scapegoat, pure and simple, for problems caused by gringos that gringos don't want to confront.

The politicians of California have, to their shame, led the anti-Mexican campaign, believing that the U.S. electorate needs reliable villains and enemies, Mexican or Japanese, to single out now that the Communists are gone. But xenophobia and racism lead to the pogrom and the concentration camp. Before going out to hunt Mexicans—as some teenage gangs have been doing—U.S. xenophobes should go see Steven Spielberg's movie *Schindler's List.*

Polish and German Jews were, however, white. The anti-Mexican phobia has a name and color: racism. This is what Governor Pete Wilson plays with when he stokes the anti-immigrant fire and excludes Mexicans from receiving compensation for earthquake damage. He sang a different tune as a senator. He demanded then that the border patrol facilitate the entry of Mexican workers to save his state's harvests—and, of course, those of his own properties.

The heart of the matter is that Mexican workers travel across the border in response to the demand of the U.S. market. California produces one-third of the nation's agricultural wealth, and 90 percent of that wealth is harvested by Mexican hands. Exclude the Mexicans at the border and California will be in real trouble.

Dianne Feinstein and Barbara Boxer, self-designated "liberal" senators, cannot ignore this. Yet they, too, call for a closed frontier, even (in Boxer's case) for a new Berlin Wall. A nice crowning gesture to the NAFTA agreement.

Of course, as a Mexican I would like my country to export products instead of people, as President Carlos Salinas repeatedly put it. Maybe one day that will happen. Just a few decades ago, Spain exported workers to France; Italy exported workers to Scandinavia. Today, Italy exports high fashion instead of low wages, and Spain exports shoes instead of feet. Yet when Mexico no longer exports workers, the United States will go on needing them, and

it will import them from other Latin American countries or perhaps from Asia. Agriculture, the hotel business, hospitals, transportation—they would all suffer without Mexican labor, as would
the U.S. wage scale.

The United States contributes to Mexico's economy in this situation: Mexican workers send back $3 billion from their earnings,
now Mexico's fourth-largest source of foreign currency. But Mexico also contributes to the U.S. economy. As I have noted, Mexico,
before the crisis, imported billions of dollars' worth of goods an-
nually from the United States, and Mexican imports from the Rust
Belt transformed a trade deficit in that area into a trade surplus.

Perhaps Jorge Bustamante, the active and courageous defender
of human rights on the border, is right when he proposes that
Mexico should enforce a one-day boycott of U.S. goods.

We can each hurt the other. It would be better if we understood
each other. The California politicians who fan the flames of racism
and xenophobia are playing with a very dangerous fire. It is un-
seemly for the Clinton administration to join this opportunistic
chorus. Both nations should recognize that Mexico and the United
States are parties to bilateral fluxes in the labor market. This economic and social problem cannot be solved by police measures.

Mexico is glad to have its excess labor migrate, and the United
States is glad to manipulate cheap Mexican labor, chastising it in
days of crisis, accepting it in boom times, and always maintaining
the police fiction of an impregnable frontier.

But do our two governments truly want to negotiate this problem or merely play possum for as long as possible? The realities of
worldwide economic integration should put things in their rightful
place.

More and more, international agreements will protect the rights
of migrant workers, the lives of those who, like Dario Miranda,
are shot in the back for no crime other than looking for a job.

Instead of manipulating illegal immigration, favoring it in good
times and blaming it in hard times, let us, Mexicans and Americans, work together toward a rational understanding of the factors
in both the bilateral and international labor markets.

Proposition 187 in California is an unsound proposition. Financially, legally, medically, socially, politically, and humanly aber-

rant, it exacerbates the issues instead of solving them, and it serves only narrow-minded demagogic electoral agendas, not the national interests of Mexico or the United States. It sets the stage for a police state, for stool pigeons and witch-hunters.

Let us keep the whole picture in mind.

Mexico has not done enough to stem the tide of workers to the United States. Its economic weaknesses, as well as the deep injustices in its society, are only the passive faults of my country: Mexico has also lacked active policies to invest in the regions from which most of the migrant laborers come to the United States. These regions are perfectly identifiable and should be targeted by the Zedillo administration for agro-industrial development.

But the United States should also heed John Kenneth Galbraith's warning in *The Nature of Mass Poverty*: "Were all the illegals in the United States suddenly to return home, the effect on the American economy would . . . be little less than disastrous. . . . Fruits and vegetables in Florida, Texas, and California would go unharvested. Food prices would rise spectacularly. Mexicans wish to come to the United States, they are wanted, and they add visibly to our well-being."

Proposition 187 would deny this. But I would deny Proposition 187 on *legal* grounds: it is unconstitutional to deprive the children of undocumented immigrants of a public education. I would deny it on *financial* grounds: California now spends just over a billion dollars a year to educate immigrant children, but by applying Proposition 187, it would lose nearly $16 billion a year in federal-aid programs to education. I would deny it on *social* grounds: it will throw thousands of children into the streets, where they will be fodder for the unscrupulous. And finally I would deny it on *financial* grounds: undocumented workers in the United States spend $29 billion more in taxes than they receive in services; workers come looking for work, not for welfare.

What Mexico and the United States have yet to reach is a sound bilateral agreement that stipulates without lies or hypocrisy the number of legal migrant workers the U.S. economy is ready to receive each year and establishes their right to cross the frontier, the places where they will work, the length of their stay, and their registration with U.S. trade unions. They would work only in sectors where they would not displace U.S. workers—a very large sector, by the way: restaurants, hospitals, transportation, hotels, domestic services, and numerous agro-industrial activities.

This, in itself, would not stop illegal immigration, but it would add a powerful force to those resisting it, the registered workers themselves. The onus would then be on the Mexican government to provide economic opportunities for workers in Mexico, on the United States government to protect the admitted workers' legal status and rights, and on the unions to protect the migrant workers as they do their own.

I believe that Mexico and the United States must look to their own strengths to overcome these problems and heighten the opportunities offered by our intimate relationship.

Mexico is still the thirteenth-largest economy in the world. It has ceased to be a monoproductive semicolonial economy. Oil was responsible for 80 percent of Mexican exports in 1982, but today, 80 percent of our exports are nonoil: sophisticated and diversified electrical machinery and vehicles, telecommunications equipment, apparel, and accessories.

Mexico should build on the strength of diversification to further NAFTA II, while the United States should heighten its incomparable advantages: its adaptability to change, its mobility, its perpetually shifting patterns of employment, and the fact that, after all, its economy is twenty times larger than Mexico's.

Where will the nations of North America focus their energies in a new, post–cold war global economy? How can we shape that new reality in favor of our own people but without damaging other people? Can we keep the global economy from breaking into warring trade blocs? Can we give political will and imagination to new international institutions so as to harness the present anarchy of shifting speculative flight capital? Can we set an example of shared substantive growth based on savings, productivity, and unemployment?

Beyond all these questions, an essential fact remains: Mexico and the United States are neighbors, permanent neighbors.

At times, perhaps, the United States would like to see Mexico disappear over the horizon and drift to the South Seas. At times, too, Mexico would like to see the United States shrink to a more humane size and use its power less arrogantly, with a greater sense of proportion and of the inevitable passing of glory and sharing of the human condition, which includes loss, pain, and death. But the United States will not break off like an iceberg and float to the North Pole. We are destined to live together.

Our challenging border is a scar: Mexico lost half its territory to the United States in the war of 1847, an unjust war denounced then by Lincoln and Thoreau and only by Robert F. Kennedy a hundred years later. The scar must close. The border must not bleed again.

It is inevitable that such a lopsided relationship should cause frictions. But in the aftermath of the Mexican Revolution, and especially during the fruitful coincidences of the Roosevelt and Cárdenas administrations, the U.S. and Mexico decided that, even if conflict was inevitable, negotiation should be the rule. This philosophy has survived the numerous strains in U.S.–Mexico relations. As Mexico, for the first time since Pancho Villa invaded Columbus, N.M., in 1916, becomes a hot electoral issue in the U.S., Washington and Mexico City should sharpen the wits of their respective diplomacies: everything can be negotiated, no single issue should poison the relationship as a whole.

We do not choose our parents or our neighbors. But we do choose our friends. We must find ways to live together, cooperate, understand our differences, respect them, but also work for all the things that build our friendship, our common interests, our mutual responsibilities.

Let us be able to exclaim one day: "Mexico and the United States, so close to each other and so close to God."

Home in Veracruz

Until his twenty-forth birthday, my father, Rafael Fuentes, lived in Jalapa, the capital city of the Gulf state of Veracruz, at 7 Lerdo Street, a sprawling townhouse inhabited only on the upper floors, since the lower spaces were reserved for carriages, storage space, and a gym that my father and his brother arranged as a playhouse where they could stage their own versions of their favorite novels, *The Three Musketeers* and the rest of the D'Artagnan saga.

When my father went to Mexico City in 1925 to take his exams for the Mexican foreign service, he left a notebook in which he wrote in green ink, with his wide-nibbed pen, *Good-bye, Jalapa dearest.*

He left behind a city that was warmly his. This was a provincial capital with annual balls in the casino and happy weekends in the hacienda of La Orduña, which I visited as a child and which smelled of orange blossoms. It was the Jalapa of La Moderna, the bookshop owned by Don Raúl Basáñez, where you could get the latest novelties from London, Paris, and Madrid, especially the illustrated glossies that set the fashions. You went with your sweetheart to the Victoria moviehouse to see the latest films by sensational Italian vamps like Pina Menichelli, Francesca Bertini, and Giovanna Terribili-Gonzalez. Artistically inclined young ladies bought sheet music at the Casa Wagner, facing Juárez Park. On sultry afternoons, foamy refershments were offered at the soda fountain run by Don Antonio C. Baez, who assured his clientele, even then, "This factory does not sweeten its drinks with zaccharin" (always with a z).

Ladies were urged to bathe with Salmones, the supreme rose-colored soap that El Fénix sold at the sole department store, Salmones and Successors. They were held in and supported by La

Ópera girdles, while gentlemen flocked to the tailor shop of Don León Moro on the first block of Zamora Street.

This was the Jalapa that witnessed the most-talked-about wedding of the 1920s, when the aristocratic Mexican lawyer Don Javier Icaza married Señorita Ana Güido and brought to Jalapa the first Isotta-Fraschini ever seen in the state of Veracruz, parking it at the very foot of the cathedral steps.

A nostalgic city of eternal drizzle over red-tiled roofs. Grillwork balconies and tall green front doors. Bursting flowers. Jalapa that is no more.

The budding writers of the early century were devoted to the Mexican symbolist poets Enrique González Martínez, Luis G. Urbina, and Amado Nervo. But their greatest enthusiasm was for Veracruz authors, the novelist Rafael Delgado and the mustachioed, lion-maned poet Salvador Díaz Mirón, who taught literature at the preparatory school and terrified his pupils by setting a pistol on his desk and reciting his own sonorous poetry while shaking his leonine locks:

> *Miraculous the landscape! Chromatic the mists*
> *That roll in fusible flakes until a breath*
> *dissolves them!*

My father went to this same preparatory school after learning the basics from the mythic Misses Ramos, two spinsters who were already elderly in 1911 and went on to teach the three Rs to members of my own generation such as Miguel Alemán Velasco.

These were turbulent times in Mexico, and my grandmother Emilia Boettiger often told me how, when the shots of the revolutionary cavalcades were heard near Lerdo Street, she would pile mattresses on top of her three offspring—my uncle Carlos, my aunt Emilia, and my father, Rafael—and wait for the cavalry and the firing to pass.

My father belonged to a group of military cadets organized to defend the port of Veracruz from the Yankee invasion of 1914. I have a photograph of these young men, my father among them, in high-buttoned dark blue tunics and French kepis, rifles ready to protect Veracruz from the invader. They were fourteen-year-old kids. The port fell before they could get to it from Jalapa, but everyone in Veracruz wept over the courageous sacrifice of the Naval Academy cadets who fell to Yankee bullets.

To leave Jalapa was to leave behind all these memories—the joys, the sorrows, the families.

The Fuentes family came from the Canary Islands in the mid– nineteenth century, and in Veracruz they joined the Vélez family. The most celebrated matron of this branch was my grandfather's mother, Clotilde Vélez, who was attacked by *bandidos* as she trav- eled by stagecoach from Mexico City to Veracruz and who, rather than give up her wedding rings, had two of her fingers chopped off by a mean machete.

My grandfather Rafael, a hawk-eyed, hawk-nosed gentleman given to boater hats and buttoned boots, became director-general of the National Bank of Mexico in the port of Veracruz, and there he wed his youthful bride, my grandmother Emilia, a beautiful eighteen-year-old from the lake city of Catemaco, where her father, Philip Boettiger Keller, had arrived in the 1860s from Darmstadt, Germany, and founded a prosperous coffee plantation. Emilia had three sisters: María, who was to become a locally famous poet in the hot, picturesque townships of Los Tuxtlas; Luisa, who married a powerful general from Oaxaca state; and Ana, a natural child of my blond, blue-eyed grandfather, who was herself very dark, very sweet, and much loved by her half sisters.

My father was born in the port city and always remembered the smell of brine rising from the docks in front of the family house, yet another grand affair that I admire in old photos, full of Vic- torian splendor, bibelots, and wicker furniture. The thermom- eter never fell below seventy and the humidity was infernal, but my grandmother had a sure formula: ceiling fans, thick white walls, the rumor of running water, and extremely hot coffee. The weather, she used to say, was merely a state of mind.

The family moved from Veracruz to Jalapa in 1908, on the eve of the Mexican Revolution. My aunt Emilia collected Chinese por- celain dolls and played Chopin waltzes before she turned thor- oughly modern, bobbing her hair and taking up tennis. And my uncle Carlos, my namesake, was a very promising young man, at the age of nineteen the editor of a literary review called *La Musa Bohemia* and advertised as "Jalapa's sole journal." I do not know if this implied quality or quantity, but reading the issues, I find a balance of poetry, criticism, politics, and youth. As another uncle, Fernando de Fuentes, later Mexico's first professional film director and one of its most famous ones, wrote in the magazine, "My youth is now my only shield in the voyage of life."

Fragile shield of youth, continually exposed to passion, disillusionment, death . . . and politics. In its issue of 16 September 1914, the magazine proclaimed, "The Revolution has triumphed!" But on 6 January 1915, *La Musa Bohemia* halted publication: "Lacking any source of print, since communications with Mexico City are interrupted, we are forced to suspend publication of our magazine for as long as the lack of communication persists, which will be brief, according to the information given to us by an officer of the Constitutionalist Army."

It was, perhaps, a bad omen. My talented young uncle Carlos Fuentes, author of poems, essays, and political editorials, went to study in Mexico City at the age of twenty-one, and ten days later he was dead of typhus, then an uncontrollable disease. So my father's departure to enter the foreign service left my grandparents in a state of terrible anguish. Pain, said my grandmother, is a sacred river that runs unseen.

But my father took with him, forever, the wound of his dead brother. He gave me his brother's name and from childhood surrounded me with books, in homage, I feel sure, to the hope represented by that Carlos Fuentes, the second family member of that name, as I am the third, and my young son, who paints, writes poetry, and makes movies, is the fourth.

We all come from Jalapa, where now a street is named after my father, a man of infinite tenderness, rectitude, and patriotism, who dedicated his life to serving Mexico abroad. I have no doubt that his breathless teenage expectation of going to fight in Veracruz marked him forever, since throughout his long diplomatic service, from 1925 to 1970, he did not let a day go by without protecting and promoting, one way or another, the national interests of Mexico.

He was formed by our provincial hearth, Jalapa, where he was a founder, student, and very young professor of the newly created state law school, from which he graduated in 1925 to enter the foreign service. His first post was as a lawyer for the Mexican–U.S. commission created to study claims brought by citizens of one country against the other. My father was sent to the wounded frontier, and I have a photo of him with one foot in Nogales, Sonora, and the other in Nogales, Arizona, symbolizing the geographic fatality that we are charged with transforming into political will, a sense of justice, and friendly dealings. Today, when Mexico's northern border once again bleeds through the wounds of xenophobia and anti-immigration hysteria, it is good to remember that we will always have conflicts with the United States but should never allow one issue to cloud the whole relationship. All differences should be solved in a spirit of justice and dignity.

Mexico has been a testing ground of legal ideas and diplomatic imagination for the Americas. My father contributed in both areas during the presidencies of Plutarco Elías Calles and Lázaro Cárdenas, in Washington during the ambassadorship of Francisco Castillo Nájera and the nationalization of Mexico's oil resources, as a delegate to the Inter-American conferences at Buenos Aires (1936), Lima (1938), and Chapultepec (1944), and as a high official of the Foreign Ministry during the presidencies of Manuel Ávila Camacho, Miguel Alemán, and Adolfo Ruiz Cortines.

"Your father is a man without froth," Mexico's great polymath the writer Alfonso Reyes (with whom my father served when Reyes was ambassador to Brazil in the 1930s) once told me, and I believed him. An essential, substantive man, infinitely respectful of others, starting with his wife and children, gifted with a spontaneous sense of humor, animated by a desire to know, to understand the other fellow's point of view, to adapt to foreign cultures, convinced as he was that Mexico was not an isolated, somber mesa but an open coast, exposed yet generous, exactly like his home in Veracruz, facing a sea of exchanges and communications.

My father taught his children and his grandchildren that Mexico was a land of capacious inclusion, not of mean-spirited exclusion, a country created thanks to many contributions, Indian, African, European. Vigilance, awareness, warmth in personal life but also, in public life, concern for the country's values, Mexico's vigorous culture, its rich history. All this he taught us.

Young, thin, nervous in his first diplomatic posts in Rio de Janeiro, Panama City, and Washington, D.C. Serene, elegant, wise in his final embassies in the Netherlands, Portugal, and Italy. I always see in him nevertheless the fourteen-year-old boy who took

up a rifle and was ready to march to Veracruz and defend
Mexico. His credo was my own, the beliefs that Mexico has proclaimed throughout its history because they reflect that history.
Self-determination, nonintervention, national sovereignty, graceful
solutions to controversies. These permanent values of Mexican foreign policy were my father's guiding principles, his professional
commandments. He was part of a brilliant generation of Mexican
diplomats—among them Manuel Tello, Sr., Francisco Icaza, Luis
Quintanilla, Jaime Torres Bodet, Pablo Campos Ortiz, José Go-
rostiza, Roberto Córdoba, and Luis Padilla Nervo. For all of them,
diplomacy was identical to the defense of the country and the
Revolution.

Mexico had fought for ten years, losing a million lives and
countless riches, in order to implement changes that could no
longer wait. These included agrarian reform, a devolution of lands
to the villages, and recovery of the nation's natural resources—all
of them contained in article 27 of the constitution. Article 123
consecrated labor protection, since the Revolution was born not
only in the countryside but in the mines and factories. And policies
for education, health, and the infrastructure were devised so that
the national economy, ideally balanced between public and private
interests, would grow without our weaker citizens being forgotten
and not giving only the stronger the human resources for prosperity. We wanted Mexicans who were better educated, healthier,
with more purchasing power. This is a lesson we have to learn
over and over.

Yet this generous program was attacked and hindered over and
over by internal reactionaries, aided yesterday as they are today by
armed thugs and professing as they still do that the Indian and
agrarian populations were hindrances to progress. Flaunting racism
of a type we still see, they looked to extermination of the country's
ethnic groups as the route to modernity, transforming the very
concept of modernity into a caricature of exclusions.

Attacked from within, Mexico was also attacked from abroad
by interests hurt first by the agrarian reform and later by the oil
expropriation. Mexico was put in the dock by U.S. Secretary of
State Frank B. Kellogg for its "crimes against humanity." What
were these crimes? Giving land to the dispossessed, the alphabet to
all children, hospitals to the sick. The task of defending Mexico

became that of the generation following my father's as well. Its most brilliant stars were Jorge Castañeda, Sr., foreign minister in the 1980s, and Alfonso García Robles, who was awarded the Nobel Peace Prize in 1982.

The next generation is my own, and I say all this because I understand and want it to be understood that a man always belongs to the men and women with whom he was formed and with whom he acted together in life. I belonged to the midcentury generation at the law school of the National University of Mexico. Along with my comrades, I lived through an age as difficult, in its own way, as that of the Revolution had been for our parents. Just as difficult but far more sterile: these were the decades of the cold war and its hermetic division into irreconcilable spheres, its Manichean comfort in easily distinguishing the good and the bad, and its sacrifice of humankind's rich political, social, and cultural diversity at the altar of two frozen ideologies in which we did not recognize who we were or what we wanted to be.

Many members of my generation served Mexico abroad with distinction, notably José Juan de Olloqui as ambassador in Washington and twice in London; Porfirio Múñoz Ledo, Mario Moya Palencia, and Víctor Flores Olea as representatives to the U.N.; Miguel Alemán as roving ambassador; Enrique González Pedrero as ambassador to Spain; and Javier Wimer as our last chief of mission to fractured Yugoslavia. We saw it as our duty to persevere in the defense of our principles, supporting the rights of the weak against the aggressions of the strong. We argued for the independence of the Mexican armed forces when we were pressured to conclude undesirable alliances. Throughout the cold war, Washington wanted an Inter-American Defense Force formed to combat "Communist aggression," which Mexico steadfastly opposed, since it would have brought Mexican armed forces under de facto Pentagon command to fight battles that might have been incompatible with Mexico's national interests, let alone her national independence. We spoke out for each nations' right to give itself the forms of government it chose, recognizing that revolutions are a source of legality—in Mexico, in the United States, in France, in Russia, in China—and that foreign pressure cannot force us to conduct our external relations according to criteria that are not our own. But above all we felt that our creative duty was to offer diplomatic imagination and legal frames of reference to solve conflicts in our two most immediate zones of interest, Central America and the Caribbean. In this strict sense, Mexico never defended Cuba, Guatemala, El Salvador, Panama, or Nicaragua against U.S. intervention. We were merely defending Mexico, defending ourselves.

For these successive generations, the words *sovereignty, independence, dialogue,* and *negotiation* were not empty. They made the deepest sense. They make sense today, when Mexico and Latin America should hasten to fill the diplomatic vacuum left by the end of the cold war, proposing new laws, institutions, and practices for a truly renovated world order. Latin America has done so throughout its independent history, ever since Bolívar proposed an American amphictyony in Panama in 1826. Now, after the end of the cold war, we should act again to advance an international order that takes into account the policies of developing regions, not only highly industrialized ones. If we do not, the powerful nations will impose their own order on us.

The new generation of Mexican diplomats, many of them studying at the University of Veracruz, has the same international duty as we and our fathers, which is to defend Mexico through law, diplomacy, negotiation, and dialogue.

We are not an island apart. We are coming into the world. And once more the world, while aspiring to an order of collective security, is fracturing in civil wars, commercial strife, racism, xenophobia, genocide, and resurrected fascism. The comfortable certainties of the cold war are gone; many people, left without ideological roofs over their heads, find renewed security in religious fundamentalism, ethnicity, or chauvinist resentment.

But, one must admit, some also recover the lost refuge of their cultures and memories in art, history, and literature and in true religious culture, which is not dogmatic but, as Milan Kundera says of Christian Central Europe, a memory to which we all belong—even atheists—because without it we would be shadows without substance, reasoners without vocabulary. . . .

All of this, furthermore, takes place in a world of economic integration, instant communication, and rapid technological expansion. How shall we wed the local values of identity with the universal values of communication? Young men and women of today, in Jalapa, in Mexico, throughout Latin America, must answer this question in their own ways. One of the answers is called culture, for culture, the Spanish philosopher José Ortega y Gasset taught us, is simply our response to the challenges of life.

We are not an island apart. We integrate ourselves into the world. This is why, more than ever, we must remember that true independence arises only among independent nations and requires the nourishment of memory, continuity, culture, and, yes—why not?—symbols.

When faced with foreign arrogance, we Mexicans must always answer with the strength of the law. But if we are to defend ourselves outside, we must first of all be zealous defenders of the law in our own land. And to defend ourselves, both inside and outside Mexico, the best weapon is democracy—fair elections supervised by impartial electoral authorities, economic policies that do more than show results on the blackboard, that recognize that bringing them to the concrete human being, his family, his environment is the true justification of economic life. The external defense of Mexico from inside Mexico passes today through federalism and separation of powers, speedy and effective justice, and respect for the regional, ethnic, and cultural diversity of our country. Decentralization does not weaken us; it strengthens us because it brings out the vast potential of each village, each city, each state.

We have much to achieve in Mexico and in the world. We can act on aspirations like those of my father and his generation because the world still needs peace, justice, diplomatic imagination, and the will to negotiate. The fortresses of the old bipolar world are crumbling, and each one of us suddenly belongs to a world of multiple centers. In each of these centers, there are many naked feet but also many shoulders covered by the mantle of history— half ermine, half rags—many heads crowned by the jewels of a culture created in the New World by descendants of Indians, Africans, and Europeans. The road has thorns, and they will wound us. But if we are guided by the lights of our civilizations, we will not lose our way.

Mexican civilization was born in Veracruz, in the lands of the Olmeca, in the pyramid of El Tajín, and in the Spanish foundation of La Antigua. We come from our home in Veracruz. We can go home again to Veracruz.

Veracruz has been the port of entry, transit, and exit of all our cultures. The Spanish Conquest entered Mexico through Veracruz, that Conquest which soon became a Mexican counterconquest—mestizo, syncretic, an Indian victory in its form, names, racial components, and its constant sanctifying of the world. Here the Indian cultures adapted to European architecture, the art of the Baroque, European literature, and European law. All of this began in Veracruz. But Veracruz became not only a European port of entry but also the port of transit from China and the Philippines to Spain. Acapulco received silks and spices from the East that were then shipped overland and sent from Veracruz to the ports of Cádiz and Seville.

When, as a child, I visited my grandparents in Veracruz, I imagined that the ocean waves that came to us from the Mediterranean returned there. I wish I had been a child with my father in Veracruz. He used to tell me how, as a seven-year-old, he would wait with his own father, my grandfather, for the arrival, on the first Friday of each month, of the *paquebot* from Le Havre, which brought to Veracruz the latest novels by Paul Bourget and Anatole France, as well as those voguish journals *La Vie Parisienne* and the *London Illustrated News*. These were their lifeline to the world.

I wish I had been a child with my father in Jalapa, a city described by the wife of the Marquis Calderón de la Barca, the first Spanish ambassador to independent Mexico, as a city of flowers. "There are flowers everywhere, flowers in the shops and in the windows and, above all else, one of the most splendid mountain views of the world," wrote Fanny Calderón de la Barca in her beautiful memoir *Life in Mexico*, written in English (she was Scottish) and published in 1843. Jalapa is a city "covered with roses," she concluded.

No wonder that another eminent traveler, the German scientist Alexander von Humboldt, described Jalapa as "a city famous for the sweetness of its climate and its eminently romantic site." This must have been one of the first times that the word *romantic* appeared in the vocabulary of Mexican culture; the term *romanticism* was introduced in Europe only in 1803, the very year that Baron von Humboldt visited Jalapa. The word continues to signify passion, a yearning to give life to the past, the burning desire to recover the unity of each person, fragmented by time, compromise, oblivion, and, sometimes, cruelty and disdain.

To come home to Veracruz, to Jalapa, is a way of furthering my father's destiny while fulfilling my own. The child is father of the man, said Wordsworth. And he was right, for the child is always the prophet of his fate but also the visionary of his past. Immortality, says the poet, broods over us. But eternity, William Blake wrote, is in love with the works of time. Now, in Jalapa, back in Veracruz, I like to find the origin of the works of time that each man, each woman, throughout his or her life, contributes to the common history of the human race. I earlier quoted the line from Quevedo, "Only the fleeting lasts and endures," and there is a beautiful echo in Wordsworth: "That nature yet remembers what was so fugitive." This is my claim to time, my fugitive memory.

II : MY SPANISH HERITAGE

In 1936 Spain was abandoned. German planes arrived in Morocco in July and Italian planes landed in Mallorca in September, and in August the European democracies, England and France, decided to abstain from opposing the Spanish Fascists. This neutralist sandwich—irresponsibility on rye, renunciation with mayo—culminated in Munich and, naturally, led to World War II.

But Mexico never abandoned Spain. Mexico was always at the side of Spain and its people, Spain and its culture, Spain and its possible democracy. Mexico was on the side of Spain and its revolution, in the sense that the Andalusian philosopher María Zambrano gives to that controversial word: "Revolutions, all revolutions, have until now consisted only of an annunciation, and their vigor must be measured by the eclipses and the falls they withstand." In the calvary of Spain, Mexico embraced the wounded body of the mother country and offered it the shelter of her own land. Mexico received more than 200,000 Spanish refugees after the fall of the republic in 1939. During Spain's civil war, Mexico tried to bring light to the Spanish eclipse, and after the war, she maintained a policy of open arms and kept faith in a free republican Spain.

I have always felt that the difference between the Franco and Hitler dictatorships is that the Nazi tyrant was able to abduct the totality of Germany's cultural life inside Germany without leaving a single dissident voice that was not forbidden, extinguished, or exiled, whereas Franco, for all his efforts at intimidation, repression, and, in many instances, death, could not completely eliminate Spanish culture inside (or outside) Spain. Sometimes going underground, often using Aesopian language, the culture inside Spain managed to develop strategies of survival, formulas of democratic continuity and symbolisms—soon apparent in the poems of Blas de Otero and José Hierro, the novels of the Goytisolo brothers, Juan García Hortelano, and Rafael Sánchez Ferlosio, and in the films of Luis García Berlanga and Juan Antonio Bardem. All of them announced a better future for Spain, embraced its fallen body, lit bonfires along the painful road.

But in yet another, equally vast measure, the light, the faith in the annunciation, took place in the Spanish exile, especially in the Mexican exile. The miracle of this exile was that Spaniards in Mexico were always protected, present, integrated into two homelands, Spain and Mexico: Mexico in Spain, Spain in Mexico.

This was no mean trick, given the depths of anti-Spanish sentiment running through Mexican history since the Conquest in 1519–21. Hispanophobia in Mexico, aroused first by the Conquest, then sustained by three centuries of colonial rule and finally by independence after 1821, did not have a leg to stand on after the republican migration. The new Spanish arrivals were not the cruel conquistador Pedro de Alvarado or the royalist hangman Calleja del Rey. They were not even that figure of fun Don Venancio, the Spanish grocery owner who wears a beret, smokes a stinking cigar, and minds the store by sleeping on the counter. After 1939, the best of modern Spanish culture arrived in Mexico, forcing Mexicans to admit that they were part of that culture and that if they refused to understand this they would never be complete, never be themselves, true Mexicans not only in body but above all in soul.

Yes, overcoming anti-Spanish prejudice in Mexico is not an easy task. We have been incapable of understanding the Conquest for what it really was—a shared defeat: certainly the defeat of the conquered Indian world but also the defeat of the Spanish conquerors insofar as they were new men, men of the European Renaissance, whose promise was defeated by Spanish royal absolutism and the stringent dogmas of the Inquisition and Counter-Reformation. We also failed to see the Conquest as merely the prelude for a counterconquest, in which the New World truly earned its name through a process of mixing bloods—Indian, black, and European—that managed to avoid the hypocrisy and puritanism of the Anglo-Saxon colonizations.

In 1521 the Aztec banners fell in Tenochtitlán while the flags of the Castilian communities fell at Villalar. The middle-class Span-

iards who defeated Moctezuma were the same middle-class Spaniards defeated by Charles V. There is here a brotherhood deserving
of further investigation, clouded over as it may be by triumphalist
dogmas of racial, political, and religious orthodoxy.

In the Spain of our independence, we must see beyond the crass
errors of the decadent Bourbon monarchy to the common heritage
of the liberal constitution signed at Cádiz in 1812, as well as to
the common fortunes shared by Spain and Spanish America during
the turbulent nineteenth century. Instead of joining together in the
powerful community of Spanish-speaking nations proposed to
Charlies III by Count Aranda in the eighteenth century, we divorced, turned our backs on each other, and nevertheless shared a
destiny of defeats. We lost Cádiz, and by losing Cádiz we lost
democracy. We won instead pendulum oscillations between dictatorship and anarchy, and in the middle of both we discovered
our own corpse. Here lies one-half of Spain, said the great
nineteenth-century Spanish social critic and journalist Mariano
José de Larra, and the other half killed it. The equation can readily
be reversed.

Larra's lament was born of the disaster of 1898, the war with
the United States, which not only dealt a death blow to the Spanish
empire in the Americas but gave birth to the United States empire
in our hemisphere. Both Spain and the United States found their
destiny in the Caribbean. Spanish America did not see this com-
munality of destiny. Perhaps only the Nicaraguan poet Rubén
Darío understood it fully, when he identified us as "the cubs of the
Spanish lioness."

The Spanish civil war and the Mexican embrace were recogni-
tions that compensated for the mutual ignorance of the past. But
I would like to speak of my own experience as a young student
and budding writer in the Mexico of the 1940s and 1950s, since
I would not be myself, nor would I have written anything, without
the presence, stimuli, and, on many occasions, tutelage of what
came to be known as pilgrim Spain, *la España peregrina.* My youth
is inseparable from the love and friendship of the poets Bartra and
García Ascot, the philosopher Ramón Xirau, the novelist Max
Aub, the publicist Jaime Múñoz de Baena, the statesman Juan Si-
meón Vidarte, the critic Carlos Blanco.

I wish to highlight a few basic teachings that I received then and

celebrate today with true enthusiasm. The Spanish émigrés renewed the cultural life of Mexico at all levels: the Colegio de Mexico became our first modern center of study and the Fondo de
Cultura Económica our greatest publishing house; architecture, art
criticism, musicology, film, theater, but above all higher learning
and creative writing were given extraordinary impetus by the Spanish republicans.

In the School of Philosophy and Letters, then housed within the
beautiful colonial walls of Mascarones, José Gaos had just translated Martin Heidegger's *Being and Time* into Spanish (long before
it received an English-language translation). With great lucidity,
Gaos—with his strong face that seemed hacked into shape by a
hatchet, his small glasses, bald head, powerful swimmer's body—
communicated to his students a vision of human movement that
went beyond dialectics to maintain what he called *la ronda*; this
was *doing the rounds*, a vigilant watch that avoided dialectical
dogmatism and the rigidity menacing Marxist thought, which Gaos
respected as a philosopher but did not adore as a true believer. But
la ronda of José Gaos also helped dissipate the potential fogginess
of Heidegger's Germanic thought, giving it a bit of Mediterranean
sun and, even, solitude—*sol y soledad*.

Sun, solitude, soil. I remember a great lecture by Gaos in which
he spoke of art as truth transformed by work. The movement of
truth to art through work simultaneously builds a world and discovers an earth. But the land, which is also our roots, means obscurity, profoundity, a mystery that never completely reveals itself.
We only know the earth thanks to the world; the world roots itself
in the land but, like the tree, spreads up toward history, and its
branches are called possibility, pluralism, alternative.

Gaos's lectures taught me that creativity consists in convoking a
universe more than in slavishly reproducing it. Based on reality—
the root, the land—the work of art creates a world that did not
exist before. Art is born from history but also creates history, starting with the history of the work of art itself.

Eduardo Nicol, in the same historic building in Mascarones,
gave a superb course on the philosophy of Nikolai Hartmann. Bald
like Gaos but short and dapper, Nicol had quite a following among
the young women who flocked to hear him. If Gaos's eyes were
myopically dreamy, those of Nicol pierced right through his eye-

glasses with mixed benevolence and ferocity. He made a distinction between personal life, collective life, and historical objectivism. Hearing him say this, I made my own dazzling discovery: we are complete beings only if we attend to the objective world that surrounds us, respecting it without making a fetish of it; but at the same time we must value the subjective world that inhabits us, enrich our individuality but avoid the sin of solipsism, which is the sin of confusing perception with reality. Above all, we must find the point of equilibrium between objectivity and subjectivity. Nicol, following Hartmann, found it in what he called collective life, which became for me the place of encounter between myself, my material world, and my cultural world. From then on, I realized I could not aspire to become a complete man if I did not explore the crossways of my person and my society, standing in the material world but shaking hands through culture. Hence, at its very root, this book I am writing and you are—I hope—reading.

Luis Cernuda and Emilio Prados, the two marvelous poets who came to Mexico in the great tide of the war, gave me and my generation another lesson, that of language, body, and idea united.

The modest and tender Prados lived in a tiny apartment on Lerma Street. With his long gray hair and clouded eyes, he was the magical hermit of my own neighborhood, Colonia Cuauhtémoc. Prados taught us to think about our bodies, to enlarge them by inquiring about the limits of the flesh. Prados imagined the borders of the carnal by conjugating the flesh with the voice, with time, with solitude, with memory, and with death. He inquired about flesh with voice and answered, "My body is silence." With loneliness: "I follow my flesh through my hope, not through my knowledge." With time: "The hour drowned in the sea." With memory: "Memory is the study of the lessons of dream." With death: "My body without image."

In contrast, Cernuda was arrogant and stylish to a fault. His tiny mustache, slicked-down hair, and tweedy outfits gave him a British look. Indeed, he had taught at Cambridge, where the splendid beech tree under which he wrote in the summers still stands at Emmanuel College. Yet behind his distant facade shimmered the most ardent and luminous passion of modern Spanish poetry. Again, as with Prados, Cernuda offered us the glory and the sacred nature of our bodies, but side by side with other, mute dangers.

Both Prados and Cernuda were homosexuals, and their sexual choice startled many puritanical Mexicans. More important, both poets rescued the great sensual vitality of Spanish letters, repressed by several centuries of Inquisition and Counter-Reformation. In their works these prohibitions came crashing down, the freedom of the body was verbally restored, and the ghosts of the great Spanish sensualists of the Middle Ages and the Renaissance—Fernando de Rojas, the Arcipreste de Hita, Francisco Delicado, María de Zayas—were reborn and reincarnated.

Our own astonished, youthful bodies saw themselves reflected in Cernuda's poetry, where they lay "on a bed of sand and abolished chance." Cernuda's bodies were like water, which though always identical to itself, is always moving on. This line by Cernuda brought back to life the line I quoted earlier by the great seventeenth-century poet Quevedo: "Only what is fugitive stays and endures." Quevedo also said, in the Golden Age of Spain, "I shall be dust, but dust in love." From our own time, Cernuda answered, "If, down here, we are anonymous statues, shadows of shadows, of misery, of misty precepts," the "ingrate amorous enterprise" manages nonetheless to reveal an eternally prefigured world, identifying each of us with "the races when they celebrate birthdays." Epiphany is reached only if we never forget that the body celebrates its ceremonies "in a half-made, cold, and clumsy bed," as it yearns for a "distant sleeping form."

Many great Spanish teachers formed me and my generation at the law school—the sociologist Luis Recaséns Siches; Niceto Alcalá Zamora, who taught us procedural law; the criminal lawyers Rafael de Pina and Mariano Ruiz Funes. But I and many others owe our greatest debt to Manuel Pedroso, the former president of the University of Seville. In his classes he taught me and my friends— Miguel Alemán, Víctor Flores Olea, Enrique González Pedrero, Mario Moya, Sergio Pitol—the richest, deepest, and most unforgettable lesson of the human being as political animal, bearer of civilizations, creator of public spaces, and agent of justice and coexistence. Don Manuel's courses on political theory and international law were like an exalted agora, a spiritual assembly in which politics ceased to be the art of the possible and became the possibility of art. Seen as creativity by Pedroso, politics created the city and its institutions as spaces where the material world, the subjective world, and our community with others—what Gaos and Nicol had taught us—could meet. The art of the city: such was Pedroso's political philosophy, the art of living together and in public, respectfully, in tolerance, with mental clarity. Opposed to the rote learning that then dominated the teaching of political theory— from Plato to Pareto in twelve easy lessons—Pedroso chose only three books during the whole academic year and asked us to read them seriously: Aristotle's *Politics*, Machiavelli's *The Prince*, and Rousseau's *Social Contract*. Circling around these three suns, said Pedroso, everything else would fall into place, attracted by the magnetic fields of the Athenian, the Florentine, and the citizen of Geneva. Writing during the agitated days of Mexican political life recorded in this volume, I have recalled the insistence with which Pedroso repeated Rousseau's famous phrase "In the end, it all comes back to politics." We cannot imagine Jean-Jacques saying, "In the end, it all comes back to technocracy."

I met the fifth Spanish master I want to evoke—Luis Buñuel— only later, when I had finished my time at the university. Still, the great Aragonese filmmaker, as deaf as Goya, but like Goya gifted with the thousand eyes of the mythical Argos, brought together all my Spanish lessons. Buñuel's surrealism was superior to the Parisian variety because it had roots in the tradition of his culture and was a critical response to it. His fiery gaze on the world was like Goya's, the gaze of the dream of reason bringing forth monsters. And if his ears were as deaf as Goya's, it was because he had been deprived of hearing by the ceaseless drums of Easter played in his native town, Calanda (introduced into many of his films as the sole musical commentary). His poetic pessimism came from Fernando de Rojas's 1499 masterpiece *La Celestina*: the world is endless agitation, and its movement leads only to death. His moral optimism, in contrast, came from Cervantes: we leave our village, we go out into the world, the world defeats and humiliates us; but we answer the world, You are wrong—the windmills *are* giants and the wooden horse Clavileño *can* fly. My fiction is my truth.

Buñuel, one of the greatest artists of the twentieth century, feeds on the great culture of Spain and gives it its most contemporary, most radical meaning, which is that of embracing the other, recognizing the marginal being, remembering the forgotten ones—*los olvidados*—admitting the obscurity of desire but offering every single man, woman, and child the chance to save themselves through others. Salvation through recognition of the forbidden, forgotten, disdained, persecuted: *Tristana, Nazarin, Viridiana.*

None of these lessons of Spain in exile is alien to the present-day life of Mexico, Spain, or the world. As in *la ronda* of José Gaos, the world does not end, history is not over. World and history only change, circulate, return, ascend in spirals, and are always borne by the actors of history—we, all of us, the men and women who create and transmit history.

As in Eduardo Nicol's axiology, the meeting of man, matter, and culture depends on our being free to encourage such a reunion, not abandoning it to fatality. As in Manuel Pedroso's idea of the state, fatality can be overcome only through legal will, political action, and the judicial process. The Spanish republic fell, after all, because it defended these values—law, justice, a policy for all—and its defeat was, in spite of all, its victory. The annunciation of the child republic, as María Zambrano called it, became real, finally, via the curving roads of dialectics, the calling forth of cultural values, and the historical perseverance of present-day democratic and pluralistic Spain. Yesterday Mexicans saw Spain as a cruel stepmother, a toothless hag sitting on the church steps, begging alms, smelling of urine and incense. Today she looks as desirable as Marilyn Monroe. Even better, Spain has become our European sister, the bridge between Latin America and the EEC. Where did the good sister, the beautiful sister, come from? From Spain's good history, the history of the courts of Aragon, the communities of Castille, the constitution of Cádiz, and the republic of 1931—defeated many times, persevering, resistant. Ortega y Gasset wrote a famous book about "invertebrate Spain," in which he complained of the Spanish inability to see the nation as a whole: he complained that a vision of the national situation was lacking, events were not seen in their true perspective, and collective reality was lost in a shuffle of myopic regionalism and arrogant individualism. Yet it is precisely in these extremities that Spain manages, despite the evil moods of the times, to create a countertime, a reality founded by the imagination. The repressions of Inquisitorial Spain were overcome by the writers and artists of the Golden Age—Cervantes, Velázquez—and the decadence of the Bourbon monarchy by Goya and the writers of 1812, notably Jovellanos and Blanco White.

Today's democratic Spain has been made vertebrate by suffering, spilled blood, hope, and memory—exactly like Don Quixote, like Quevedo's lovers, like Goya's dreamers.

Buñuel's art opens both Mexico and Spain to the supreme challenge facing human beings today all over the world: how to live with those who are not like you or me. We are not alone. *Los olvidados* have arrived at our doorsteps. Civilizations meet and mix, but half the modern world refuses to acknowledge the existence of the other half. The cruel perversions of xenophobia, racism, ethnic cleansing, and religious fundamentalism return to cloud our sights and stain our hands.

Spain, Mexico, and Latin America should take stock of their historical and cultural experience. We have suffered tyrannies, repressions, massacres. We have surmounted them only by reaffirming our cultural tradition and opposing to the dark side of Hispanic history a few incomparable works of art, internationalist propositions, and, I think, a passion for justice all the stronger for having been defeated so many times. Persecution, intolerance, war against the unarmed rear their heads as the new century and the new millennium begin. Can we answer with that part of ourselves that never gives up, that writes the unwritten, says the unsaid, dreams what must be dreamed? From the depths of Counter-Reformation Spain Quevedo goes on speaking for the shared culture of Spain and Mexico: "I shall not keep silent, for never was the tongue of God mute."

CONCLUSION AND CODA :
MEXICAN TEMPI

Presto

We are now ninety million Mexicans. By the year 2000 we will be one hundred million. In 1910, when the Revolution began, we were only fifteen million. Ten years later the civil war (and many cantina brawls) had left only thirteen million, but by 1940 we had climbed back to twenty million. When I was born, in 1928, Mexico City had a million inhabitants. Now the city has as many people as the whole country back in the 1940s.

Until the late 1960s our population policy was simply, the more Mexicans the better. Had we not lost the north of Mexico, from Texas to California, because these provinces had been so sparsely populated? We had admitted settlers with airport names—Dallas, Houston, Austin—and soon they took over Texas and set the stage for the War of 1847, Polk's war, hotly debated in the United States between partisans and adversaries of additional slave states. Lincoln opposed the war in Congress and so did Thoreau, who, just like Edmund Wilson 120 years later, refused to pay taxes to support what he considered an unjust war.

So we settled for more Mexicans but no immigrants. Left to our own devices, sheltered by the traditions of machismo and the harem, we reproduced like rabbits. From the pulpits, priests forbade (and continue to forbid) contraceptive methods. Only during the 1970s did President Echeverría inaugurate a policy of demographic persuasion that managed to slow down (only relatively) a capacity for procreation that makes one imagine a Mexican chromosomal imperialism extending throughout our former territories in the U.S. Southwest and as far north as Chicago, New York, Oregon, and the Pacific (where there are numerous colonies of both legal and illegal workers from the Mexican state of Michoacán).

In 1970, each Mexican woman bore an average of six children. Today, we are down to a ratio of three children per woman. But beyond ancestral fears of the United States, beyond traditions of Aztec, Spanish, and Arab machismo, beyond agrarian loneliness, beyond sex as the only form of entertainment and children as the only proof of virility lies a constant will to survival.

On the night following the 1985 earthquake that devastated Mexico City, a U.S. television interviewer asked me to appear on his talk show. "The American public should understand that the earthquake comes on top of foreign debt, corruption, and poverty. Mexico cannot survive," he said. I answered that if the United States had suffered what Mexico has—revolutions, foreign invasions, territorial mutilation—maybe the United States would not have survived. Mexico, on the contrary, has a genius for survival.

Where does it come from? From what have I been arguing throughout this book: a population that cannot be described in an abstract manner (the "Mexican") but only in a concrete, often contradictory, yet finally fruitful way, as the result of a tension between opposites—old and new country, eternally seduced by the past and the future, by the traditional and the modern. In the exceptional moments of our history, we have been able to face both, looking clearly at the past, admitting what we are, embracing our cultural totality, and seeing ourselves in a full-size mirror. Exceptionally.

Moderato Cantabile

More than in the number of pure Indians (which is small—nine million, or 10 percent, at most, of Mexico's total population), I see an Indian country in the buried tone, the oneiric potency, the demands for justice, and the alternatives that the Indian peoples offer to our succeeding, and never fully successful, versions of modernity. One historical cycle of the Indian's history in Mexico ended with the Spanish Conquest, but their own cultural cycle went on. "The sentinels of silence," they were called in an Oscar-winning documentary made by Plácido and Manuel Arango. The repertory of our urban insufficiencies, of our own version of Western culture, awaits us silently in the Indian world, which has become the secret repository of all that we have forgotten and disdained: ritual intensity, mythic imagination, caring for nature, the relationship with death, communal ties, the capacity for self-government.

Indian traditions inform and identify the Mexican majority, which is mestizo, the result of at least two dimensions of the racial and cultural encounter of Europe and America. Mexico is not, strictly speaking, a Catholic country. It is a *sacred* country. The experience of the sacred in my country, which comes from the dawn of time, constantly challenges our capacity to imagine. Paradoxically, it is one of the most modern traits of our culture; being the oldest, it now faithfully reflects the ambivalent relationship of our own times to the sacred. Religious temperament without religious conviction has branded some of the greatest works of the twentieth century; those of Camus, Buñuel, Bergman. The search for the sacred within a secular civilization has led to great and anguished explorations of faith in the novels of Graham Greene, François Mauriac, and Georges Bernanos, and in the philosophy of Simone Weil, Pierre Teilhard de Chardin, and Reinhold Niebuhr. Milan Kundera goes on to say something very important in his *Testaments Betrayed*: Communism could not create a viable culture in Central Europe, because it banished the language of Christianity, without which Europe is left speechless, a stuttering ghost.

Radically sacred, the religious world of the Mexican Indian does not escape this modern ambiguity. On the one hand, it possesses a hermetic totality, as embodied in the statue of the supreme Aztec deity, the mother goddess Coatlicue, she of the skirt of serpents, an impenetrable monolith, headless, composed of radical sacred otherness: snakes, skulls, fangs, lacerated hands, skulls. No Venus this, not even the Virgin Mary; no sexual openings here, only the wounds of the sacred. Or, as Borges once wrote, "in agreement with divine—that is, inhuman—laws. . . ."

On the other hand, the actual life of the Indian peoples, its concrete manifestations, immediately wins a margin of creativity over the sacred totality of religious and political power. In this, a Mexican Indian myth resembles, again, the literature of Borges. The Argentinian author first sets up a Platonic abstraction—the total library, the total universe (which in Borges are synonymous)—and then subverts its totality through an invention of detail (a garden of labyrinths, a man who suffers from total recall and must whittle down his memory to a manageable number of items, an obscure French notary who rewrites *Don Quixote*, etc.). The Indian culture of Mexico, captured by time, a servant of time, frees itself from totalitarian, sacred time through imagination—the work of art and vital custom—becoming instead the mistress (the lover) of time.

This is the supplication of Mexico's Indians: Do not forsake us; if you abandon us, you abandon yourselves. Use your imagination, bring forth your sense of continuity, and try to survive as we have survived. Give us and give yourselves balance between nature and progress, between using and preserving nature, between life and death. Give life on earth a sacred value, deprive the false gods of their sacred aura, since we—the Indians—could not do it.

We have tried to answer this telegram from the depths of time with the capacity for survival I have mentioned before. But one of the greatest pains of Mexico is the gigantic loss of energy put into the tasks of pure survival. Half of Mexico's population is young. Out of ninety million Mexicans, fifty million are eighteen or younger. These children and teenagers are beautiful, intelligent, hardworking—and they exhaust their energy in useless pursuits. Our growing economic crisis has thrown many of them out of homes and schools. Just a few years ago they could hope to pass their youth studying in schools and, with luck, in colleges. Now, many of them must abandon school at the age of ten or eleven and go out into the streets to wash windshields at busy intersections, juggle balls, swallow fire, join criminal gangs, and survive, helping their families and justifying it as part of the Mexican attachment to clan, family solidarity, ties of blood, bonds of emotion. They join a mass of poor in a country where more than forty million people live in poverty, at least twenty million in dire poverty.

Such are the extremes of the sacred and the profane, the poverty of wealth and the wealth of poverty, that continue to determine the tensions of societal life in Mexico. Between the ruins of the past and the garbage of the future, Mexico tries to create a livable space in the present. The cultural experience of the Revolution gave us a vision and an impulse. Mexico's modern artists and writers are descendants of the Revolution but also show a personal and collective Mexican capacity to transform experience into knowledge. The members of a whole new civil society, perhaps the real protagonist in this book—professional people and public servants, entrepreneurs and workers, campesinos and women, cooperatives, unions, and associations, as well as one of Latin America's largest, most ambitious, stabilizing, and energetic meritocracies—have determined the growth of modern Mexico. They are certainly the protagonists in Mexico's present crisis.

Although the Mexican Revolution may have identified the totality of our past, it did not give us, in return, the needed identification of culture with democracy or with social justice. Today we are torn between a healthy identification of the nation and its culture and the two factors menacing that identity. Thanks to the national identity it achieved in the postrevolutionary decades, Mexico, for the time being, does not face Balkanization, separatism, fractures such as those that have divided the former Soviet Union and the former Yugoslavia or that menace the United Kingdom, France, Spain, and Canada. But unfortunately, Mexico's unity will be dramatically altered if we lose control of the growing differences between northern Mexico, relatively prosperous, ever more modern, impulsive, decentralized, self-sufficient, well-informed, and integrated with the United States, and southern Mexico, ever poorer, enslaved, without horizons, where the worker in the coffee fields or lumberyards lives on a dollar a day plus the portion of alcohol needed to keep him happy but brutish.

Andante

The north–south fracture is the biggest danger I see in my country's future. This division can be overcome only through social justice and democratic politics. The one and the other, in turn, can be obtained only by dynamic and pluralistic actions in Mexico's civil society. Democracy begins right there, where workers are savagely exploited or manage to organize themselves autonomously. Enrique González Pedrero is right when he demands a democracy that starts in the municipalities and town halls, a democracy that begins by respecting the vote in Mexico's smallest and most isolated villages. Democracy can integrate the other identities that might be lacking in the spheres of modernity, we must all face and integrate the profane and the sacred, market economics and state interventionism, nationalism and globalism. Ruins or garbage stare at us:

being Walter Benjamin's angel, facing all of history as ruins, is perhaps better, if crueler, than ending contentedly in the junkyard. Mexico is a nation made by its wounds. A nation, Emile Durkheim wrote, is the result of the loss of previous centers of identification—clan, tribe, family—and the urgent need to create new ones. A society cannot live without a center that identifies it and permits it to adhere, if not to clan, tribe, or family, then to nation. Nationalism, said the late Ernest Gellner, created nations, not the other way around. It took existing cultures and transformed them into nations. Culture precedes the nation, and culture can organize itself in many ways, but nations and nationalism are a product of modernity. They rose to fill the void left by the crumbling of the medieval order, the Christian civitas hammered to death by Luther on the church door at Wittenberg and buried by the demands of the new European kingdoms born of the Renaissance, of colonial expansion and religious conflict. The new states had to be justified; nationalism became their justification, the nation their legitimation; and both—nation and nationalism—are the response, says Isaiah Berlin, to a wound inflicted on society.

Mexican nationalism is the response to numerous and successive wounds, each of them the result of the loss of a center to adhere to. The first was the loss of the Indian center. The fragile Aztec political structures were destroyed by the Spanish Conquest, but the graver aspect of the loss was that of the religious world, the Indian world vision. The response to this loss was more cultural than political: the equally fragile laws and institutions of the Spanish colony mattered less than the new religious adherence promoted by a Christianity strengthened by syncretism with the old Indian faiths.

The second loss was that of the artificial "independent" nation, which simply prolonged the political order of colonialism. Between 1821, when Mexico achieved full independence from Spain, and 1854, the date of the liberal, or reform, revolution, the socioeconomic relationships of the colonial period no longer counted on their former religious justifications. And the substitute legitimations—national independence, the republic, legality, territorial unity—were shattered by the United States' victory of 1847. Santa Anna's dictatorship proved unable to defend Mexico against territorial dismemberment. Juárez and the liberals tried to give sense back to the ideas of law and the state, but they had to suffer and overcome a second foreign blow, the French invasion and Maximilian's short-lived empire. The restored liberal republic of Juárez shunned the religious legitimation and substituted legal and economic legitimation. Its name was democracy. Identified with the nation, democracy should be a value superior to cultural diversity (Indian, Spanish, Catholic, syncretic, Baroque . . .). Like the rest of Latin America, Mexico chose civilization, understood as European, urban, progressive, legalistic, and romantic, over barbarism, understood as agrarian, Indian, black, Iberian, Catholic, and Scholastic. The condition for sustaining such an identity was political freedom, that is, democracy. The new center of adherence would be based on Civilization = Democracy.

The Porfirio Díaz dictatorship wanted to give us civilization without democracy. But it only gave more barbarism than ever to the Indians, peasants, and new working class. The economic factor of the equation was protected: development without freedom. Mexicans finally rejected this formula, as well as the cultural discrimination that went with it.

The price to be paid for the Mexican Revolution's effort to recognize the totality of the country's past was that none of the components of our history could be sacrificed. When, for example, the Revolution tried to sacrifice the religious components of our culture during the so-called persecution of the Calles years (dramatized by Graham Greene in *The Power and the Glory*), it failed miserably. Instead, the revolutionary government ably manipulated the forms and even the content of social justice, presenting them as a gradual promise, but also as a concrete accomplishment on which to sustain its domination of national politics.

The most recent Mexican wound was opened on 2 October 1968, when the Díaz Ordaz government massacred several hundred students in Tlatelolco Square in Mexico City. The previous fifty years of legitimations crumbled. The government no longer represented a central adherence to the Revolution. Lack of democracy and lack of development became the new Mexican wound. It is open. The old adherences are broken. The questions are many. Nationalism or globalism? Isolationism or integration? Sovereignty or subservience to the United States? Political democracy or economic development? Or, of course, democracy with justice *and* growth? These questions are at the center of Mexico's present debate. How are we going to answer them?

Allegro, Ma Non Troppo

The history of Mexico and Latin America is that of a deep cleavage between a vigorous continuous culture and a fragmented, failed, weak political and economic life. To breathe the culture's vigor into political and economic institutions would be the primary answer to our present-day dilemmas.

Throughout the tumultuous history I have evoked in this book, Mexico's answer has been to associate culture with nationalism. It was thought in the postrevolutionary period that this identification (the nation is its culture, the culture is the nation) would close all our historical wounds. It was understood that culture had to have a political correspondence, and this was with the nation.

But the nation, as I have said, is not an eternal concept. Gellner reminds us that we can feel culture identified with other political structures besides the nation. And when, as in the case of Mexico, the state and its party both identify themselves with the nation, the culture is uncomfortable with this excessive, overly familiar, at times even incestuous proximity. When, in the now-distant past, the successes of the national state were extended to the PRI and vice versa, both could propose national unity as a value and culture as an ornament. But when both political and economic failure is the only gift of the state-party twinship, the culture can no longer fool itself, at least on one count: the nation itself is no longer synonymous with the state. Since 1968, the vices of the PRI have been grievously attributed to the state and, by extension, to the nation. This is how the PRI has become an obstacle not only to democracy but to the state and, in the measure that it is our state, to the nation.

In democratic countries, mistakes and successes are finally more or less evenly distributed among political parties that alternate in government. In Mexico, all triumphs and all failures have been attributable to one party, and that party is the state and that state is the nation. During the past quarter century the vices have all but drowned the virtues of this system. Still, throughout this long process, roughly between 1917 and 1967, Mexican nationalism could not be faulted for an aggressiveness like European or Japanese nationalism of the same period. *Ein Volk, ein Reich, ein Führer; La Terre et les Morts; Il Sacro Egoismo*—these war cries of German, French, and Italian nationalism have no equivalents in Mexico. More modestly, we have spoken of national unity, with the internal purpose of justifying the hegemony of the party-state and the external purpose of defending ourselves against another, far more powerful, and all too proximate nationalism, that of the United States of America. In other words, Mexican nationalism has been defined, to a very large degree, by U.S. nationalism.

Sometimes, Mexico and Latin America (which begins in Mexico) have seen the United States as a benevolent, democratic, good-neighborly Dr. Jekyll. More often, we have seen it as our Mr. Hyde, the monster wielding the big stick, arrogantly following the dictates of Manifest Destiny, unilaterally intervening against hypothetical European interference in the name of a doctrine no one in Latin America has ever subscribed to: the Monroe Doctrine.

The response to Dr. Jekyll, especially among middle- and upper-class Mexicans, has often been a result of the following reflections: The United States has been successful at everything that we Mexicans have failed at. Americans adapt to the means necessary to achieve modernity, while we are steadfastly loyal to our archaic cave. They are democratic; we are authoritarian. They are prosperous; we are eternally poor. They are efficient; we are useless. Mexico is a national failure living next to the biggest success story of the modern age: the American empire, democratic, prosperous, and free. Nationalism should be buried, this attitude proclaims. We should see in the United States our new center of identity, capable of healing, once and for all, our national wounds. The severe wounds in U.S. society are promptly dismissed, though they more and more resemble our own: moral, economic, and social fissures reflective of an almost universal breakdown of urban civilization—drugs, crime, violence, homeless people, denial of women's rights, an aged, crumbling infrastructure. But the pro-Americans in Mexican society do not disguise their hope that Mexico can become a sort of undeclared fifty-first state of the Union. Good-bye, problems. Welcome, success, prosperity, democracy.

This passive response garners no respect either in the United States itself or among most Mexicans. And not only because, for most Americans, if you behave like a slave you are treated as such; you are respected only if you speak on your feet and face-to-face. The passive response does not deserve respect, because it merely displaces Mexico's problems without solving them. Back in the 1950s I wrote a short story in which Mexico gains admittance to the United States, puts all its problems at Washington's feet, and is promptly expelled. The United States has enough troubles of its own without taking on Mexico's. In my story, Mexico is offered its former territories in the Southwest as compensation for its expulsion. It accepts them all—except Texas.

Should Mexico abandon its nationalist policies in this era of growing globalization? Let me answer this way: There can only be an interdependent world of independent nations. Sovereignty is not, and has never been, an absolute concept. It is, and has always been, more the exception than the rule. But the essence of sovereignty—the existence of a national center of decisions—still holds. There is a boundary that you cannot cross without destroying your own identity. Is a nation a daily plebiscite, as Ernest Renan proclaimed? Is is a continuous loyalty to certain territorial, political, and cultural unity, a sum of values that inform and justify the very notion of nation and nationalism? Any state, whether democratic or authoritarian, can fit Renan's description. Hitler practiced this century's most aggressive form of internal and external nationalism with the support of the majority of Germans. Leonard Barnes long ago defined Britain as a nation that would have to choose between democracy or empire; the United States has been a democracy within, an empire without. Sweden is a democratic *nation*, Iraq is an authoritarian *nation*. Renan's definition is not enough, especially in an age of conflicting jurisdictions, when international, regional, national, tribal, linguistic, and religious loyalties battle for the souls of men and women at the levels of both the global and the local village. The global village offers the temptation of access to high technology, economic integration, and instant information; the local village promotes adherence to earth and hearth, memory, tradition, values. Both can be damaged by the ugly sins of xenophobia, racism, "ethnic cleansing," religious fundamentalism, and the fundamentalism of the marketplace. No viable international order will arise without first considering this growing anarchy.

Mexico's temptation to find refuge in its own nationalism is, in these circumstances, understandable but not sufficient. Another, more demanding form of identification between the culture and the politics of our country awaits us. Where shall we find the political complement, the qualitative improvement that will save both our nation and its culture? Anti-Americanism is not enough. Most Mexicans today are far more sophisticated than their ancestors were in judging both the bad and the good of the United States. Never has the interdependency of the two countries been as great. Never has the U.S. presence—both its vulgar commercial offerings as well as its superior literary, musical, artistic values— been more evident in Mexican life. And never have Mexican values—from family bonds to gastronomy, all kinds of religious, linguistic, and societal forms—been more present in the United States. Mexico is filled with Pizza Huts and, horror of horrors, Taco Bells, but salsa now outsells ketchup in the United States. Who's afraid of Mickey Mouse? Not I, for one, when I consider that thirty million Spanish-language speakers live in the States. Not I, when I consider that Mexico can organize a show called *Thirty Thousand Years of Mexican Art* and the United States can do nothing comparable. Is Mexico, then, more of a menace to the United States than the United States is to Mexico? Certainly not. Cultures perish in isolation and bear fruit through contact with one another. Let us not fear cultural contamination. We are all of us living through stages in the unending process of *mestizaje* that created Greece from and against Asia, Rome from Greece, and modern Europe from Greek, Roman, and barbarian influences. Throughout Latin America, consciousness of this fact has grown. We all consider ourselves parts of multiracial and multicultural societies, Indian, black, European, mestizo.

That this cultural consciousness has not yet been translated into stronger political institutions is, as I have said, our greatest drawback. How will we create centers of identification within Mexico, so that we do not have to look for them elsewhere—and how will we remain open as well to the influence of life-giving external contacts?

The unfulfilled promise of all our modernizing projects is called democracy. The time has come to give it to ourselves, before its absence serves the United States and its nationalism, whether democratic or imperial, as a pretext to impose its own politics on us. Besides, Mexico must renew its economic development, which can no longer do without its political shield, democracy, or its social shield, which is justice, or its mental shield, which is culture.

Traditionally, we have identified yet another triad, that of nation, territory, and state, as coresponsive unities. But the singularity of culture is the element that gives plurality to the whole, for culture is a singularity achieved only through diversity. In this sense, all culture is democratic. Nation and territory, nation and state can coincide in a unified manner. But nation and culture can be elements of identity and unity only if their variety is respected and can manifest itself freely.

After all, the bearer of culture is society as a whole, and a society is as pluralistic as its culture. If the society and its culture are both pluralistic, should not its politics also be? How else can they be authentically representative?

Democracy as a center of identification, coherent with culture and society, should allow us to close the wounds of our history by ourselves. On the basis of democracy and justice within, my country should be able to move with greater security on the broad stage of the forthcoming century. I do not identify nationalism with the defense of the nation. But I do search for values that defend the society, the culture, and the individuals that compose and create both.

Like most other Latin American writers, I have been a purveyor of hope and even of utopia for our societies over the past forty years. We have also been critics of our political realities. We have tried to respond to the definition I came up with in my novel *Terra Nostra*: Reality is a sick dream. Today, I must admit that the country I believed in and hoped for is farther from my reach than it was when I was thirty years old. But maybe it is closer to the grasp of our young people. In any case, old or young, we must go on proposing projects born of our imagination and our will, the offspring of our memory and our desire. A difficult task: Mexico continues to be an infinitely complex culture, nation, society, incipient democracy. All our times demand consideration before we take the plunge into a new time for Mexico.

Adagio

The difference between Mexico and Argentina, says my friend the Buenos Aires novelist Martín Caparrós, is that Argentina has a beginning and Mexico has an origin. The Argentine nation, recalls Tomás Eloy Martínez, author of the mesmerizing *Santa Evita*, is constantly refounded, breaking with a past it dislikes and starting all over again, shedding its "barbarisms"—Indian and black traditions, the brown Argentina of the interior, petty tyrants and brutal dictators—in order to enshrine its migrant, white, European, weightless, transparent "civilizations." The result is that the brown, "shirtless" nation and its worst devils refuse to die, waiting in the shadows and reappearing in cyclical fashion, dashing the dream of civilization and drenching Argentina once more in murder, folly, and blood.

If Mexico has an *origin*, it is by definition difficult to establish. This is the difference between it and of *beginning*. Mythical, memory-laden, dreamlike, set in a time of creation, of dual gods and immemorial migrations, an origin comes back to the present with a demand that is a gift: Include, do not exclude. We are ungoverned beings, as the Brazilian novelist Nelda Pinion writes; we are barely out of the caves and have not yet learned how to explain all our emotions. That is why we write and paint and sing and film so powerfully. Our culture is inclusive. Why are our writers and artists so imaginative and our politicians so unimaginative? Perhaps this book provides, if not a definitive answer, at least some clues.

Mexico is now set between two forms of modernity. Exclusionary modernity, drawn from Western models, banishes all that it does not understand. Inclusive modernity understands, especially after the Chiapas rebellion, that there are many ways of being "modern," of being contemporaneous with one's own values. Exclusionary modernity refuses the magic and mystery of a country far more attractive because of what we do not know about it than because of what we do know. Let this idea color what I have said in this book: it is impossible to penetrate all the mysteries of Mexico, it is challenging to attempt to do so, it is humbling to attempt in writing.

Many Mexicans conceive only of a Western model of development as the way to be "modern." But the genius of Mexico has consisted in preserving the values of progress without ceasing to affirm the right to mystery, the right to astonishment, the right to an unending shock of recognition. Order is the anteroom of horror. Mexico constantly perverts both—order and horror—with the temptation of chaos, the dream at the edge of a cliff, the ritual of a people bent less on telling us what we already know than on discovering what we ignore.

In his beautiful volume of essays *The Gods of Mexico*, C. A. Burland was the first to see in the art of ancient Mexico the form of the mandala, a circular symbol representing the universe, manifesting itself formally in drawings based on a system of four rectangles around an empty circle. With these sometimes highly intricate drawings, we attempt complex and numerous approximations to the reality of time and nature.

In ancient Mexico, the mandala of water signified the several origins of a fluid world. Tlaloc was the god of water, and his kingdom, Tlalocan, was suspended on the clouds, just a little distance above the earth. In contrast to Western gods, each described as a unified whole, the four sources of power in Tlaloc were both contradictory and complementary. From the East came the golden rain of morning. At noon the waters turned blue as they moved southward. At dusk the world was flooded by the red rainfall of the West. At night crops fell, mowed down by the black rain of the North.

Yet this description is itself a simplification, since we must immediately add that in ancient Mexico each direction of the compass had its own four cardinal points, so that the South had its own east and west, north and south, the North its own north and south, east and west, and so on. If we keep multiplying the directions of each new direction, we find ourselves immersed in a maximum concretion of the infinite. Since the very idea of the infinite is terrifying, we must step back, returning to the simpler orientations of the mandala. A center unifies this immense variety of time and space. Yet if space can be as visible as it wants to be, time must continue to be a mystery.

Not a passive mystery but more of an invitation to re-create time. Thus its radical modernity. Condemned by "modern" exclusionists to the shadows of superstition, the old time of Mexico

comes back to life with the absolute powers of an oblivion that
suddenly becomes an announcement. Einstein says the same thing
as the builders of the Zapotec center at Mitla, in Oaxaca do: Geometry is not something inherent in nature but a product of the
mind. All measure of time and space is relative, not fatally linear and
logical. The position of an object in space is defined by its relation to
another object. The temporal order of objects is not independent of
the position of the observer of the event. And Heisenberg adds, as if
he, too, were reading the patterns at Mitla: The presence of the observer introduces indeterminacy into the system. The observer cannot be separated from a point of view. He thus is part of the system.
And so, finally, an ideal closed system is impossible.

Mexican time, old and new, is rooted in this oldest of memories,
in this radical and inclusive novelty. It is constituted by them as it
constitutes them.

Vivace

We fall into the positivist vice when we try to avoid the mystery
of Mexico. We become solemn logocentrists. We identify reason
with civilization. We must heed Gellner's warning. It is disastrous
to avail oneself of reason in order to escape culture: "We cannot
escape a contingent, history-bound culture, and we cannot vindi-
cate it either" (*Reason and Culture*). But we can at least attempt
to reconcile the individual with his or her culture.

Mexican positivists identify reason with civilization, not with
culture, and civilization is for them white, Western, and rational,
even in its dialectical madness. We have revered all forms of trin-
itarian thought, from Catholic dogma to the dogmatic triads of
Auguste Comte and Karl Marx. So let us behave sagely for a moment and state that Tlacaelel and Hernán Cortés are the fathers of
Mexico. Tlacaelel, the éminence grise of the Aztec state from the
reign of his brother Moctezuma I to that of the emperor Ahuizotl
in 1480, created the first Aztec administrative structures and invented the power systems that have ruled Mexico right down to
this day: authoritarian centralism, obedience from the top down,
submission from the bottom up, legitimacy derived from the prestige of the past and the promise of the future, but each selectively
proposed.

A fifteenth-century Orwellian, Tlacaelel destroyed all memories that were noxious to the Aztecs, kidnapped the Toltec cultural inheritance, promised happiness in the future, and demanded sacrifice in the present. This power behind the throne imposed the ritual of offering human hearts to the gods, against the wishes of the more humane, Toltec-inspired functionaries of the realm, whom he then put to death. Tlacaelel is at the heart—begging your pardon—of a totalitarian system that was humanized only by its need to exhibit the mantle of Toltec culture, deemed superior to that of the Aztecs, who were described by their more civilized contemporaries as uncouth barbarians, people without a face. It is this memory that Tlacaelel radically excluded and destroyed.

The divine couple Cortés and his mistress La Malinche preside over the feasts of our birth—baptism, communion, and confession—as something new and different: "Mexico." Cortés is the founder of the mestizo world. He is far more complicated than he appears in Rivera's cartoons. He wants to save something of the world he is forced to destroy in order to achieve an impossible personal power that the royal absolutism of Spain will not grant him. He opens the door to Baroque syncretism, Scholastic politics, redemption without human sacrifice although with divine sacrifice, and wealth without divine sacrifice but with much human sacrifice.

Yet we do not accept our father and mother, Cortés and La Malinche. We react to them with shame, anger, jealousy, repentence, all mixed, all mestizo. They turn us, in the words of Juan Rulfo, into a "living rancor." We turn instead to the phrases and names that give us a different sense of history and renewal, memory and hope—independence, reform, revolution; Hidalgo, Juárez, Madero. Still, they quickly become only the names of streets, statues, squares. Yet they are the answer to the wound of the Conquest. They are Revolutions. That is, they are, according to the oft-quoted María Zambrano, annunciations, "and their vigor must be measured by the eclipses and falls they withstand." Just like Christianity.

Are Christianity and Revolution our true breeding grounds? Perhaps, but only when they are animated by the fires of the sacred, of myth and language, and—thanks to the verbal bridge—to the promise of democracy. When Mexican culture joins its sacred fire to its democratic ideal, it creates the imagination of civil society, a Mexican democracy with dreams, with nights, with sex. Yet the power of Tlacaelel continues, even if it now speaks Spanish. Thus do fatalism and challenge constantly face each other in Mexico.

The mandala of time opens up in four directions yet returns to a center called simultaneity. A country of simultaneous times, where past is present and all of history happens, or can happen, at this very moment. The colors of the Stone Age are fixed in the most ancient stones, and the Coras repeat rituals that are always enacted at the origin of time. Neon lights and candles to the Virgin, skyscrapers next to shanties, supermarkets near garbage dumps. Mercedes-Benzes run races with burros and the TV antenna is the new cross of faith. The god of fire is a little boy spitting flames in exchange for a few centavos. But couples love each other next to the walls of ancient convents, the veterans of the Revolution survive surrounded by memories, and all the ages of man can be stored in the eyes of a very old man or a very young child, all the graffiti of history can be read in the scars of a provincial wall, and the creation of the world is happening at this very moment, in the jungles, the stones, or the lights of Mexico.

For all these reasons, because of all these images, the rationalist need to find a beginning or an end to Mexican time frightens me. The greatness of Mexico is that its past is always alive. And not as a burden, except for the most primitive of modernizers. Memory saves it, filters, chooses, but it does not kill. Memory and desire both know there is no living present with a dead past and no future without both: a living present transformed into a living past. We remember here, today. We desire today, here. Mexico exists in the present, its dawn is occurring right now, because it carries with it the wealth of a living past, an unburied memory. Its horizon is also today, because today does not diminish the force of Mexico's living desire.

Yes, we are more than calendars. We know that nothing has an absolute beginning or an absolute end. If, in a sense, Mexico continues to be a Renaissance country, it is because it refuses the tyranny of either reason or magic—our extremes—and instead celebrates the continuity of life. A multiple life, bearer of the past we ourselves created, inventor of a future we ourselves imagine. We must not tie ourselves to any dogma, any essence, any exclusive goal. We should rather embrace the emancipation of signs; the human scale of things; inclusion; the dreams of others. This, I think, is the only way to found, every day, a new Mexican time.